Related Books of Interest

WebSphere Application Server Administration Using Jython

by Robert A. Gibson, Arthur Kevin McGrath, Noel J. Bergman
ISBN: 0-13-700952-6

The first start-to-finish guide to Jython scripting for WebSphere administration, this book's practical techniques and downloadable scripts can help you improve efficiency, repeatability, and automation in any WebSphere environment.

This book's expert authors begin with practical introductions to both WebSphere Application Server administration and Jython, today's powerful, Java implementation of Python. Next, they cover a broad spectrum of WebSphere management tasks and techniques, presenting real, easy-to-adapt solutions for everything from server configuration and security to database management.

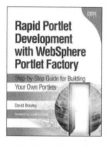

Rapid Portlet Development with WebSphere Portlet Factory
Step-by-Step Guide for Building Your Own Portlets

by David Bowley
ISBN: 0-13-713446-0

Expert developer David Bowley walks you through several of today's most common portlet development scenarios, demonstrating how to create powerful, robust portlets quickly and cost-effectively. Each walkthrough contains all the step-by-step instructions, detailed guidance, fast answers, and working sample code you need to get tangible results immediately.

As the best resource available on WebSphere Portlet Factory, this book reflects Bowley's unsurpassed experience constructing large enterprise portals. Bowley covers everything from back-end integration to user interface and AJAX techniques, helping you choose the right builder tool for each task and define high-level instructions that generate superior code artifacts. His example projects are simple enough to understand easily, but sophisticated enough to be valuable in real-world development.

Related Books of Interest

WebSphere Business Integration Primer
Process Server, BPEL, SCA, and SOA

by Ashok Iyengar, Vinod Jessani,
and Michele Chilanti
ISBN: 0-13-224831-X

Using WebSphere® Business Integration (WBI) technology, you can build an enterprise-wide Business Integration (BI) infrastructure that makes it easier to connect any business resources and functions, so you can adapt more quickly to the demands of customers and partners. Now there's an introductory guide to creating standards-based process and data integration solutions with WBI.

WebSphere Business Integration Primer thoroughly explains Service Component Architecture (SCA), basic business processes, and complex long-running business flows, and guides you to choose the right process integration architecture for your requirements. Next, it introduces the key components of a WBI solution and shows how to make them work together rapidly and efficiently. This book will help developers, technical professionals, or managers understand today's key BI issues and technologies, and streamline business processes by combining BI with Service Oriented Architecture (SOA).

IBM WebSphere DataPower SOA Appliance Handbook

by Bill Hines, John Rasmussen, Jaime Ryan, Simon Kapadia, Jim Brennan
ISBN: 0-13-714819-4

IBM WebSphere DataPower SOA Appliance Handbook begins by introducing the rationale for SOA appliances and explaining how DataPower appliances work from network, security, and Enterprise Service Bus perspectives. Next, the authors walk through DataPower installation and configuration; then they present deep detail on DataPower's role and use as a network device.

Using many real-world examples, the authors systematically introduce the services available on DataPower devices, especially the "big three": XML Firewall, Web Service Proxy, and Multi-Protocol Gateway. They also present thorough and practical guidance on day-to-day DataPower management, including monitoring, configuration, build, and deploy techniques.

Related Books of Interest

WebSphere Engineering
A Practical Guide for WebSphere Support Managers and Senior Consultants

by Ying Ding
ISBN: 0-13-714225-0

In *WebSphere Engineering*, author Ying Ding shows how to maximize the WebSphere platform's reliability, stability, scalability, and performance for large enterprise systems. You'll find insightful discussions of each option and strategy for managing WebSphere, including practical guidance on making the right tradeoffs for your environment.

Coverage includes

- Planning, hiring, training, funding, and building a world-class WebSphere engineering support organization
- Implementing tight standards and consistent, comprehensive processes for managing the entire WebSphere engineering life cycle
- Creating optimal testing environments, administering parallel testing pipelines, and managing testing workloads
- Empowering production support teams with knowledge, system privileges, and the right tools

Executing SOA
Bieberstein, Laird, Jones, Mitra
ISBN: 0-321-18579-X

The New Language of Business
SOA & Web 2.0
Carter
ISBN: 0-13-195654-X

SOA Governance
Brown, Laird, Gee, Mitra
ISBN: 0-13-714746-5

Dynamic SOA and BPM
Fiammante
ISBN: 0-13-701891-6

The Greening of IT
Lamb
ISBN: 0-13-7155083-0

Enterprise Master Data Management
Dreibelbis, Hechler, Milman, Oberhofer, van Run, Wolfson
ISBN: 0-13-236625-8

Enterprise Java Programming with IBM WebSphere, Second Edition
Brown, Craig, Hester, Pitt, Stinehour, Weitzel, Amsden, Jakab, Berg
ISBN: 0-321-18579-X

Getting Started with IBM® WebSphere® sMash

Getting Started with IBM® WebSphere® sMash

Ron Lynn, Karl Bishop, and Brett King

IBM Press
Pearson plc
Upper Saddle River, NJ • Boston • Indianapolis • San Francisco
New York • Toronto • Montreal • London • Munich • Paris • Madrid
Cape Town • Sydney • Tokyo • Singapore • Mexico City

Ibmpressbooks.com

Note to U.S. Government Users: Documentation related to restricted right. Use, duplication, or disclosure is subject to restrictions set forth in GSA ADP Schedule Contract with IBM Corporation.

IBM Press Program Managers: Steven M. Stansel, Ellice Uffer
Cover design: IBM Corporation
Associate Publisher: Greg Wiegand
Marketing Manager: Kourtnaye Sturgeon
Acquisitions Editor: Katherine Bull
Publicist: Heather Fox
Development Editor: Kendell Lumsden
Managing Editor: Kristy Hart
Designer: Alan Clements
Project Editor: Lori Lyons
Copy Editor: Water Crest Publishing
Indexer: Lisa Stumpf
Compositor: Nonie Ratcliff
Proofreader: Apostrophe Editing Services
Manufacturing Buyer: Dan Uhrig

Published by Pearson plc
Publishing as IBM Press

IBM Press offers excellent discounts on this book when ordered in quantity for bulk purchases or special sales, which may include electronic versions and/or custom covers and content particular to your business, training goals, marketing focus, and branding interests. For more information, please contact:

U.S. Corporate and Government Sales
1-800-382-3419
corpsales@pearsontechgroup.com.

For sales outside the U.S., please contact:

International Sales
international@pearson.com.

The following terms are trademarks or registered trademarks of International Business Machines Corporation in the United States, other countries, or both: IBM, the IBM logo, IBM Press, Tivoli, and WebSphere. Java, JavaScript, JDK, JRE, JVM, and all Java-based trademarks and logos are trademarks of Sun Microsystems, Inc. in the United States, other countries, or both. Microsoft and Windows are trademarks of Microsoft Corporation in the United States, other countries, or both. Linux is a registered trademark of Linus Torvalds in the United States, other countries, or both. Other company, product, or service names may be trademarks or service marks of others.

Library of Congress Cataloging-in-Publication Data

Lynn, Ron.
Getting started with IBM Websphere sMash / Ron Lynn, Karl Bishop, and Brett King.
    p. cm.
Includes index.
ISBN-13: 978-0-13-701970-0
ISBN-10: 0-13-701970-X
1. Web site development. 2. WebSphere. I. Bishop, Karl. II. King, Brett, 1968- III. Title.
TK5105.8885.W43L96 2010
006.7--dc22

                          2010030753

ISBN-13: 978-0-13-701970-0
ISBN-10: 0-13-701970-X

Text printed in the United States on recycled paper at Courier-Westford, Westford, Massachusetts.

First printing September 2010

Thank you to all the developers out there who are tired of complex and cumbersome development, and those who had enough desire to do something different and, dare we say it, fun. We wrote this book for you. We hope you enjoy developing in WebSphere sMash using Groovy, PHP, normal Java, and JavaScript with Dojo. None of us can stand to write classic JEE applications anymore. If that doesn't speak to the value of this product, nothing does.

Contents

Acknowledgments

Ron Lynn

First and foremost, I would like to thank my family—Jeannette, Rowan, Evelyn Claire, and Sophia—for putting up with all the hours I spend tucked away in my office. Thank you also to Katherine's daughter Maria for keeping her mommy sane (sort of) during this project. Last, but not least, thanks to Madison, my constant companion, for sleeping in my office while I work.

Karl Bishop

I'd like to thank my family—my wife Cheryl, and my awesome kids Matthew and Aubriana. It still amazes me that you put up with me being so continually distracted by work and this book for so long. I love you all! I'd also like to thank all my friends down at the Residence Inn in Orlando, Florida, where I spent way too much of my life during the writing of this book.

Brett King

I would like to thank my family for their support and understanding during my time on this project. In particular, I would like to thank my father, who passed away during the writing of the book, for his encouragement and guidance throughout my life.

From Us All

The authors would collectively like to thank the following people: The co-authors, for putting up with and encouraging each other throughout this experience. It's been a long process, but we finally finished. We'd also like to thank Katherine Bull for the huge amount of time she has spent on this project. Thank you to Kendell Lumsden for all the fantastic editing and working with technical reviewers. Thank you to Lori Lyons and Sarah Kearns for copy editing the book—wow, what a nice job. Thanks also to our managers at IBM for your support and encouragement.

Finally, thank you to all our technical reviewers: Doug Phillips, Joey Bernal, Ulf Feger, Madhu Chetuparambil, Roland Barcia, Kevin Dzwonchyk, Manu T. George, Jacek Laskowski, and Edward Slattery. Your comments and suggestions made the book better than it ever would have been otherwise.

About the Authors

Ron Lynn is a Senior Software Engineer on the IBM® Web Enablement and support team. He is currently working on internal projects utilizing WebSphere sMash. Ron joined IBM June 1995, as an indentured graduate student and has yet to return to academia. As an IBM neophyte, he spent his time working on a now-defunct project called Knowledge Utility (KnU). KnU allowed for exploration of many technologies and theories, from a then little-known language named Java™ to knowledge representation to what we now call portals and portlets. This led him to develop portlets for IBM Business Partners and proselytizing portals to the world. After landing on the Web enablement and support development team, Ron formalized his expertise into building portal applications in support of IBM's biggest customer, IBM. The team's fast pace and ever-changing project line-up is a fertile environment for forging applications out of the latest IBM products and technologies, which led him to work with Web 2.0 technology and WebSphere sMash.

Ron's primary passion for his job is the multiplicity of skills it draws upon from the mathematical, theoretical, scientific, and engineerical to the personal, magical, and artistical. The constant variety and juggling keeps him forever learning and wondering what will smite him next—though there are dark times when he muses if he'd have the same passion for his work were he a juggler in the circus.

Ron calls a small farm in the San Joaquin Valley of central California home, where he lives with his fabulous wife, darling children, a great dog, and several cats of undetermined disposition. When he's not bent over his computers, he spends his time as a father, husband, knitter, dressmaker, tailor, welder, carpenter, painter, plumber, gardener, pool boy, fine furniture builder, farmer, mechanic, writer, mad scientist, and water gun target. He loves to see the angelic delight on little faces as the latest in rocket launchers, onagers, or robots work wonderfully or fail fabulously. He doesn't even mind the eventual chastisement when his lovely wife discovers the mess that the dog must have made. (Sorry Madison—someone had to take the fall.)

Karl Bishop is a Senior Software Engineer with IBM. He works for the Web enablement and support group within the IBM Software Services for WebSphere for IBM. As the name implies, his group develops and supports many internal IBM applications. His technical focus of late has been in Web 2.0 technologies in general, and the Dojo toolkit in particular. Karl has worked for IBM for close to 12 years. Before that, he spent another dozen years honing his geek credentials at another computer company in California. Karl currently works out of his house, hidden away in the Sandhills near Pinehurst, North Carolina—no, he doesn't play golf—but professes to be an original "Florida Cracker" by heart and birth.

When he's not pounding away at the keyboard, Karl enjoys being the cool dad and husband. Karl likes to play with his son, Matt, building Lego's and other contraptions. With his daughter, Aubri, he plays games, critiques her artwork, and generally goofs off. Other family enjoyments include biking, swimming, gardening, and playing disc golf. Karl also enjoys brewing when time permits and quaffing craft beers just about anytime. When work gets to be too much, the Bishop family frequently heads up toward the Appalachian mountains or the beach. Come on kids, we're off to Boone—Tweetsie Railroad and the Mellow Mushroom are calling.

Brett King is a Senior Software Engineer with IBM, working on the WebSphere Commerce product. He is currently working on social networking enhancements to the product using WebSphere sMash. Prior to WebSphere Commerce, Brett was a developer on WebSphere sMash. Brett has been a software developer at IBM for almost 20 years, working in such varied areas as networking software, pervasive computing, and grid computing. He has been fortunate to work with advanced technologies throughout his career, including WebSphere sMash. He has particular interests in finding ways for developers to be more productive, whether through better tools or better software engineering processes, such as agile development.

Brett grew up in rural Pennsylvania but he has lived in the Research Triangle area of North Carolina since graduating from Lehigh University. In his free time, Brett has a wonderful wife, two kids, and a multitude of hobbies to keep him busy. He especially enjoys reliving his childhood through his own kids. Always eager to tap into his creative side, Brett enjoys playing role-playing games, constructing miniature terrain sets, and modding his muscle car. Brett also enjoys travel, with favorite destinations being places with historical significance, the homes of remote family members, and anywhere the Pittsburgh Steelers are playing.

Introduction

IBM® WebSphere® sMash is a platform for the rapid development and deployment web applications using popular web technologies. It quickly enables developers to go from concept to production in a fraction of the time required by traditional platforms and web application models. Developers can use the dynamic scripting languages Groovy and PHP to speed development and still have Java™ as the underlying system language for extension development. Add to this easy development of Representational State Transfer (REST) services and rich AJAX interfaces. This is a platform that excels at quickly getting Web 2.0 applications built. To speed deployment, the runtime environment is integrated, so there is no "server environment" to deploy to. Applications can be built to run standalone on any machine. This makes IBM WebSphere sMash an ideal platform for the development of situation applications.

Situational Applications

Situational applications are defined by Wikipedia as follows:

A **situational application** is "good enough" software created for a narrow group of users with a unique set of needs. The application typically (but not always) has a short life span, and is often created within the group where it is used, sometimes by the users themselves. As the requirements of a small team using the application change, the situational application often also continues to evolve to accommodate these changes. Although situational applications are specifically designed to embrace change, significant changes in requirements may lead to an abandonment of the situational application altogether—in some cases, it is just easier to develop a new one than to evolve the one in use.

Given the constantly changing business landscape, situational applications provide the ideal instrument for constant adaptation. As a platform for situational application, WebSphere sMash provides an ideal mix of features and flexibility allowing for rapid application development.

Rapid Application Development

The use of dynamic scripting languages is well acknowledged to improve software developer productivity. Groovy and PHP both have many build-in and reusable components and allow developers to create function with fewer lines of code. The use of dynamic scripting languages along with the integrated runtime environment also speeds the develop-compile-test loop by removing the need for compilation. Developers need to make changes only to their scripts, and IBM WebSphere sMash detects and executes the changed code. This sort of rapid development means that applications can be continuously tested and available to testers or end users even while an application is still being developed, extended, or evolved. Applications can also be rapidly changed as the situation dictates. This type of continuous application adaptation fits the constantly changing business landscape perfectly.

IBM WebSphere sMash Development Process

IBM WebSphere sMash has been developed using a community-driven commercial development process. This means that most of the development efforts are done in the open and are transparent to all parties through a community-based website. The community website hosts the IBM WebSphere sMash incubator project, Project Zero. Project Zero is the technology for which the IBM WebSphere sMash product is derived. IBM encourages everyone to participate by contributing to the open discussions around the product development, features, functions, and bugs. The community website provides tools to facilitate participation. The tools include forums, a wiki, a bug-reporting tool, a developers blog, and access to the source repository. You can even download the latest stable and experimental versions of the product. This begs the question: Which version should I use?

Available IBM WebSphere sMash Offerings

IBM WebSphere sMash is available in four different offerings. The offerings range from fully supported with an IBM commercial license and extended features to bleeding-edge nightly builds of the latest and greatest code. The four offerings are summed up in Table 1.1.

Table 1.1   IBM WebSphere sMash Offerings

Offering	Features	Availability
IBM WebSphere sMash	Stable, production version of Web-Sphere sMash with a Standard IBM Commercial license.	Available for purchase from www.ibm.com/software/ webservers/smash/
IBM Reliable Transport Extension for WebSphere sMash	Stable, production version of Web-Sphere sMash with a Standard IBM Commercial license. This version extends WebSphere sMash with features for reliable messaging and communication.	Available for purchase from www.ibm.com/software/ webservers/smash/
IBM WebSphere sMash Development Edition	Stable, community version of Web-Sphere sMash with a license that allows for development and limited deployment.	Available for free from www.projectzero.org/ download/
Project Zero	Experimental version of WebSphere sMash with features not yet available in the stable versions.	Available for free from www.projectzero.org/downl oad/latest.php

From this list of offerings, it should be fairly easy to match up what level of investment you're looking for. Most developers start with the IBM WebSphere sMash Development Edition unless they're looking for the cutting-edge enhancements or would like to peek into the future. When the developers have established that WebSphere sMash is their preferred platform for development, the business would then invest in the production-ready and supported versions.

What Is Covered in This Book?

This book covers a wide range of topics of interest to software developers. The intent of this book is to supplement and expand upon the information available on the projectzero.org website and in the product documentation. Each chapter includes concrete examples and demonstrations of how to use the technology presented. You can find much of the code from this book at the IBM Press Books website: ibmpressbooks.com/sMash. We open the book by discussing installation and development environments. From our own experience as software engineers, we see that these are important aspects for the adoption of any new development environment. After we learn about installation and the available development environments, we move into a chapter that outlines a complete application. This chapter is intended to stand by itself and give you a quick introduction to the complete WebSphere sMash development cycle. After that, we dive into the details of many different aspects of WebSphere sMash. This book is by no means comprehensive. We've included what we believe to be important aspects to get you going and give hints into where there's more to be uncovered. We hope you enjoy this book and find it to be useful in learning WebSphere sMash.

Installing the IBM WebSphere sMash CLI

In the Introduction, we talked about the four different IBM WebSphere sMash offerings. For the purposes of this book, any version should be appropriate. So, feel free to download the latest Project Zero build or the latest IBM WebSphere sMash Developer Edition. Before we do that, though, let's prepare our Java development environment.

First Things First: Java Development Environment

Prior to installing the sMash CLI, you must ensure that you have a functional Java SE Development Kit (JDK™) version 5 or 6 installed. It is important to remember that you cannot use the Java SE Runtime Environment (JRE™) to develop with sMash. The AppBuilder development environment requires libraries found only in the JDK and not in the JRE. This is a common problem with first-time users. You may choose to use either the JDK from Sun or IBM. They can be found in the locations in Listing 1.1.

Listing 1.1   Locations of Supported JDKs

```
IBM: http://www.ibm.com/developerworks/java/jdk/
Sun: http://java.sun.com/javase/downloads/index.jsp
```

After you have downloaded a JDK, install it per the instructions provided for your operating system. The following steps show the configuration using the Linux® command line. For Windows® users, you need to open a command prompt and alter the statements appropriately. When installed, you can verify your JDK installation by running the commands in either Listing 1.2 or Listing 1.3.

Listing 1.2   Linux Java Version Check

```
$ java -version
java version "1.6.0"
Java(TM) SE Runtime Environment (build pxi3260sr3-20081106_07(SR3))
IBM J9 VM (build 2.4, J2RE 1.6.0 IBM J9 2.4 Linux x86-32 jvmxi3260-
20081105_25433 (JIT enabled, AOT enabled)
J9VM - 20081105_025433_1HdSMr
JIT  - r9_20081031_1330
GC   - 20081027_AB)
JCL  - 20081106_01
```

Listing 1.3   Windows Java Version Check

```
C:\>java -version
java version "1.6.0"
Java(TM) SE Runtime Environment (build pwi3260sr2-20080818_01(SR2))
IBM J9 VM (build 2.4, J2RE 1.6.0 IBM J9 2.4 Windows XP x86-32
jvmwi3260-20080816
_22093 (JIT enabled, AOT enabled)
J9VM - 20080816_022093_1HdSMr
JIT  - r9_20080721_1330ifx2
GC   - 20080724_AA)
JCL  - 20080808_02
```

The output shown in the listings indicates that I am running the IBM JDK version 1.6.0 on a Linux x86 platform. If running the Sun JDK, a similar output will be shown. The important thing is that you get JDK version information back and not some random error. Now that we have the JDK installed and have ensured that it is working, we can move on to downloading and installing WebSphere sMash.

Installing the Command-Line Interface

The installation for IBM WebSphere sMash is very easy. At a high level, you simply need to download the zip file and unzip it, set up a proxy server if needed, and test the installation. IBM WebSphere sMash is highly modular. It uses the ivy dependency manager (see http://ant.apache. org/ivy/) to manage dependencies for each application. Every application has tremendous flexibility to include only the modules the application needs. Developers also have the ability to create reusable modules for other applications to use.

For the purposes of this book, it is fine to download the latest stable WebSphere sMash Development Edition driver or the experimental Project Zero driver. You can download either from the Project Zero website (see Figure 1.1).

Figure 1.1   Project Zero website

The website, projectzero.org, will change over time, but you can find the download link to retrieve the zip file from the site. Remember, it is http://projectzero.org.

After you have the zip file on your computer, you need to unzip it using whatever extraction tool you have available. Unzip the contents into a directory of your choosing. The zip file has a base of zero, which you want to retain. In these samples, I am using a top-level directory called development located under my home directory. In the following, replace the location shown with your preferred directory:

```
unzip ~/Downloads/zero_<version>.zip -d ~/development/
```

Of course, if you're using a different operating system, your unzip command and paths will look different. After the files are extracted, you should end up with a directory structure similar to that shown in Figure 1.2 under your target directory.

The final step to finish the installation procedure consists of setting up your environment to include the location to the JRE and the Project Zero binaries. This will be accomplished by manipulating the PATH environment variable appropriately. Placing these commands in your normal login environment ensures that everything is ready to go the next time you log in. This is an optional step, but will save you the hassle of having to specify full paths when running the Zero command line. Examples of these paths for Linux are shown in Listing 1.4.

Figure 1.2   Zero directory structure

Listing 1.4   Example Linux Paths

```
export JAVA_HOME=/usr/lib/jvm/java-1.5.0-ibm-1.5.0.8/jre
export ZERO_HOME=~/development/zero
export PATH=$JAVA_HOME/bin:$ZERO_HOME:$PATH
```

For Windows users, you can set the environment variables by accessing the Control Panel > System > Advanced tab > Environmental Variables. Then, in either the user or system areas, add/edit the following values, as shown in Listing 1.5. Be sure to adjust the directory paths to match your actual environment.

Listing 1.5   Example Windows Paths

```
JAVA_HOME    C:\Program Files\Java\jdk1.6.0_16\jre
ZERO_HOME    C:\development\zero
PATH         %JAVA_HOME%\bin;%ZERO_HOME%\bin;%PATH%
```

This completes the basic installation of IBM WebSphere sMash. The next section discusses setting up proxy support. However, if your connection to external websites doesn't require you to use a proxy, skip the proxy section and continue to the section on testing your installation.

Activating HTTP(S) Proxy Support

The command-line interface (CLI) retrieves modules from remote repositories. For the command-line interface to do this, Java needs access the Internet. If you use a proxy server to access external websites, you need to set up the proxy server for IBM WebSphere sMash. If you don't know if you use a proxy server, skip this section and try testing your WebSphere sMash installation. If you receive an unknown host error message, you probably need to come back to this section and set up your proxy server. The easiest way to do this is to edit the zero script file for Linux or zero.bat file for Windows in the installation directory.

Open the script file or the batch file that is appropriate for your platform in your favorite text editor. At the top of the file, there are comments that direct you to uncomment particular lines and update the values (see Listing 1.6 for Linux and Listing 1.7 for Windows).

Listing 1.6   Linux Zero Script Fragment Demonstrating Proxy Configuration

```
# proxy support -
#    uncomment the following line( and the export ZERO_OPTS) and
#    update proxy values
# ZERO_OPTS="$ZERO_OPTS
        -Dhttp.proxyHost=myProxyHost
        -Dhttp.proxyPort=myProxyPort
        -Dhttps.proxyHost=myProxyHost
        -Dhttps.proxyPort=myProxyPort"
# export ZERO_OPTS
```

For Linux, uncomment by removing the # sign at the start of the ZERO_OPTS line and the start of the export line. Set the proxy variables to the appropriate values, and your proxy is set up.

Listing 1.7   Windows Zero Batch File Fragment Demonstrating Proxy Configuration

```
rem proxy support -
rem    uncomment the following line and
rem    update values to add proxy settings.
rem set ZERO_OPTS=%ZERO_OPTS%
-Dhttp.proxyHost=myProxyHost
-Dhttp.proxyPort=myProxyPort
-Dhttps.proxyHost=myProxyHost
-Dhttps.proxyPort=myProxyPort
```

For Windows, uncomment by removing the rem at the start of the set ZERO_OPTS. Set the proxy variables to the appropriate values, and your proxy is set up.

Now that your proxy is set, we can continue on and sanity test our IBM WebSphere sMash installation.

Test Your IBM WebSphere sMash Installation

The quickest way to verify that your IBM WebSphere sMash installation is installed correctly is to run a version check. To do this, open a command line and change directories to the zero installation directory. In this directory, there is a script for Linux named zero and a batch file for Windows named zero.bat. On the command line, type zero version. If your installation has been done properly, you should see output similar to Listing 1.8.

Listing 1.8   Output from the "Zero Version" Command on Windows

```
C:\temp\zero>zero version
CWPZT0901I: The following module(s) are not currently in the local
  repository:
        zero:zero.cli.tasks:[1.0.0.0,)
CWPZT0902I: Trying to locate the module(s) using one of the config-
  ured remote repositories
CWPZT0545I: Retrieving zero.cli.tasks-1.1.1.1.30731.zip from host
http://www.projectzero.org/sMash/1.1.x/repo/base
CWPZT0545I: Retrieving zero.kernel-1.1.1.1.30725.zip from host
http://www.projectzero.org/sMash/1.1.x/repo/base
CWPZT0600I: Command resolve was successful
Command-line Version:  1.1.1.1.30719 20090908 2152
Command-line Information:
        Name: zero.cli
        Version: 1.1.1.1.30719
        Location: C:\temp\zero
        Modulegroup: stable

        Dependencies:
                zero:zero.cli.tasks:1.1.1.1.30731 (userhome)
                zero:zero.kernel:1.1.1.1.30725 (userhome)

The java command path is
C:\bin\ibm-java-sdk-60-win-i386\jre\bin\java.exe

java version "1.6.0"
Java(TM) SE Runtime Environment (build pwi3260sr2-20080818_01(SR2))
IBM J9 VM (build 2.4, J2RE 1.6.0 IBM J9 2.4 Windows XP x86-32
jvmwi3260-20080816_22093 (JIT enabled, AOT enabled)
J9VM - 20080816_022093_lHdSMr
JIT  - r9_20080721_1330ifx2
GC   - 20080724_AA)
JCL  - 20080808_02
```

This listing came from a Windows-based machine, so the output will look slightly different than what you might see on a Linux machine. Also, the versions and paths will be appropriate for the version of IBM WebSphere sMash you downloaded, the version of Java you're using, and the paths you have selected for installation.

You should notice at the top of the output that IBM WebSphere sMash automatically retrieves certain modules from the remote repository. Namely, it retrieves the CLI tasks and the zero kernel modules. These modules are necessary for IBM WebSphere sMash to run and, if successfully downloaded, indicate that you have connectivity to the remote repository.

If you receive errors during the download of these modules, you need to fix those errors before moving on. An easy test to see if you have connectivity to the repository is to take the URL listed in the output in Listing 1.8 and plug it into your web browser. In Listing 1.8, the URL we'd use is the following:

```
http://www.projectzero.org/sMash/1.1.x/repo/base
```

This URL will be different depending on the version of IBM WebSphere sMash you are using. If you have access to the URL from your web browser, but see errors using the zero version check, you probably need to go back to the proxy section and set up a proxy server for IBM WebSphere sMash to use.

When the zero version check works, you can get started using the command-line interface.

Getting Started with the Command-Line Interface (CLI)

In the next chapter, we look at various development environments, including the command-line interface (CLI). Let's take a quick look at the CLI now just to get acquainted with it. As we saw, the CLI is a module retrieved from a remote module repository. There are many commands available, but don't let this scare you. The CLI is very helpful. To get a list of available commands, type the following:

```
zero help
```

The results of typing this into the command line can be seen in Listing 1.9.

Listing 1.9 Results of the "Zero Help" Command

```
Usage:  zero [main-opts] <task> [task-args]
main-opts:
  -d             enable minimal logging
  -v             enable all logging
  -l=<file>      use the given file to output log to

compile        Compiles all Java source files under the module's
/java          directory.
create         Creates a new module in the current directory.
help           Prints the documentation for the given command.
modulegroup    Manage modulegroups.
package        Packages the module as a zip file.
```

```
publish            Publish the module to your local repository.
repository         Manage repositories.
resolve            Determine the module's dependencies.
rollback           Reverts the effects of the last resolve or update.
search             Finds and prints all matching modules in the reposi-
                   tory.
switch             Switch the module group.
update             Resolves a module to its latest dependencies.
version            Displays version information
```

As you can see, there are a bunch of available commands. Each command may have arguments that it can be given, but again the command line is very helpful. You need only to type the following to get help on a particular command:

```
zero help <command>
```

For example, if we use zero help search, we get the results shown in Listing 1.10.

Listing 1.10   Results of "Zero Help Search" in the CLI

```
Usage:

zero search <org:module[:revision]> [-remote] [-json]

The command uses the current module group to find in the local re-
pository for a module that matches the given <org:module:revision>
value and prints its search results. If no module name is given, the
command will print information about all available modules. You can
also use the -remote option to tell the command to search the remote
repository instead of the local one.

If the -json option is used the report is formatted as a JSON docu-
ment.

The return codes for this command are:
0 - success
1 - command failed
```

The search command enables you to search for modules in the repository. There are commands to create new IBM WebSphere sMash applications, start and stop applications, package applications, and many more. Spend some time familiarizing yourself with the commands, and we'll take another look at the CLI in the next chapter.

Conclusion

In this chapter, we learned how to install IBM WebSphere sMash and how to test that installation. We also started working with the command-line interface (CLI) and became familiar with the available commands. In the next chapter, we're going to take a look at three different development environments that you can use to develop IBM WebSphere sMash applications. The first is a web browser-based environment called AppBuilder that is built into IBM WebSphere sMash. The second is an Eclipse-based development environment. Finally, we'll come back to the CLI and take a look at what else it can do.

Choose Your Development Environment

Introduction

WebSphere sMash offers three different development environments: AppBuilder, Eclipse, and a CLI environment. AppBuilder is a fully functional web-based application development environment. It is lightweight, easy to use, and comes with WebSphere sMash as a sMash application. Eclipse is a full-feature development environment that is very popular the world over. WebSphere sMash offers a plugin for the Eclipse environment that enables developers to use the full Eclipse suite of tools to help develop WebSphere sMash applications. Finally, there is a CLI environment that enables developers to utilize their own tooling suite to develop WebSphere sMash applications. This gives developers a broad range of development options and the ability to set up and configure an environment in which they are comfortable.

AppBuilder

The AppBuilder environment is the quickest and easiest way to get started with WebSphere sMash and comes included with your WebSphere sMash installation—how nifty that you can build WebSphere sMash applications with a WebSphere sMash application! The AppBuilder uses a lightweight browser-based environment and provides some nice features, including a drag-and-drop client designer for the Dojo Toolkit and a graphical editor for Assemble Flow (see Chapter 11, "Framework Components"). Generally, the AppBuilder is a great way to get your feet wet and implement small projects.

Getting Started

After you have installed WebSphere sMash, you can start the AppBuilder by running the appbuilder command from the command line in the zero directory. The first time this script is run, it will resolve and download all the needed packages; when that has completed, you should be presented with the usage for the script, as shown in Listing 2.1.

Listing 2.1   appbuilder Usage

```
Usage: appbuilder command
where command is one of:


open    Starts the AppBuilder (if not already started) and
        opens it in a browser
start   Starts the AppBuilder
stop    Stops the AppBuilder
status  Prints the started or stopped state of the AppBuilder
update  Updates the AppBuilder with the latest dependencies
version Prints the AppBuilder version information
help    Prints this help message
```

Run appbuilder open from the CLI, and the AppBuilder opens in your default browser. Your development can begin, as shown in Figure 2.1.

As you can see, there are several quick help lists to get you started: Create a new application, open an existing application, and copy a sample.

Sample Applications

A great way to get started with WebSphere sMash is to take a look at the samples that are available. To do that, click Create from repository link. The Create from Repository dialog box appears, as shown in Figure 2.2. Note that you need an Internet connection for this to work because AppBuilder connects to the WebSphere sMash repository to retrieve a list of available modules. When you type **demo** into the text box, the list of modules will be filtered to show only available sample applications. The modules that are filtered are the features that can be added to your WebSphere sMash application. We'll look at some of them later in the book.

From here, you can select any of the sample applications. There are a number of sample applications that demonstrate different aspects of WebSphere sMash. Choose any application that interests you and click Create. AppBuilder will now create a new application from the repository and open up the MyApplications page, where you can explore the application or run it as described later in this chapter. Before we do that, though, let's take a look at how to create an application from scratch.

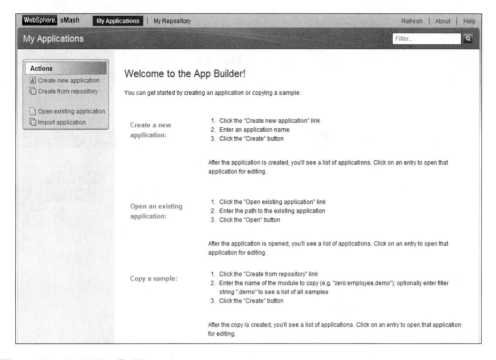

Figure 2.1   Initial AppBuilder screen

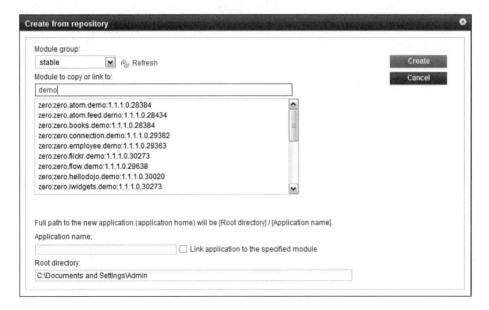

Figure 2.2   Create a sample application from the repository.

Creating a New Application

To create a new application, start by clicking the Create new application link in the left navigation bar, as shown previously in Figure 2.1. This link pops open a dialog box, which enables you to type in an application name and choose a path in which to store your application, as shown in Figure 2.3.

Create new application

Full path to the new application (application home) will be [Root directory] / [Application name].

Application name:

Root directory:

C:\Documents and Settings\Admin

Description:

Module group:

experimental   Refresh

Create

Cancel

Figure 2.3   Create new application dialog

Type in an application name and the path where you want it to store the application. We used "Test application" for our application name. You may use any name you'd like, but the images all reference "Test application." After your new application has been created, it will be displayed in your My Applications list, as shown in Figure 2.4.

Sort by: Name ∨ | Status | Path

Test application

http://localhost:8080/
C:\zero\appbuilderTest\

Module Group   experimental
Tags   ZeroProject

Figure 2.4   My Applications list

Editing Applications

From the application list, you can do several things. By clicking the name of the application or the pencil icon, you can start editing your application. Click the green arrow to start the application and the last icon to the right to package your application for deployment onto another machine. If you start editing the application, you'll see several tabs that enable you to do everything from editing files and managing dependencies to debugging the running application. Figure 2.5 shows the initial display when you first begin to edit your application.

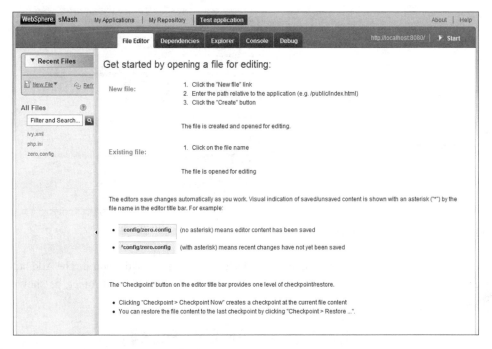

Figure 2.5   Initial application edit display

From the initial File Editor tab, you can create and edit any of the files in the application. By clicking the filename in the left navigation bar, you can start editing the given file. Likewise, you can create new files by selecting the New File link in the left navigation bar. The File Editor tab opens context-sensitive editors for each type of file. For example, there is a drag-and-drop HTML editor that has the Dojo Toolkit support. This feature makes it easy to quickly lay out your HTML client pages.

Adding Dependencies

The Dependencies tab enables you to resolve and manage your project dependencies. In Figure 2.6, you can see that the project starts with a dependency on zero.core. The zero.core module is the base module that WebSphere sMash needs to run.

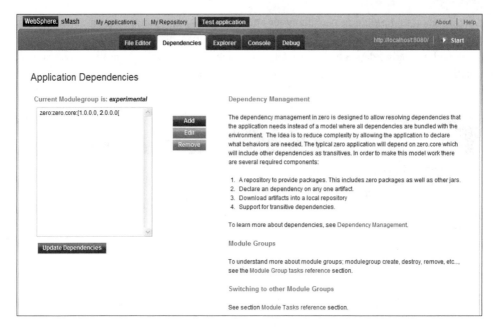

Figure 2.6   Dependencies tab

You can add a dependency on another package by clicking the Add button. The Add button opens a dialog that displays several packages that can be added to the project, as shown in Figure 2.7.

Figure 2.7   Add Dependency dialog

After a dependency is added, it shows up in the list of application dependencies. You can, of course, remove and update dependencies on the main Dependencies tab. The Explorer tab is a file explorer that allows you to explore the application's directory and look at files in a read-only mode. The Console tab provides a command-line console for controlling various aspects of the project, such as starting and stopping the application and resolving dependencies. The Console is a web-based CLI environment and can be used like the CLI environment we discuss later in this chapter. The last tab is the Debug tab. The Debug tab gives the application developer the ability to set breakpoints and look at variables while the application is running. This is a powerful aspect of the AppBuilder environment. Breakpoints can be set at any place in the code and variables inspected to determine their state at that point in the code.

Finally, when your application is complete and you'd like to deploy it to another machine, you'll need to package it up. This is made very easy in the AppBuilder. Simply return to the My Applications page and click the Package button (it looks like a little window with an arrow pointing to it), as shown earlier in Figure 2.4. This button enables you to package your application in a zip file that will be stored in the application's export directory. There is an option to package the application as a standalone application. This packages the WebSphere sMash runtime in with the zip file so that there will be nothing but the application to install.

Overall, the AppBuilder is a nice lightweight environment for developing WebSphere sMash applications. Because the AppBuilder comes included with WebSphere sMash, it is easy to get started with it and costs no additional time to set up. This feature of WebSphere sMash is constantly evolving, so it's worth looking at in each new release of the product.

Eclipse

Eclipse is an open source-integrated development environment used by many professional developers. There are more than a thousand commercial and open source plugins created for Eclipse that enhance the development environment. It is intended for experienced developers and teams with plugins for several source control systems, database access, and a plethora of others to help with development tasks. WebSphere sMash offers a plugin for Eclipse that allows a developer to create, build, and export WebSphere sMash applications in Eclipse. Installation instructions for the plugin can be found on the Project Zero website (http://www.projectzero.org).

Sample Applications

As with the AppBuilder, you can create a sample application from the repository. This is a good way to get a feel for various features of WebSphere sMash. To create a sample application, go to File > New > Project and choose Examples > WebSphere sMash Examples > WebSphere sMash Sample Application, as shown in Figure 2.8.

After you press the Next button, a list of sample applications will be retrieved from the repository, as shown in Figure 2.9.

Figure 2.8   Create a sample application.

Figure 2.9   List of sample applications

As before, this list is retrieved from the remote WebSphere sMash repository, so you'll need an Internet connection to populate this list to. After you select a sample, click Next and then Finish, and the sample application will be created in your current workspace. After it has been created, you can poke around and take a look at the sample, edit it, and run it as is discussed later in this chapter.

Creating a New Project

Creating a new project in Eclipse will be familiar to those who have used Eclipse before. Go to File > New > Project and choose a WebSphere sMash application; then click the Next button (see Figure 2.10).

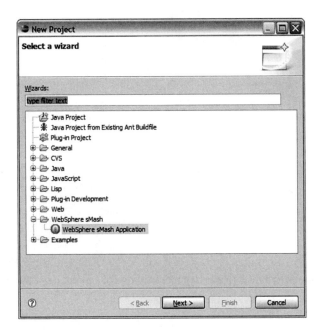

Figure 2.10   New Project dialog box

Next, you'll be prompted to type in a project name, and you'll have the option to select a location for the project. When you have completed those tasks, press the Finish button. You'll now have a newly created project in your workspace ready to edit or run. If you browse through the project structure, you'll find many project-related files to browse or edit. To run the application, right-click on the project and select Run As > WebSphere sMash Application, as shown in Figure 2.11.

When the project is started, the Eclipse console window displays messages to indicate that the application was started and on which port the application is listening.

Figure 2.11   Running the application inside Eclipse

Adding Dependencies

To add dependencies, you need to double-click the ivy.xml file inside the project. To do this, expand the project and then expand the config directory, as shown in Figure 2.12.

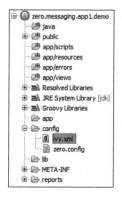

Figure 2.12   Add dependencies by opening the ivy.xml file.

After the ivy.xml file is double-clicked, it will open in a dependency editor. Within this editor, you can click the Add button to add dependencies to the project, as shown in Figure 2.13.

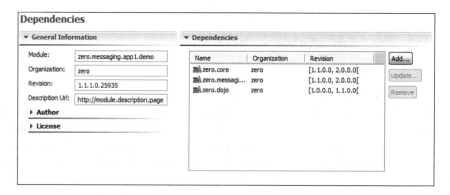

Figure 2.13   Eclipse dependency editor

Clicking the Add button opens the Dependency Selection dialog, shown in Figure 2.14. From here, you can add specific dependencies to your project that will be stored locally. These dependencies add particular features to your WebSphere sMash application—for example, the zero.dojo dependency. It gives the application access to Dojo JavaScript™ libraries objects that have been created by the WebSphere sMash team for use in your applications.

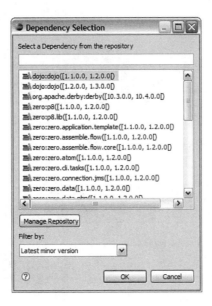

Figure 2.14   Dependency Selection dialog

If you don't see the particular dependency you need, click the Manage Repository button to find additional dependencies located in the remote repository. Figure 2.15 shows the Manage Repository dialog.

On the left side of the Manage Repository dialog, you can see the modules that you currently have locally stored. On the right side, you can search for new modules that you'd like to add locally. Then you can add them to your dependency list for use by your own applications.

Finally, when your application is finished, you'll want to package it for distribution. To do this, we right-click the project again and select Export. This opens up the Export dialog. In that dialog, we need to select the WebSphere sMash Export Wizard, as shown in Figure 2.16.

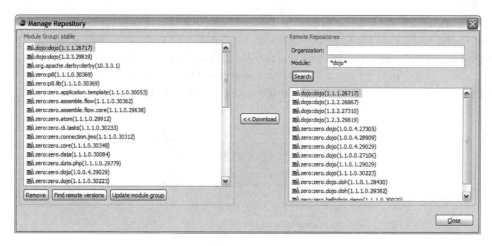

Figure 2.15   Manage Repository dialog

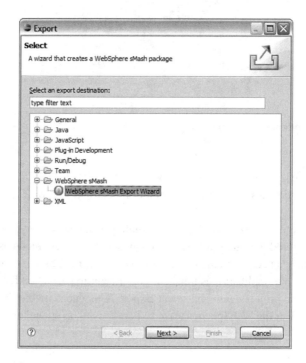

Figure 2.16   Export dialog

After the correct wizard is selected, press Next. This opens the WebSphere sMash Export Wizard, as shown in Figure 2.17.

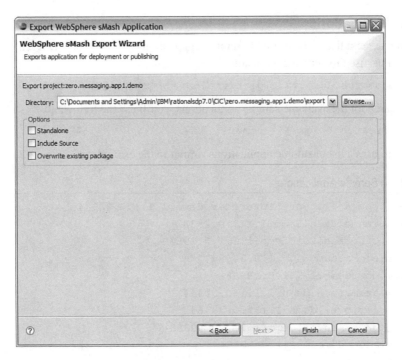

Figure 2.17   WebSphere sMash Export Wizard

From this wizard, you can set the export directory and various options for export, including Standalone, which packages the WebSphere sMash runtime with the application. After your options are selected, click Finish, and a zip file of your application will be created in the chosen destination directory.

Command-Line Interface Environment

The CLI environment is useful for developers who have an established tool chain that they'd like to keep using. It is also the perfect match for build servers and continuous integration servers.

With WebSphere sMash installed, you can also get right into developing from the command line. The first thing you may need to do is run zero resolve. The resolve command will retrieve any needed modules that you haven't previously retrieved. Open a terminal or command window and go to the directory where WebSphere sMash was installed, run the resolve, and wait for it to finish. You may also need to resolve path issues with Java. Typically, these are solved by setting the JAVA_HOME environment variable and verifying that the java executable is in the PATH environment variable. The resolve command will retrieve any needed modules that you haven't previously retrieved.

Sample Applications

Next, you can get a list of the available sample applications from the local and remote repositories. To do this, use this search command:

```
zero search <org:module[:revision]> [-remote]
```

To search for the available sample applications, you'll use the following:

```
zero search "*demo*" -remote
```

This returns a list of sample applications similar to the example in Listing 2.2.

Listing 2.2   Sample Applications

```
zero:zero.openajax.contentprovider.demo:1.1.1.0.28384
zero:zero.connection.demo:1.1.1.0.29382
zero:zero.officemonitor.demo:1.1.1.0.29638
zero:zero.books.demo:1.1.1.0.28384
zero:zero.flow.demo:1.1.1.0.29638
zero:zero.atom.feed.demo:1.1.1.0.28434
zero:zero.employee.demo:1.1.1.0.29363
zero:zero.phpemployee.demo:1.1.1.0.29363
zero:zero.atom.demo:1.1.1.0.28384
zero:zero.openid.demo:1.1.1.0.30292
zero:zero.messaging.broker1.demo:1.1.1.0.24952
zero:zero.iwidgets.demo:1.1.1.0.30273
zero:zero.flickr.demo:1.1.1.0.30273
zero:zero.suggest.demo:1.1.1.0.30023
zero:zero.travelrequest.demo:1.1.1.0.30227
zero:zero.hellodojo.demo:1.1.1.0.30020
zero:zero.messaging.app1.demo:1.1.1.0.25935
zero:zero.kicker.demo:1.1.1.0.26427
zero:zero.openajax.demo:1.1.1.0.29638
zero:zero.messaging.app2.demo:1.1.1.0.25935

CWPZT0600I: Command search was successful
```

As you can see, there are a number of available samples. You can create these applications locally by using the create command. This retrieves the sample from the remote repository and stores it locally for you to use:

```
zero create <name> from <org:module:revision>
```

In this case, let's pick the kicker sample application:

```
zero create zero.kicker.demo from zero:zero.kicker.demo
```

This command created a new directory in the current directory named zero.kicker.demo. If you browse that directory, you'll notice that the sample application has been created with the same structure and files as the other two environments. You can use the text editor of your choice to edit the files and save them. In the next section, we learn how to run applications from the command line in more detail.

Creating a New Application

The next step is to create an application of your own. If you go back to the WebSphere sMash directory, you can create a new application by using the create command again, as follows:

```
zero create myApp
```

Notice that creating an application from scratch does not require the use of the "from" clause to specify the module from which we're creating the application. This has again created a new directory—the myApp directory—with our application's base structure in it. The new application is already complete and ready to run. To run the application, we need to change only to the directory and issue the start command, as follows:

```
zero start
```

When the command has been executed, it returns a message that tells you the URL and port on which your new application is listening—for example:

```
Application started and servicing requests at
http://localhost:8080/
CWPZT0600I: Command start was successful
```

Again looking at the directory structure, you'll see all the same files that you would have seen in the AppBuilder and the Eclipse environments. WebSphere sMash applications are dynamically built so that you can make changes, and the results will generally be seen immediately within the running application. The only exception to this rule is changes to the zero.config file, which requires a restart of the application by issuing a stop command followed by a start command. To stop the application, you need to issue only the stop command, as follows:

```
zero stop
```

This stops the application, closing any resources that were opened.

Adding Dependencies

At some point during the course of developing an application, you'll need to add new dependencies to your project. To do this from the command line, you'll need to open up the ivy.xml file in the config directory of the application and add a dependency line, such as the following:

```
<dependency org="zero" name="zero.timer" rev="[1.0.0.0,
  2.0.0.0["/>
```

The preceding line would add a dependency on the zero.timer module. After this dependency is added, you should once again issue the resolve command; then you can use the module in your code. To execute the resolve command, return to the root of your application directory and issue the following:

```
zero resolve
```

This retrieves the module from the remote repository, allowing it to be used in your application.

Deploying Your Application

At some point, you'll want to package your application for deployment on other machines. To do this, use the package command:

```
zero package [shared | standalone]
```

By default, the application is packaged as shared and stored in the export directory. A shared application package is one that is deployed into a WebSphere sMash runtime environment. That is a server that has WebSphere sMash already installed, whereas a standalone application is one that includes the WebSphere sMash runtime as part of the package. No matter which path you choose, they are both compressed into zip files and stored in the export directory. Finally, if you need help navigating the WebSphere sMash CLI, you need to use only the help command:

```
zero help <command>
```

Enter any zero command, and all help that is available will be retrieved. To see a list of available commands, enter only the zero command. The help also shows the return codes and what each means to allow for easier development of scripts. As you can see, the command line is easy to use, powerful, and scriptable. The CLI can integrate with nearly any tool chain that you are already using.

Conclusion

We have looked at three different development environments for WebSphere sMash. The App-Builder is a built-in environment that is supplied with WebSphere sMash and enables developers to get started quickly. It works well for learning WebSphere sMash and can be used for small and quick application development. The Eclipse plugin development environment is an established, well-known environment with a lot of features. It has many plugins for source control and other team-oriented activities. This environment is well suited for teams of developers on any size project. Finally, we looked at the CLI environment. Individual developers may prefer this environment because it offers the most flexibility in tooling use and scripting capabilities. The CLI environment is well suited for use on build and continuous integration servers. With all these options for development, you're free to choose whichever suits your needs.

dler

create a simple WebSphere sMash application using
demonstrated simple file serving in a WebSphere
lex application, we need to understand the structure
In this chapter, we look at how to use conventions in
ult behaviors that can save you time and code. Web
odels, and we show you how to easily create *handlers*
htly more complex application to illustrate some of
a number of topics to help you quickly create appli-
in later chapters.

ut

development environments is "convention over con-
where possible, convention should be used to define
tion allows developers to take advantage of common
fy only where their application differs from the norm.
ufficient; where it is not, configuration is required.
onstructed using sets of conventions. We will try to
explain how to bypass the conventions using config-

s is the directory layout of a WebSphere sMash appli-
tion in Chapter 2, "Choose Your Development Envi-
l directories were automatically created for you. This

directory structure was copied from an application template. That application template defines what it means to be a WebSphere sMash application. The WebSphere sMash tooling assumes that all applications follow this template.

In general, you should not change the predefined directories or try to circumvent their intent. Use them as intended, and you will be on the "happy path" to a working application that is easy to understand, maintain, and extend. The exception to this rule might be if you have an existing application that you are trying to port to a WebSphere sMash environment. However, even in that scenario, you may find that it is easier to use the WebSphere sMash default directory structure.

Here is a tree view of a typical WebSphere sMash application directory structure:

```
+---.zero
|    +---private
|    \---shared
+---app
|    +---errors
|    +---models
|    |    \---fixtures
|    +---resources
|    +---scripts
|    \---views
+---classes
+---config
+---export
+---java
+---lib
+---logs
+---META-INF
+---public
\--reports
```

Source Directories

The most important directories in a WebSphere sMash application are app, public, and possibly java. These are the directories where you will put the majority of your application code. The other directories are supporting directories.

Some directories are automatically made available to client applications through a file-serving handler—that is, the files in these directories are published and available to web requests on the application's port. We identify these directories so that you are aware that these files are visible to users, applications, and browsers.

- The `public` directory (file-served) is where you put the files that you want to publish through HTTP or HTTPS. This directory is the primary directory for your web files. Place all of your public HTML, CSS, and JavaScript™ files here.

- The `app` directory contains a set of subdirectories that provide a structural convention for building your application.

- The `app/errors` subdirectory (file-served) is a published directory that contains web files that render error pages. The error pages are typically written in HTML, Groovy, Groovy templates, or PHP. If you want to create a custom error page to handle the HTTP error code 404 (FILE_NOT_FOUND), for example, you would create the file in this directory. You can find additional details about this directory in Chapter 6, "Response Rendering."

- The `app/models` directory contains Zero Resource Model (ZRM) model files and *fixtures* (initial data for priming your database). ZRM is a WebSphere sMash framework for quickly generating REST-based applications. A ZRM model defines the schema for your REST resources.

- The `app/resources` directory (file-served) contains the *handlers* that respond to REST requests for your application's resources. Handlers are written in Groovy or PHP. You can write handlers in Java as well, but the Java files are put into the java directory rather than here.

- The `app/scripts` directory contains script files (for example, Groovy and PHP) that are used as library files. These files aren't served directly. You access them from your published files in other directories.

- The `app/views` directory (file-served) contains files for rendering a view in an app that follows the Model-View-Controller (MVC) pattern. The files can be written in Groovy, the Groovy template language, or PHP.

- The `app/zwidgets` directory (file-served) contains Dojo widgets. Dojo widgets are JavaScript widgets written using the Dojo JavaScript framework.

- The `app/iwidgets` directory (file-served) contains iWidget widgets. iWidgets are web-served widgets that are described in an XML file using the iWidget metadata format.

- The `java` directory is where you put your Java source files. You should, of course, put your source files in subdirectories corresponding to their Java package, just as in other Java environments.

Supporting Directories and Files

When you create a WebSphere sMash application, a lot of functionality is enabled for you out-of-the-box. Some of this functionality appears in the supporting files and directories created for your application. Depending on the development tool you're using, some of these files and directories are hidden. They typically start with a dot and are managed by WebSphere sMash processes. You won't usually need to worry about them, but we describe them here for completeness.

- The `.classpath` file contains your app's Java classpath. This file is generated for you automatically when your application is *resolved*. Application resolution is a process for determining and locating the specific code packages your application needs to run. Any classes compiled from Java or Groovy files or contained in JAR files in your `lib` directory are automatically included in the classpath.

- The `.project` file enables your application to be imported into Eclipse as a project.

- The `.zero` directory contains a number of intermediate files that are generated by WebSphere sMash. For example, it contains the `.zero/private/resolved.properties` file, which contains a list of the specific dependency files located for this application the last time it was resolved. The `.zero` directory also contains files with application runtime state.

- The `classes` directory contains compiled Java classes.

- The `config` directory contains, obviously, your application's configuration files. There are a number of important files in here. However, configuration is covered in much more detail in Chapter 4, "Configuration Files Explained."

- `config/ivy.xml` describes the external modules on which your application depends. It also declares the name and version of your application if you choose to package it as a module.

- `config/php.ini` contains configuration options, such as logging and extensions, for PHP-based applications. More details can be found in the php.ini file itself.

- `config/zero.config` is the primary configuration file for your application. You can configure your application's port, database connections, and security rules in `zero.config`.

- The `lib` directory is where you put standalone Java JAR files that you want to use in your application. You don't need to put JAR files in here that are already bundled into one of your external dependencies.

- The `logs` directory contains log files for your application. By default, you get a rotating set of trace and log files (`error-0.0.log` and `trace-0.0.log` are the newest) and an HTTP access log.

- The `reports` directory contains a detailed report of which external modules were found when your application's dependencies were resolved. To view the report, open up the .xml file in this directory in a web browser. You should see a nicely formatted report.

REST

You now know what a WebSphere sMash application looks like on the file system, but we haven't actually described what an app looks like from an architectural perspective. Although there are a number of ways to design a WebSphere sMash app, there is a prevailing and preferred architectural style. That style is REpresentational State Transfer, or REST.

REST is a term and concept that was introduced by Roy Fielding, one of the authors of the HTTP specification. REST is an architectural style that gets back to the basics of HTTP. The interface of a RESTful application is defined in terms of standard HTTP methods and structures. This approach contrasts protocols like SOAP or RPC, where interactions with services are embedded in message bodies. By using HTTP as it was intended, a developer gains advantages in interoperability, cacheability, and scalability.

RESTful HTTP applications describe application data and state as URI-addressable resources. State is not stored in session objects or cookies. Clients interact with these server-based resources using standard HTTP methods: GET, PUT, POST, and DELETE. REST applications are often compared to database applications, which offer a CRUD (Create, Retrieve, Update, and Delete) interface. The HTTP methods are used to provide a CRUD interface on the REST resources.

WebSphere sMash has conventions for describing resources with URIs, and conventions for interacting with those resources using HTTP methods. These conventions can be overridden through configuration if necessary.

Relative URIs for WebSphere sMash resources take this form:

```
/resources/<resource-collection>/<resource-id>
```

For example, if we have a resource that describes a collection of bookmarks stored on the server, the relative URI to address that collection could be `/resources/bookmarks`. To address a specific bookmark within that collection, we might use a URI like this:

```
/resources/bookmarks/10240
```

You might notice that the relative URI starts with `/resources`. It's not a coincidence that there is a subdirectory in a WebSphere sMash application's `app` directory called `resources`. It's a convention. The `/app/resources` directory contains pieces of code called *handlers* that "handle" requests for resources in the /resources URI namespace. Again, by convention, the filename of the handler corresponds to the resource name for which it handles requests. In our bookmarks example, we might have a "bookmarks" handler written in the Groovy language. The file structure would look like this:

```
app/resources/bookmarks.groovy
```

Table 3.1 lists HTTP methods and how they are interpreted in a REST application.

Table 3.1   HTTP Methods

Action	HTTP Method	URI Format with Sample
List resources in a collection.	GET	/resources/<resource-collection> /resources/bookmarks
Retrieve a particular resource.	GET	/resources/<resource-collection>/<resource-id> /resources/bookmarks/10240
Create a new resource.	POST	/resources/<resource-collection> resources/bookmarks

Table 3.1   HTTP Methods

Action	HTTP Method	URI Format with Sample
Update a resource.	PUT	/resources/<resource-collection>/<resource-id> /resources/bookmarks/10240
Delete a resource.	DELETE	/resources/<resource-collection> /resources/bookmarks/10240

REST with the Zero Resource Model (ZRM)

How do you create a REST application with WebSphere sMash? There are actually a few different ways, but, like most programmers, we start with the easiest. WebSphere sMash provides a framework for developing REST applications called the Zero Resource Model (ZRM).

Some application frameworks start at the database level and work their way up to the client application. Other frameworks start at the GUI and work their way down to the database. ZRM starts in the middle.

Earlier in the chapter, we discussed an application that managed a collection of web bookmarks. We already described what the URI structure of the bookmark resources might look like; now let's look at describing the data structure of the bookmark resources. Defining your *resource model* or data structure is the first step in writing a RESTful app with ZRM. In ZRM, the data structure is described using JSON syntax.

JSON (also known as JavaScript Object Notation) is a language-independent data format that happens to be extremely easy to parse with JavaScript. As such, it is an ideal data format for REST applications, which often have JavaScript clients. JSON is also pretty easy for humans to read.

JSON data is defined using arrays, objects, and name-value pairs. JSON arrays are delineated with square brackets, and JSON objects are delineated with braces. When passing JSON to or from a REST service, you should generally pass a single JSON objects rather than a list of discreet parameters for ease of parsing. We discuss how to parse JSON objects in JavaScript later in this chapter. For more information on JSON, see http://www.json.org.

Now, let's build on our earlier example. First, we need to create an application, using one of the tools described in the previous chapters. For simplicity, we use the command line interface. Create an application called Bookmarks, using the following command:

```
zero create Bookmarks
```

Note that the application name can be anything; it doesn't need to correspond to the name of the resource handler or resource model.

For our bookmarks model, we will start simple. We need a URL, a name, and a category. The model, by convention, is a .json file placed in the /app/models directory. So, we create a file called `/app/models/bookmarks.json` in our Bookmarks application directory. The content of the file is a JSON object that looks like Listing 3.1.

Listing 3.1 Bookmarks Model

```
{
    "fields": {
        "url": {
            "label": "URL",
            "required": true,
            "type": "string",
            "description": "",
            "default_value": "",
            "max_length": 1024
        },
        "name": {
            "label": "Name",
            "required": true,
            "type": "string",
            "description": "",
            "default_value": "",
            "max_length": 80
        },
        "category": {
            "label": "Category",
            "required": false,
            "type": "string",
            "description": "",
            "default_value": "",
            "max_length": 50
        }
    }
}
```

The three fields we defined are `url`, `name`, and `category`. Each field has some self-explanatory metadata that describes the field. The one piece of metadata that might need further explanation is the label. The label is used by clients to present the field to the user, typically in a form or a table. The label is meant to be more human-readable than the field name itself.

The model is used to generate database tables for your resources. Before we can do that, though, we should create some sample data to put into the database. The initial data that we want to put into the database is called a *fixture*, so it gets put into a file named /app/models/fixtures/ initial_data.json. Again, this filename is the convention used by ZRM. The format of the file is a JSON array of resource instances. Note that the "type" field refers to the name of the model file, "bookmarks" (see Listing 3.2).

Listing 3.2   Bookmarks Fixture

```
[
    {
        "type": "bookmarks",
        "fields": {
            "url": "http://www.ibm.com",
            "name": "IBM",
            "category": "Software Companies"
        }
    },
    {
        "type": "bookmarks",
        "fields": {
            "url": "http://projectzero.org",
            "name": "Project Zero",
            "category": "Development"
        }
    },
    {
        "type": "bookmarks",
        "fields": {
            "url": "http://groovy.codehaus.org",
            "name": "Groovy",
            "category": "Development"
        }
    }
]
```

Now that we've created our model file and our initial data file, we can tell WebSphere sMash to automatically create a database for us. There are a couple of steps involved here. The first step is to declare that our application is going to use the ZRM libraries. This is called declaring a dependency.

Declaring a Dependency

WebSphere sMash uses a dependency management system called Ivy. WebSphere sMash applications and libraries are packaged into Ivy *modules*, which are just ZIP files containing code and an Ivy metadata file that describes the package and the modules it requires. The Ivy metadata file is called an "Ivy file" and is always named ivy.xml. The modules that are required by the package are called *dependencies*.

In our scenario, we want to declare that our bookmark application requires the ZRM libraries. The ZRM libraries are stored in an Ivy module called zero.resource. Most of the modules supplied by WebSphere sMash have zero. as a prefix. To add zero.resource as a dependency, we must edit our application's Ivy file.

If you are using the WebSphere sMash CLI, edit the /config/ivy.xml file and add the line in **bold**, as shown in Listing 3.3. This entry should be entered as a single line in the file. We provide a more in-depth explanation of Ivy configuration files in the next chapter.

Listing 3.3   Ivy Configuration File

```
<ivy-module version="1.3">
  <info module="Bookmarks" organisation="zero" revision="1.0.0">
   <license name="type of license" url="http://license.page"/>
   <ivyauthor name="author name" url="http://authors.home.page"/>
   <description homepage="http://module.description.page"/>
  </info>
  <publications>
    <artifact type="zip"/>
  </publications>
  <dependencies>
   <dependency org="zero" name="zero.core" rev="[1.0.0.0,      \
3.0.0.0 ["/>
    <dependency org="zero" name="zero.resource"
    rev="[1.0.0.0, 3.0.0.0["/>
  </dependencies>
</ivy-module>
```

If you are using App Builder or Eclipse, you can either edit your ivy.xml file source as shown previously, or add the zero.resource dependency using the UI. In App Builder, dependencies are added using the Dependencies tab. If you are using Eclipse, opening ivy.xml opens up an editor that lets you add dependencies. Before the dependency can be added to your application, it must be downloaded to your computer from an Ivy *remote repository*. If the zero.resource module is not already in your *local repository* (on your computer), it can be downloaded by clicking on My Repository (see Figure 3.1). When searching for the remote file, specify "zero" as the organization and "zero.resource" as the module.

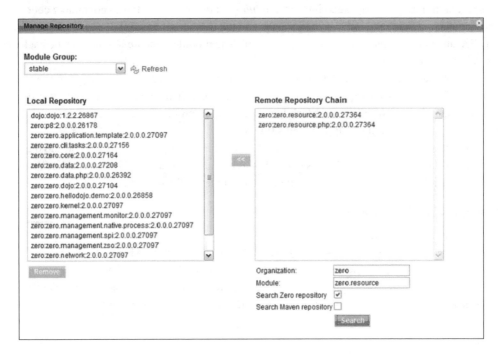

Figure 3.1   My Repository

After you have added the `zero.resource` module as a dependency to your application, you must *resolve* your application. "Resolve" is an Ivy term that means, "find all of my application's dependencies." In AppBuilder and Eclipse, the resolve step happens automatically when you add the dependency to your application. From the command line, after editing your ivy.xml, you must execute

```
zero resolve
```

from your application's root directory. The `resolve` command attempts to find the `zero.resource` module in your local repository. If it can't find it, you get an error message and are instructed to run `zero update` instead. When you run `zero update`, the command finds the appropriate `zero.resource` module in the remote repository and downloads it. The application is resolved once the download is complete. When your application is resolved, it can make use of the ZRM libraries.

Virtual Directories

An important feature of WebSphere sMash's dependency system is the concept of *virtual directories*. When an application starts up, a virtual directory of the application and all of its dependencies are created. When WebSphere sMash needs to find a file in the application, it looks in the application's directory first, followed by the same directory in each of the application's dependencies. For example, if an HTML file in the application's /public directory attempts to load the file library.js from the server, WebSphere sMash's static file server first looks in the application's /public directory. If it can't find the file there, it looks in the /public directory of all of the dependencies until the file is found.

Synchronizing a ZRM Model

As part of dependency resolution for the zero.resources module, the WebSphere sMash command line within your application is enhanced with some new features. The new commands added by the zero.resource dependency take this form:

```
zero model <subcommand>
```

You can execute

```
zero model help
```

within your app's root directory to see a list of the subcommands (duplicated here for your convenience):

```
dumpdata      Dumps data from the ZRM database into files
loaddata      Loads data from specified files into the ZRM
              database
reset         Restores the ZRM database to the initial state
sql           Writes the SQL that manages the database arti-
              facts
sync          Create database artifacts and load initial
              data
```

The command that we are interested in at the moment is *sync*. The sync command synchronizes the model with the database. From a WebSphere sMash command-line interface in your application's directory or from the command prompt in the App Builder, execute the following:

```
zero model sync
```

This command creates database tables from the bookmarks.json model file and populates the tables with data from the initial_data.json file should it exist. By default, the tables are created using an embedded Derby database.

Event Handling in Groovy

We now have a database that reflects our model and contains some interesting data. So, how do we get a REST interface to our data? We have to create a *resource handler*. We mentioned handlers previously. "Handler" is a WebSphere sMash term for a piece of code that responds to events within the application's lifecycle. A handler that responds to HTTP requests for resources is called a resource handler.

Resource handlers, by default, are put into the /app/resources directory. Handlers can be written in Groovy, PHP, or Java. For writing simple handlers, Groovy is hard to beat. Because Groovy is a scripted language with minimal syntactic overhead, you can write very concise handlers. In fact, our first handler is going to have a single, short line. In your application's /app/resources directory, create a file called bookmarks.groovy. In the file, put this line:

```
ZRM.delegate()
```

This line tells ZRM to handle all requests for the "bookmarks" resource, by filename convention. We don't need to declare any imports. The dependency resolution step we performed earlier let Groovy know where to find the ZRM libraries.

ZRM.delegate() is set up to handle the five LCRUD requests for our bookmarks resources. LCRUD is CRUD with an additional (L)ist semantic. With this one line, we are now able to process GET, PUT, POST, and DELETE requests for our bookmarks. Let's try it out.

Running the Application

You can start your bookmarks application as described in the last chapter. We haven't done anything to create a client yet, but we can use the browser to interact with some of our new REST APIs. From your browser, browse to the following:

```
http://localhost:8080/resources/bookmarks
```

This URL issues a GET request to the bookmarks resource handler. Because "bookmarks" is a resource collection, it performs a "List" on the bookmarks resources. The results vary by browser, but you will either see the response displayed in the browser or be asked to save the response as a file. The result is a compact JSON-format representation of the bookmarks resources. If you would like a more human-readable result, you can edit your config/zero.config file and add the following line:

```
/config/json/prettyPrint=true
```

Note that there is no need to restart your application. Most configuration changes are detected on the next client request. Simply repeat the request for the bookmarks resource, and you get a response that looks like Listing 3.4.

Listing 3.4   Bookmarks Response

```
[
    {
        "url": "http://www.ibm.com",
        "name": "IBM",
        "category": "Software Companies",
        "id": 100,
        "updated": "2008-12-18 00:30:29"
    },
    {
        "url": "http://projectzero.org",
        "name": "Project Zero",
        "category": "Development",
        "id": 101,
        "updated": "2008-12-18 00:30:29"
    },
    {
        "url": "http://groovy.codehaus.org",
        "name": "Groovy",
        "category": "Development",
        "id": 102,
        "updated": "2008-12-18 00:30:29"
    }
]
```

From the response, we can see that the ID of the first entry is 100. Note that the IDs were automatically created when the initial_data was populated. We can now request individual resources by using the ID in the URL, as follows:

```
http://localhost:8080/resources/bookmarks/100
```

This URL issues a GET ("Retrieve") request and returns Listing 3.5.

Listing 3.5   Bookmark GET Response

```
{
    "url": "http://www.ibm.com",
    "name": "IBM",
    "category": "Software Companies",
    "id": 100,
    "updated": "2008-12-18 00:30:29"
}
```

If you'd like to try out the REST APIs using the browser, you can use the "Poster" Firefox Add-on (https://addons.mozilla.org/en-US/firefox/addon/2691). To create a new bookmark, you issue a POST using values like those shown in Figure 3.2.

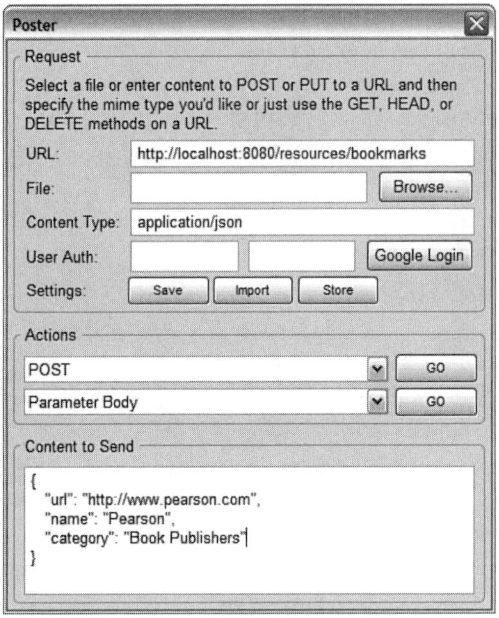

Figure 3.2   Posting with Poster

To modify a bookmark, you specify the ID of the bookmark in the URL. The Action would be PUT, and the content would include all the nongenerated fields, as shown in Figure 3.3.

To delete a resource, specify the bookmark ID in the URL and set the Action to Delete. No parameter body is needed.

Explicit Event Handling

In the preceding example, we took the "happy path" and let ZRM handle everything for us. Of course, there are situations where we need more control. You may need to handle your own GET, PUT, POST, and DELETE requests. For example, what if your REST interface needs to store the data in a file or a legacy database? In that case, we would need to implement our resource handler, bookmarks.groovy, using a pattern similar to Listing 3.6.

Figure 3.3   Putting with Poster

Listing 3.6   Resource Handler for Explicit Event Handling

```
def onList() {

    // Retrieve the list of bookmarks from the
    // data store and put into a java.util.Map
    def bookmarks =  ...

    // Create the response
    request.status = 200
    request.json.output = bookmarks
    request.view = 'JSON'
    // The render method tells Zero to render
    // the output using the JSON renderer
    render()
}
```

```
def onCreate() {
    // Use the WebSphere sMash JSON decoder to
    // decode the JSON-formatted bookmark
    // request.input[] is a short-hand reference
    // to the input data stored with the request
    // in the Global Context.  The Global Context
    // stores application state.
    def jsonBookmark = zero.json.Json.decode(request.input[])

    // Create the id for the bookmark entry and
    // add the entry to the data store
    def bookmarkId = ...
    def data = ...

    // Set a response header in the request object in the
    // Global Context
    request.headers.out.Location = getRequestedUri(false) + '/' +
    \ bookmarkId
    // Set the HTTP response code
    request.status = 201
    request.json.output = data
    request.view = 'JSON'
    render()
}

def onRetrieve() {
    def bookmarkId = request.params.booksmarksId[]

    // retrieve the bookmark from the data store based on the id
    def data = ...
    // Create the response
    if (data) {
        request.status = 200
        request.json.output = data
        request.view = 'JSON'
        render()
    }
    else {
        // Not found
        request.status = 404
```

```
    }
}

def onUpdate() {
    def bookmarkId = request.params.bookmarksId[]

    // Retrieve the requested bookmark from the
    // data store based on the Id
    def data = ...
    // Update the data in the data store
    ...
    // Set the response code
    request.status = 204
}

def onDelete() {
    def bookmarkId = request.params.bookmarksId[]
    // Delete the entry based on the Id
    ...
    // Set the response code
    request.status = 204
}
```

The preceding example shows five methods: onList, onCreate, onRetrieve, onUpdate, and onDelete. These five methods define the convention for a resource handler. You don't need to have your handler inherit from a parent class; you just need to implement these methods. By implementing these methods, you have complete control over how the requests are processed.

Event Handling in PHP

WebSphere sMash also supports PHP, of course. PHP makes a fine alternative to Groovy for writing resource handlers. For ZRM-based resource handlers, use the dependency zero.resource.php rather than zero.resource:

```
<dependency org="zero" name="zero.resource.php"
  rev="[1.0.0.0, 3.0.0.0["/>
```

For our resource handler, we create /app/resources/bookmarks.php with the content in Listing 3.7.

Listing 3.7   PHP ZRM Resource Handler

```php
<?php
    zrm_delegate();
?>
```

If we want to handle events individually in PHP, we need to create a class with the same name as the resource in our resource handler file (with capitalization). So, for bookmarks.php, we would do something like Listing 3.8.

Listing 3.8   Explicit Event Handling in PHP

```php
<?php
class Bookmarks {
    function onList() {
        // Retrieve the list of bookmarks from the data store
        $bookmarks = ...

      // build the response
      zput('/request/status', 200);
      zput('/request/view', 'JSON');
      zput('/request/json/output', $bookmarks);
      // The render_view method tells WebSphere sMash to render
      // the output using the JSON renderer
      render_view();
    }
     function onCreate() {
        // Use the WebSphere sMash JSON decoder to
        // decode the JSON-formatted bookmark
        $bookmark = json_decode($HTTP_RAW_POST_DATA);
        // Create the id for the bookmark entry and
        // add the entry to the data store
        $bookmarkId = ...
        $data = ...

        // Set a response header in the request object
        // in the Global Context
        $location = get('/request/path') . "/" . $bookmarkId
        zput('/request/headers/out/Location', $location);
        zput('/request/headers/out/Content-Type', 'text/json');
        echo json_encode($data);
```

```php
        zput('/request/status', 204);
    }
    function onRetrieve() {
        $bookmarkId = zget("/request/params/bookmarksId");
        // retrieve the bookmark from the data store based on the id
        $data = ...
        // If data is found, create the response as JSON
        if (isset($data)) {
            zput('/request/headers/out/Content-Type', 'text/json');
            echo json_encode($employeeRecord);
            zput('/request/status', 200);

        } else {
        // Page not found
            zput("/request/status", 404);
        }
    }
    function onUpdate() {
        $bookmarkId = zget("/request/params/bookmarksId");
        $bookmark = json_decode($HTTP_RAW_POST_DATA);
        // Retrieve the requested bookmark
        // from the data store based on the Id
        ...
        // Update the data in the data store
        ...
        // Set the response code
        zput("/request/status", 204);
    }
    function onDelete() {
        $bookmarkId = zget("/request/params/bookmarksId");
        // Delete the bookmark from the data store based on the Id
        ...
        // Set the response code
        zput("/request/status", 204);
    }
}
?>
```

Event Handling in Java

When performance is important, Java can be used in place of Groovy for event handling. We discuss Java in more detail in later chapters, but the pattern is similar to Groovy and PHP. You need to create a class with a null constructor to handle the requests, with naming corresponding to the resource. So, we could create `java/bookmarks.java` like Listing 3.9.

Listing 3.9   Java Event Handler

```java
public class Bookmarks {
    public void onGET() {
...
    }
    public void onPOST() {
...
    }
    public void onPUT() {
       ...
    }
    public void onDELETE() {
...
    }
}
```

Creating a Client

So far, we've covered the basics of creating a simple RESTful service. What we need now is a client that end users can use. Earlier we used Poster, which is quite useful for unit testing our services. However, for some odd reason, end users are not usually very happy formulating JSON messages in Poster. If we were to release our application with Poster as the front-end client, the Human-Computer Interaction people would probably faint. We can create our user interface using three primary technologies: Groovy Templates, PHP, and Dojo.

Earlier in this chapter, we learned that, as part of the application directory structure, there are a few client-oriented directories. Of particular interest at this point is the `public` directory.

Groovy Templates

Using Groovy templates, we can create a client that accesses the RESTful service on the server side. Groovy templates are very much like JSPs. They embed Groovy code inside HTML. Groovy script elements are surrounded by "<%" and "%>" and expression elements by "<%=" and "%>". In the `public` directory, create a file named `groovy.gt`. We'll start by simply displaying the contents of our bookmark database. To do this, we start by calling the GET method on a connection to our service, as shown in Listing 3.10.

Listing 3.10   Calling the GET Method

```
Connection.Response resp =
    Connection.doGET("http://localhost:8080/resources/bookmarks")
```

This connection retrieves a response object. The body of the response object is a String representing a JSON object, the same JSON object we saw earlier in this chapter. After we have turned the JSON object into a map suitable for iteration, we iterate over the map and output the contents (see Listing 3.11).

Listing 3.11   Decode Results and Display

```
resultData = Json.decode(resp.getResponseBodyAsString())
for(bookmark in resultData)
{
  %><tr>
    <td><%=bookmark.url%></td>
    <td><%=bookmark.name%></td>
    <td><%=bookmark.category%></td>
    <td><a href="?delete=<%=bookmark.id%>">delete</a></td>
  </tr><%
}
```

We could have made the bookmarks into anchors, which would make this little application more useful. It is easier to demonstrate in type by making a simple table. You might have noticed that we've added a column in our data to send back a parameter to our Groovy template so that we can handle deletes of bookmarks. When the user clicks a bookmark's delete link, the page is reloaded, with an extra parameter added. To determine if we're going to be deleting a bookmark from our database, we check the request and see if the delete parameter is non-null. If the parameter is non-null, we perform the delete and redirect back to our regular view, as shown in Listing 3.12.

Listing 3.12   Delete and Redirect

```
if(request.params.delete[]){
  Connection.Response resp = Connection.doDELETE(
  "http://localhost:8080/resources/bookmarks/${request.params.delete[]}")

  //set the location and the redirect status
  request.headers.out.Location = "http://localhost:8080/groovy.gt"
  request.status = 301;
}
```

To perform the delete, we use the DELETE method and pass the appropriate RESTful URL. Notice that the `request.params.delete[]` parameter contains the ID of the entry to be deleted so that our URL ends up pointing to an individual resource. Similarly, for the CREATE operation, we create a form element with parameters to pass back to our Groovy template (see Listing 3.13).

Listing 3.13 Create Form

```
<form action="groovy.gt" method="get">
<table>
  <tr>
    <th>URL*</th>
    <th>Name*</th>
    <th>Category</th>
  </tr>
  <tr>
    <td><input type="text" name="url"/></td>
    <td><input type="text" name="name"/></td>
    <td><input type="text" name="category"/></td>
  </tr>
</table>
<input type="submit" value="Save" /><br />(* = required field)
</form>
```

As you can see, this is a very simple form that passes the parameters back to our Groovy template. In the template, we check for the required parameters and POST the new bookmark to the RESTful service (see Listing 3.14).

Listing 3.14 Create the New Bookmark

```
if(request.params.url[] && request.params.name[]){
  data = [url:request.params.url[],
          name:request.params.name[],
          category:request.params.category[]]
  Connection.Response resp = Connection.doPOST(
          "http://localhost:8080/resources/bookmarks",
Json.encode(data))
//Examine the response code here to see if there are errors. This
//should also address the asynchronous nature of the POST, so that
//the redirects do not race with the actual create.
  if("200".equals(resp.getResponseStatus())){
    request.headers.out.Location = "http://localhost:8080/groovy.gt"
    request.status = 301;
```

```
  }else{
    //do error handling
  }
}
```

We collect the data into a map and POST the JSON-encoded map to our RESTful service. Then we redirect the client back to the original page to view the results. Of course, we should do more error checking to make sure all these operations worked well. This code has a bit of a problem in that the redirect sometimes is faster than the database update, so you may need to refresh the page after a delete or a create. Point your browser to http://localhost:8080/groovy.gt. Here's what it ends up looking like (see Figure 3.4).

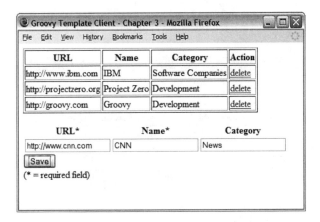

Figure 3.4   Groovy template client

As you can see, we're displaying the contents of our initial load. We can add CNN to our bookmark list by typing in the fields. After we press the Save button, we end up seeing what is shown in Figure 3.5.

Again, you may have to press Refresh because the database commit is sometimes a touch slower than the redirect. It all depends on your system. You can avoid this refresh if you ensure that the POST/DELETE operation is completed prior to redirecting. We can delete a bookmark simply by pressing Delete (see Figure 3.6).

As you can see, we've deleted the Groovy bookmark. This is how you can make a simple client to your bookmark RESTful service using Groovy templates. Let's go back and look at the same thing, but in PHP.

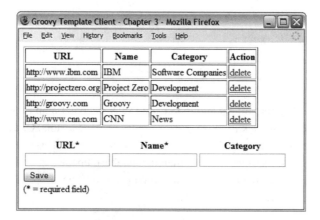

Figure 3.5   Groovy template client after Add

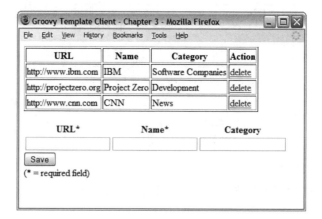

Figure 3.6   Groovy template client after Delete

PHP

To start using PHP, we have to enable the PHP feature by adding a dependency to the ivy file. You can do that in the same way you did earlier in this chapter. When you do, your ivy.xml will have an additional line:

```
<dependency name="zero.php" org="zero" rev="[1.0.0.0, 3.0.0.0["/>
```

After this feature is enabled, you need to create a new PHP file in the `public` directory for our PHP code. Let's call it php.php.

As with Groovy templates, we start by simply displaying the contents of our bookmark database. To do this, we start by calling the GET method on a connection to our service (see Listing 3.15).

Listing 3.15   GET Method in PHP

```php
$conn = curl_init("http://localhost:8080/resources/bookmarks");
curl_setopt($conn, CURLOPT_CUSTOMREQUEST, "GET");
curl_setopt($conn, CURLOPT_RETURNTRANSFER, true);
$response = curl_exec($conn);
curl_close($conn);
```

This connection retrieves a response, which is a string representing a JSON object, the same JSON object that we saw earlier in this chapter. When we have turned the JSON object into an array suitable for iteration, we process each entry and output the contents (see Listing 3.16).

Listing 3.16   PHP Decode Result and Display

```php
$resultData = json_decode($response);
foreach($resultData as $bookmark){
  echo "<tr>
          <td>${bookmark['url']}</td>
          <td>${bookmark['name']}</td>
          <td>${bookmark['category']}</td>
          <td><a href=\"?delete=${bookmark['id']}\">delete</a></td>
        </tr>";
}
```

As seen previously, we've added a column in our data to send back a parameter to our PHP script so that we can handle deletes of bookmarks. To determine if we're going to be deleting a bookmark from our database, we check the request and see if the delete parameter is non-null. If the parameter is non-null, we perform the delete and redirect back to our regular view (see Listing 3.17).

Listing 3.17   PHP Delete and Redirect

```php
if(zget('/request/params/delete')){
  if(zget('/request/params/delete')){
    $conn = curl_init("http://localhost:8080/resources/bookmarks/".
      zget('/request/params/delete'));
    curl_setopt($conn, CURLOPT_CUSTOMREQUEST, "DELETE");
    curl_setopt($conn, CURLOPT_RETURNTRANSFER, true);
    curl_exec($conn);
```

```
    curl_close($conn);
    zput('/request/headers/out/Location',
         'http://localhost:8080/php.php');
    zput('/request/status',301);


}
```

To perform the delete, we use the DELETE method and pass the appropriate RESTful URL. Notice that the `/request/params/delete` parameter contains the ID of the entry to be deleted so that our URL ends up pointing to an individual resource. Similarly, for the CREATE operation, we create a form element with parameters to pass back to our PHP script (see Listing 3.18).

Listing 3.18   PHP Create Form

```
<form action="php.php" method="get">
<table>
  <tr>
    <th>URL*</th>
    <th>Name*</th>
    <th>Category</th>
  </tr>
  <tr>
    <td><input type="text" name="url"/></td>
    <td><input type="text" name="name"/></td>
    <td><input type="text" name="category"/></td>
  </tr>
</table>
<input type="submit" value="Save" /><br />(* = required field)
</form>
```

Again, there is a simple form that passes the parameters back to the PHP script. In the script, we check for the required parameters and POST the new bookmark to the RESTful service (see Listing 3.19).

Listing 3.19   PHP Create New Bookmark

```
if(zget('/request/params/url') && zget('/request/params/name')){
  $data = array("url"=>zget('/request/params/url'),
                "name"=>zget('/request/params/name'),
                "category"=>zget('/request/params/category'));
  $conn = curl_init("http://localhost:8080/resources/bookmarks");
```

```
curl_setopt($conn, CURLOPT_RETURNTRANSFER, true);
curl_setopt($conn, CURLOPT_POST, 1);
curl_setopt($conn, CURLOPT_POSTFIELDS, json_encode($data));
$header = array("Content-type: application/json; charset=iso-8859-
1");
curl_setopt($conn, CURLOPT_HTTPHEADER, $header);
curl_exec($conn);
curl_close($conn);
zput('/request/headers/out/Location','http://localhost:8080/php.php')
;
zput('/request/status',301);
}
```

We collect the data into an array and POST the JSON-encoded array to our RESTful service. Then we redirect the client back to the original page to view the results. As mentioned previously, the redirect is sometimes faster than the database update, so you may need to refresh the page after a delete or a create. Point your browser to http://localhost:8080/php.php. It ends up looking exactly like what we saw with the Groovy template. Likewise, the delete and create operations work the same.

Dojo

WebSphere sMash provides a couple of nifty Dojo-based widgets that help us get a Dojo client up and running very quickly. We use one of those named the DataGrid to show us a table of our bookmarks. To start using Dojo, we have to enable the Dojo feature by adding a dependency to the ivy file. You can do that the same way you did earlier in this chapter. Once you do, your ivy.xml will have an additional line, as follows:

```
<dependency name="zero.dojo" org="zero" rev="[1.0.0.0,1.1.0.0["/>
```

After this feature is enabled, you need to create an HTML page in the `public` directory named dojo.html. In the newly created HTML file, there are two primary lines of HTML (see Listing 3.20). The first line defines a DataStore, which we use to RESTfully retrieve data.

Listing 3.20   Defining a DataStore

```
<span dojoType="zero.resource.DataStore" jsId="bookmarkdata"
    contextRoot="./resources"
    resourceCollection="bookmarks"></span>
```

As you can see, we point the DataStore to our RESTful bookmarks service using the `resourceCollection` attribute, and the DataStore itself takes care of all the details around making the CRUD requests. The second line, as shown in Listing 3.21, uses the DataStore to display our data in a table that has CRUD operations.

Listing 3.21   Defining a DataGrid

```
<div dojoType="zero.grid.DataGrid" id="thegrid"
    visibleFields="url,name,category"
    store="bookmarkdata"
    style="width: 500px; height: 300px;"></div>
```

In this line, the DataGrid uses the `store` attribute to retrieve data to display. We've tailored this DataGrid to show only the data columns we're interested in using the `visibleField` attribute. Point your browser to http://localhost:8080/dojo.html to take a look at your newly created Dojo client (see Figure 3.7).

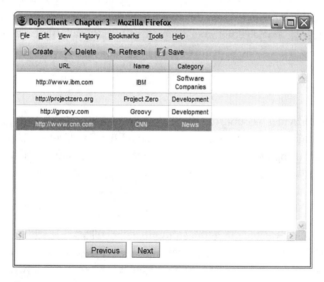

Figure 3.7   Dojo client

As you can see, the DataGrid provides all the standard CRUD operations and a nice table format for our data.

Conclusion

In this chapter, we've taken the first steps toward building real applications with WebSphere sMash. We learned about the application directory layout and how it is structured to make your applications easy to develop and maintain. We learned about how straightforward it is to create RESTful services using ZRM, Groovy, Java, and PHP. Finally, we learned how to create some clients for our REST services. Throughout this book, we'll revisit and examine, in more depth, many of the parts of what we've skimmed over here.

## CHAPTER 4

Configuration Files Explained

In the previous chapter, we talked about favoring convention over configuration. In this chapter, we discuss what to do when you need to override convention and tell the system or your application how to behave. This chapter describes exactly how to do that in the WebSphere sMash environment. This chapter gives you the "tools" and the know-how to configure the WebSphere sMash environment and your applications.

Configuration in WebSphere sMash can be roughly categorized as affecting either the application or the environment, as shown in Figure 4.1. The list of files shown is not exhaustive; it merely shows the files we will be discussing in this chapter. We defer discussion of some types of configuration, such as database, PHP, and security, to chapters that deal specifically with those subjects. In this chapter, we focus on creating custom configuration data for your application and on configuring the runtime environment.

Application Configuration

The following sections concern the settings that are specific to a single application. The files and settings involved are located within the application directory tree.

Global Context and zero.config

WebSphere sMash applications consist of a collection of related but separate modules that respond to application and user request events. All data for these events is stored in a global data structure called the *Global Context (GC)*. Although we discuss the Global Context in detail in Chapter 5, "Global Context," it is important to understand its role in configuration. The Global Context is a URI-addressable tree with predefined root nodes called *zones*. Each zone has a particular purpose. One of these zones is used for application configuration. It is called, naturally, the *config zone*, and entries in this zone are addressed using the pattern /config/<path>.

The config zone is populated at runtime by processing `zero.config` files stored in the `config` directories of WebSphere sMash modules. The majority of configuration you need to worry about as a developer of WebSphere sMash applications is contained in the `zero.config` file. Every WebSphere sMash application or module has a `zero.config` file by default, even if it's empty. When a WebSphere sMash application starts, the `zero.config` files for the application, and all its dependencies, are merged to populate the config zone of the Global Context for the application. The application can query the appropriate Global Context URI to find the configuration values it needs.

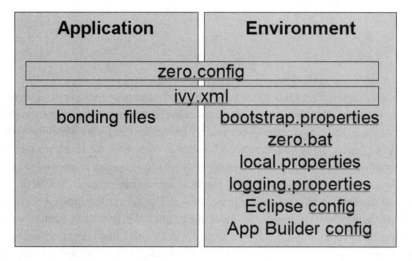

Figure 4.1   WebSphere sMash configuration

WebSphere sMash is intended to be a dynamic, script-oriented environment. As such, most configuration changes are picked up automatically when a new request comes in to the application. An application restart is not usually required.

Custom Configuration Data

For most applications, you will have some custom configuration data that you need to read from somewhere. `zero.config` is the place to put your application's custom configuration data. This file has a flexible, easy-to-use format for specifying configuration data. Users of your application will also know where to look for your configuration data, because most application configuration is consolidated in this file.

From an initial glance, the `zero.config` file looks to be a collection of key/value pairs. If you look a little closer, however, you see that it is actually a sequence of modifications to the Global Context. Each entry in the `zero.config` file consists of a Global Context key, an append or set operation, and a JSON-legal entity. The Global Context is a hierarchy of URIs pointing to JSON values, arrays, or objects. JSON values can be numbers, quoted strings, or one of the literals: *true*, *false*, or *null*. Quoted strings can use single or double quotes. You can make assignments with any of these types using the = operator or append to arrays and objects using the += operator. See Listing 4.1 for an example.

Listing 4.1   Example Assignments

```
# Comments begin with a hash mark
/config/myapp/myvar = 'test'
/config/myapp/myarray = [ 'value1', 'value2', 'value3' ]
/config/myapp/myobject = { 'attr1':100,'attr2':'hello','attr3':false }

/config/myapp/myarray += [ 'value4', 'value5','value6' ]
/config/myapp/myobject += { 'attr4':true, 'attr5':null, 'attr6':500 }
```

There are a few important rules about how these operations are processed. The statements in the zero.config for the application are processed first in sequential order, followed by statements in the zero.config files for the application's dependencies. During this processing, the first assignment for a URI wins; all other assignments are ignored. This approach ensures that your application wins when it overrides config values that are specified in dependencies. For objects, you can only append an attribute that hasn't already been set.

With the concepts of overrides, operators, arrays, and objects, you have a lot of flexibility in defining your application's configuration. If you are developing a module for use by others, you can offer extensibility through configuration. For example, someone extending your module could decorate one of your configuration objects with additional attributes that are then processed by an additional handler that is chained to yours. You could also create a wrapper application that contains database information for a specific test environment that overrides the local development database.

Variable Substitution

The zero.config file supports variable substitution within the file. This feature is useful if you have repetitive paths in your configuration or if your configuration needs to be more dynamic. These text substitutions are processed at configuration load time. In your zero.config file, you can set a substitution variable as follows:

```
<variableName> = <Global Context URI or JSON entity>
```

For example:

```
my_data = "/config/myapp"
```

You can then reference this elsewhere by using the syntax `${variableName}`. You can also reference a location in the Global Context directly using the syntax `${Global Context URI}`— for example:

```
${my_data}/myVar = "value1"
${my_data}/myVar2 = 400
${my_data}/myVar3 = ${/config/http/port}
```

Include Files

If your configuration is complex, you may want to partition your configuration by topics. Sometimes you need to include configuration information from an external file into your application's `zero.config`. For both of these cases, include files can be used. For example, WebSphere sMash provides a configuration template for security configuration for your application. To include a configuration template, WebSphere sMash provides an *include* directive. It takes the following form:

```
@include "<file name>" [JSON object of variables to define]
```

For example:

```
@include "test/template.config" {
    "param1" : "value1",
    "param2" : "value2"
}
```

The filename parameter is relative to the location of the current config file. The virtual file system is used, so files from dependencies can be included as well. If you want to locate a file in a specific dependency's directory, you can use a GC variable of the form, as follows:

```
${/config/dependencies/<dependency name>}
```

For example:

```
@include "${/config/dependencies/foo}/config/template.config"
{
    "param1" : "value1",
    "param2" : "value2"
}
```

The optional parameters in the include statement are defined as variables for use by the `include` file. The `include` file can reference them just like other variables, such as `${param1}` or `${param2}`.

WebSphere sMash security uses include files for configuration. See Chapter 9, "Security Model," for more information.

Handler Configuration

In the last chapter, we introduced the notion of event handlers. Usually, the default REST handler naming convention is sufficient to route events to your handler. However, if you want to configure nested resources, such as `/resources/users/1234/bookmarks/2002`, you need to configure a *bonding* file.

A bonding file is created with your `/app/resources` directory with the same name as your handler with a `.bnd` extension. In the preceding example, you might have the files shown in Table 4.1.

Table 4.1 Handler/Bonding Files

File	Description
/app/resources/users.groovy	Handler for users resources
/app/resources/bookmarks.groovy	Handler for bookmarks resources
/app/resources/bookmarks.bnd	Bonding file to nest bookmarks within users

The bonding file contains pseudo-code for your URI path. `bookmarks.bnd` would have the following content, based on the preceding URI structure:

```
/resources/users
/resources/users/bookmarks
```

Note that we provided the URI for users and bookmarks. Without the first line, we would not be able to handle events for the *users* resources independently of events associated with the *bookmarks* resources.

The `<handler>/<id>` pattern is implied in the bonding file. In your handler code, you can access the IDs through a Global Context URI generated in the *request* zone by concatenating the handler name and `Id`. For example, given the request URI, `/resources/users/1234/bookmarks/2002`, the following GC URI values are set:

```
/request/params/usersId = 1234
/request/params/bookmarksId = 2002
```

If, however, your desired URI path does not follow the WebSphere sMash convention of `/resources/{handler}/{id}`, you can configure a different path sequence in one of two ways. The first is to configure a bonding file; the second is to explicitly declare your handler in the `zero.config` file.

However, some handlers (such as the WebSphere sMash authentication handlers) require configuration. You might also want to create your own custom handler that is only invoked under certain conditions. If, for example, your desired URI path does not follow the WebSphere sMash convention of `/resources/{handler}/{id}`, you can configure a different path sequence.

Listing 4.2 displays an example event handler declaration, which adds to the existing list of handlers.

Listing 4.2 Example Event Handler Declaration

```
/config/handlers += [{
"events" : "GET",
"handler" : "myhandler.groovy",
"conditions": "/request/path == /myhandler|",
"instanceData" : { " testparm" : "testval" }
}
```

events is a JSON string for a single event, or a JSON array for a list of events. Valid values are as follows:

```
[ "GET", "PUT", "POST", "DELETE", "requestBegin", "re-
   questEnd", "log" ]
```

handler is a JSON string that specifies a handler file. The string can include a relative path for a Groovy script, Groovy template, or PHP script. For Groovy and PHP scripts, the path is relative to the `/app/scripts` directory. For Groovy templates, the path is relative to the `/app/views` directory. If the handler is a Java class, specify the full Java class name, like `com.myco.MyHandler.class`.

conditions is an optional expression that further filters events based on input values from the Global Context. A typical usage is to check the `/request/path` against some value. The event is passed to the handler only if it is one of the specified events and the specified condition evaluates to true. The `conditions` expression takes one of the forms shown in Listing 4.3.

Listing 4.3 Conditions Expression

```
<GC URI> == <selector pattern>
<GC URI> != <selector pattern>
<GC URI> =~ <Java regular expression>
<GC URI> !~ <Java regular expression>
!(condition)
(condition1) && (condition2)
(condition1) || (condition2)
```

The selector pattern syntax is typically specified in one of two ways: using a vertical bar or a variable substitution. The vertical bar ends a pattern match and creates the delineation between the matched URI and the request path info. If you need to match a path segment in the middle of a URI, you can use a variable substitution with braces. If you need even more complex matching, you can use a Java regular expression. When the event is routed to the handler, values will be set in the *event zone* of the Global Context corresponding to the matching URI segments. Table 4.2 displays some example conditions and how they are evaluated.

instanceData is an optional JSON object that is set as `/event/instanceData` in the Global Context.

Table 4.2 Sample Event Zone Conditions

Condition	Sample /request/path	Global Context URI	Value
"/request/path == /a/b|"	/a/b/c/d/e	/event/matchedURI	/a/b
		/event/pathInfo	/c/d/e

"/request/path == /a/b/{somevar}/c/d"	/a/b/foo/c/d	/event/matchedURI	/a/b
		/event/pathInfo	/c/d/e
		/event/somevar	foo
"/request/path =~ /a/b/.*"	/a/b/c/d	/event/matchedURI	/a/b
		/event/pathInfo	/c/d/e

Dependency Management with Ivy

In the last chapter, we introduced the WebSphere sMash dependency management system, which is based on an Apache project called Ivy. WebSphere sMash applications and libraries are packaged into Ivy *modules*, which are ZIP files containing code, and an Ivy metadata file that describes the package and the modules it requires. The Ivy metadata file is called an "Ivy file," and is always named ivy.xml. The modules that are required by the package are called *dependencies*.

From a packaging perspective, there is little difference between an application and a dependency. An application can be distributed as a module. For example, the WebSphere sMash samples are applications packaged as Ivy modules and distributed through an Ivy repository. Ivy modules are created by running the package command against an application. When the package is created, it can be published to an Ivy repository or distributed through other means.

Ivy Modules

An Ivy module is a ZIP file that is described by an ivy.xml metadata file. In a WebSphere sMash module, the ivy.xml file is embedded in the ZIP file in the /config directory. When the module is published to an Ivy repository, the ivy.xml file is extracted.

Ivy Files

Listing 4.4 shows the fields within an Ivy file.

Listing 4.4   Sample Ivy File

```
<ivy-module version="1.3">
<info module="Bookmarks" organisation="zero" revision="1.0.0">
  <license name="type of license" url="http://license.page"/>
  <ivyauthor name="author name" url="http://authors.home.page"/>
  <description homepage="http://module.description.page"/>
</info>
<publications>
  <artifact type="zip"/>
</publications>
```

```
<dependencies>
  <dependency org="zero" name="zero.core" rev="[1.0.0.0, 3.0.0.0["/>
</dependencies>
</ivy-module>
```

These fields are as follows:

- **ivy-module version**—It is important to note that the "version" attribute here refers to the Ivy version, not the version of this module. The default value of 1.3 should not be changed.

- **info**—The info stanza contains metadata about the package.

- **module**—The module attribute specifies the name of the module. By WebSphere sMash convention, the module name is identical to the application's root directory. The module name can contain alphanumeric characters and periods. Most WebSphere sMash modules have a module name that begins with zero., such as zero.core.

- **organisation**—The organisation attribute specifies the name of the organization that created the module. WebSphere sMash defaults this attribute to zero.

- **revision**—The revision attribute specifies the version number of this particular module. When other packages declare a dependency on this module, they specify a revision range that is compared against the revision attribute of matching modules. WebSphere sMash uses a four-digit revision scheme for its modules, but the default for user applications is three digits.

- **license, ivyauthor, description**—These fields are attributes that are fairly self-explanatory. The values are provided for informational purposes only. WebSphere sMash does not use these attributes.

- **publications**—The publications stanza refers to the type of files that are described by this Ivy file. In WebSphere sMash, you do not need to modify this list.

- **dependencies**—The dependencies stanza lists patterns that describe the modules on which this module depends. There is one *dependency* stanza for each module.

- **org**—The organization name of the required module.

- **name**—The name of the required module.

- **rev**—A pattern describing the acceptable range of revisions for this dependency.

Revision patterns generally take the following form:

```
[lower-bound, upper-bound]
```

The left bracket before the lower-bound means "everything greater than or equal to lower-bound." The left bracket after the upper-bound means "everything up to but *not* including the upper-bound." A right bracket would include the upper-bound. You can leave off the upper-bound and ending bracket if you only want to include modules greater than or equal to the lower bound.

The best way to specify this range is to use the same pattern as specified by the module that you are depending on. For example, if the child module uses three-stanza revisions (for example, `1.0.0`), you would specify your dependency as `[1.0.0,2.0.0]`. If it uses four-stanza revisions (for example, `1.0.0.0`), you would specify your dependency as `[1.0.0.0,2.0.0.0]`. When WebSphere sMash searches for dependencies matching the pattern, it does a numerical comparison on each individual stanza. If an individual stanza contains a letter, a string compare is used instead. The following example show how different version numbers would be compared:

```
1.0.0 < 1.0.0.0 < 1.0.0.0.29102 < 1.0.0.0.29102B
```

Resolution and Resolvers

After you have declared your application's dependencies, they need to be *resolved*. "Resolving dependencies" means telling WebSphere sMash to find specific versions of modules that match the dependency patterns declared in the Ivy file. WebSphere sMash searches a series of *local* and *remote repositories* for matching modules.

Local repositories are repositories on your local file system. They are simply directory structures that follow the Ivy format. In general, you shouldn't need to understand the format of a repository. The repository structure is managed by the WebSphere sMash tooling. Repositories can contain multiple revisions of the same module.

By default, the WebSphere sMash repository is stored in a directory called "zero-repository" under your WebSphere sMash command-line installation directory, such as c:\sMash\zero\zero-repository. Under the zero-repository directory, you will have one or two directories named "stable" and "experimental," depending on which version of the WebSphere sMash CLI you installed. The "stable" and "experimental" branches are *module groups*. Module groups are collections of version-compatible modules. "stable" contains modules that were downloaded from a stable, fully tested remote repository, whereas "experimental" contains modules that were downloaded from the most recently published remote repository.

Remote repositories come in two flavors: Zero repositories and Maven repositories. Zero repositories are Ivy-formatted repositories. Maven repositories are structured and packaged according to the Apache Maven specifications. Many Apache projects, such as Apache Commons, Xerces, and Xalan, are packaged and published in Maven repositories. WebSphere sMash can locate modules in both kinds of repositories.

Remote Zero repositories look like local repositories, except that they are HTTP-accessible. The preconfigured remote repositories are all published on www.projectzero.org. The list of remote Zero repositories at the time of this printing is shown in Table 4.3.

Note that the URL for the experimental module group will change as newer versions of sMash are released.

Table 4.3   Remote Zero Repositories

Version	Module Group Name	URL
1.0.x	stable	https://www.projectzero.org/sMash/1.0.x/repo/
1.1.x	stable	https://www.projectzero.org/sMash/1.1.x/repo/
Latest	experimental	https://www.projectzero.org/zero/monza/latest/repo/

The default Maven repository is located at the following:

```
http://repo1.maven.org/maven2/
```

To see information about your current local repository, such as its location on your local file system and which module groups are available, you can execute the following from the Web-Sphere sMash CLI directory:

```
zero repository info
```

This command will also tell you which module group is currently being used by the CLI. The CLI can only use one module group at a time. Any CLI commands will execute from modules in the currently active module group. Likewise, any applications created will be created using modules from the currently active module group. To see which module group an application is using, you can execute the following command from the application's directory:

```
zero modulegroup info
```

You can see which specific modules a module group contains by executing the following:

```
zero modulegroup list
```

If you want to use multiple module groups for different versions of your application, such as a stable and experimental version, you must make sure your CLI is pointing to the correct module group. You must switch the CLI to use the new module group:

```
zero modulegroup switch <modulegroupname>
```

After switching the command line, you can create the application using the `create` command. You can also use the `modulegroup switch` command from within an application's directory to switch the application to a new module group. In this case, the application will be resolved again against the new module group. You will probably need to run zero update to pick up compatible versions of modules from the new module group.

NOTE   The preceding instructions apply to CLI users. If you are using App Builder, module group switching is handled for you. You need to specify only the correct module group on the application creation dialog. If you are using Eclipse, the module group can be selected through the WebSphere sMash Preferences dialog.

Remote Resolvers

When you executed the `zero modulegroup info` command, you may have noticed that the list of *resolvers* was displayed. Resolvers are CLI components that are responsible for matching modules in a particular location or locations. Understanding the different resolvers will help you understand how WebSphere sMash finds dependencies for your application.

- **chain resolver**—Simply executes multiple resolvers in a particular order
- **zero resolver**—Searches a remote Ivy repository, typically stored on www.projectzero.org
- **maven resolver**—Searches a remote Maven repository

Local Resolvers

- **workspace resolver**—Looks for modules that are peers to the application that is being resolved. The workspace resolver executes first in the local resolvers. Note that the revision number in the ivy.xml does not matter to the workspace resolver. The workspace resolver considers the module name to be sufficient for a match. This behavior is of primary benefit to Eclipse users who are developing multiple related modules in a single Eclipse workspace.
- **userhome resolver**—The standard resolver that searches the application's module group in the local repository.

The first time you invoke "resolve" on an application, it executes the local resolvers followed by the remote resolvers, until all dependencies are resolved. The order looks like the following:

```
workspace resolver > userhome resolver > zero resolver > maven
resolver
```

During the resolve, the first matching module that is found for each pattern is copied into your local repository under the appropriate module group. The resolvers will resolve nested dependencies as well and inform you of any conflicts. After the resolve has completed successfully, the versions of modules that were found are written into a file called within the application at

```
.zero/private/resolved.properties
```

If you run a resolve against the same application again, it will attempt to find the specific versions of modules described in the `resolved.properties` file rather than use pattern matching. Furthermore, only the local repositories will be searched. If the CLI cannot find these versions, the resolve command will fail. You will be instructed to perform a *zero update* instead.

The purpose of the `zero update` command is to update your application to point to the latest modules in your local repository that match the patterns declared in your ivy.xml. However, what you probably want is to first update the modules in your local repository and then update your application to point to those new modules. This procedure requires executing two commands within your application's directory, as follows:

```
zero modulegroup update
zero update
```

If you want to see a detailed report of the modules that were resolved for your application, there is an XML file in your application's /reports directory with a name that matches the pattern `zero-<module>-default.xml`. If you open up this XML file with a web browser, you will get a nicely formatted report describing the specific versions of modules that were found and which resolver found them.

Finally, if your resolve or update accidentally breaks your application, you can undo the damage. WebSphere sMash maintains a history of the last `resolve` or `update` command. To undo the last command, execute the following:

```
zero rollback
```

Environment Configuration

We have discussed how to create your application configuration parameters in `zero.config` and how to declare your application's dependencies in `ivy.xml`. We will now look at how to configure your application for different environments, and at what additional configuration information your application can retrieve at runtime.

WebSphere sMash core modules provide a number of configuration URIs that are useful to developers. Some of these URIs should be set in the `zero.config` file because they are read-only at run-time. Other URIs can be read or set programmatically from your application using the Global Context APIs. The URI's type and default value, if any, are shown in parentheses below (type/default).

Useful Information About Your Application

The following configuration URIs cannot be set in `zero.config` or using the Global Context API, but they are available for your application to read as part of the config zone of the Global Context:

- **/config/name** (String)—This URI provides the name of the application. It might be important to read this value rather than use a hard-coded string, because someone could have created a wrapper around your application, giving it a different name.

- **/config/dependencies** (List)—This URI points to a list of the module names of your application's dependencies, such as `["zero.core", "zero.data"]`.

- **/config/dependencies/<moduleName>** (String)—By adding the `moduleName` of the dependency to the URI, you can retrieve the directory for that dependency.

Runtime Configuration

`zero.config` contains a number of runtime configuration URIs that are set when your application is started. Most of these values can be read (but not set) in your application using the Global Context API:

- **`/config/http/port`** (Long/8080)—Set the value of this URI in `zero.config` to configure the port that the application will listen on for HTTP requests. The value can be set to –1 if you only want the application to respond to HTTPS requests.

- **`/config/http/ipAddress`** (String)—You can set the specific IP address of the WebSphere sMash HTTP server in `zero.config` using this URI.

- **`/config/https/port`** (Long/0)—Set the value of this URI in `zero.config` to configure the port that the application will listen on for HTTPS requests. The default HTTPS port is 0, which means HTTPS is not open.

- **`/config/https/ipAddress`** (String)—You can set the specific IP address of the WebSphere sMash HTTPS server in `zero.config` using this URI.

- **`/config/runtime/mode`** (String / "development")—The default for this URI is "development". When you are ready to move your application to production mode, this value should be changed to "production" in `zero.config`. Changing the value to "production" changes request timeouts, maximum numbers of requests, and application recycle frequencies to be more suited to a production environment.

- **`/config/contextRoot`** (String)—This URI sets the context root for the application. The value is a URI path starting with a slash. The URI should be set in `zero.config`, but it can be read by an application using the Global Context API. With the context root set, requests to your application will take the form `http://myhost:8080/<contextRoot>/index.html`.

- **`/config/externalUriPrefix`** (String)—This URI can be set in `zero.config` to specify the full scheme, hostname, and port (for example, `http://www.ibm.com:8080`) for use in generating absolute URIs when the application is deployed behind a reverse proxy. The WebSphere sMash URIUtils API described in Chapter 11, "Framework Components," uses this field to generate absolute URIs.

- **`/config/id`** (String)—This URI contains the process ID of the running application. This information is useful for debugging.

Response Configuration

WebSphere sMash applications have some default behaviors for returning responses to web requests. The default responses can be overridden in `zero.config` to help you debug or optimize your application. You can also set behaviors for returning responses based on browsers requesting resources in different languages:

- **/config/json/prettyPrint** (boolean/false)—If this value is set to `true` in `zero.config`, WebSphere sMash will render JSON responses in a more legible multi-line format rather than a single-line format. These "pretty print" responses are easier to read in a browser or file editor and are useful for debugging.

- **/config/compressResponse** (boolean/false)—If you want to use gzip compression of responses, set this URI to `true` in `zero.config`. The client request will need to set the header `Accept-Encoding: gzip,deflate`.

- **/config/exitCode** (Integer/0)—If you are writing a config event handler for your application, you can set the `exitCode` to a nonzero value when you encounter an error loading the configuration. The application will terminate after the handler exits.

- **/config/fileserver/contentNegotiation** (boolean/false)—When this value is set to `true` in `zero.config`, the Accept-Language request header is used as a file extension to find an appropriate file to serve if the requested resource does not exist. The value of the Accept-Language header is appended to the filename for the search. For example, if Accept-Language was set to en, a request for sample.html would search for `sample.html` followed by `sample.html.en`.

- **/config/fileserver/defaultLanguage** (String/server language)—When content negotiation is enabled, the final option for locating an appropriate resource is to append the default language as a file extension. For example, if `Accept-Language` is set to ja and `defaultLanguage` is set to en, the search order for sample.html would be `sample.html`, `sample.html.ja`, and `sample.html.en`.

- **/config/fileserver/directoryBrowsing** (boolean/false)—If directory browsing is enabled, you will be able to use a web browser to browse virtual directories under your app's public directory. For example, `http://myhost:8080/test` would list the files and directories in the virtual directory `/public/test` of the running application.

- **/config/fileserver/expires/<.extension>** (Long/0)—The default cache expiration for static served files is 0 seconds. You can specify a maximum age for files with a particular file extension using this Global Context URI. The value is set in the Cache-Control header for files of that type. For example, putting the following statement in `zero.config` would set the max-age for .html files to 180 seconds:

```
/config/fileserver/expires/.html=180
```

- **/config/fileserver/setEtag** (boolean/true)—Setting this flag in `zero.config` causes the eTag response header to be set for served files for caching purposes.

Command-Line Interface (CLI) Config

When you first download the WebSphere sMash CLI, you get a small ZIP file with just a few files in it. This is the bootstrap code for the CLI. The first time you execute *any* zero command (even *help* or nothing), the bootstrap code will prime the local repository from the remote repository defined in `/config/bootstrap.properties`. Although you can change the information specified in `bootstrap.properties`, you will not typically need to do so unless you are using your own enterprise repository. When the CLI is bootstrapped, the `bootstrap.properties` file will not be used again.

If you are using a proxy to access the Internet, you will need to configure the proxy settings by editing the `ZERO_OPTS` line in the `zero.bat` file, as described in Chapter 1, "Installing the IBM WebSphere sMash CLI."

There are a number of other interesting configuration files for the CLI, as follows:

- **local.properties**—Enables you to set HTTP timeouts and the location of your local Ivy repository
- **logging.properties**—Enables you to set logging and tracing levels and log and trace file-handling options for the CLI

App Builder Configuration

The App Builder configuration can be found in your `<zerohome>/installed/appbuilder/config` directory. The most commonly changed configuration parameter in the App Builder's `zero.config` is the port on which AppBuilder runs. Listing 4.5 is a default `zero.config` file for App Builder.

Listing 4.5   Sample zero.config File

```
# HTTP port (default is 8080)
#/config/http/port = 8080

# Runtime mode (default is "production")
#/config/runtime/mode="development"
```

Eclipse Configuration

The WebSphere sMash Eclipse plugin requires you to configure the location of a CLI before use. This configuration is found under Window > Preferences in Eclipse. The `Zero home` field should point to the zero directory of your CLI installation (see Figure 4.2).

After the CLI location is provided, a list of available module groups are displayed in the drop-down list. Module groups are part of WebSphere sMash's Ivy dependency management system. See the section on Ivy dependencies in this chapter for more information on module groups.

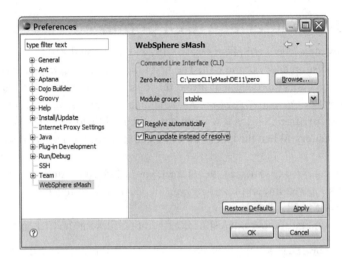

Figure 4.2   Eclipse preferences

If the Resolve Automatically check box is selected, modules in the workspace will automatically be resolved when a change is detected that would require resolution. Examples of changes that require resolution are changes to a module's ivy.xml file or creation of a new module.

If the Run Update Instead of Resolve check box is selected, resolves will automatically find the latest module dependencies in the local repository rather than the ones that were recorded during the last successful resolve.

For new users of WebSphere sMash, we recommend selecting both of these check boxes. More information on dependency resolution can be found in the Ivy dependencies section of this chapter.

JVM Configuration

WebSphere sMash uses a utility called the Zero Socket Opener (ZSO) to manage the life cycle of WebSphere sMash applications. When ZSO starts a WebSphere sMash application, it starts a new Java Virtual Machine (JVM™). You can provide ZSO with Java command-line arguments for your application by using the /config/zso/jvmargs Global Context URI in your zero.config. The format is a JSON array of properties to pass to the JVM—for example,

```
/config/zso/jvmargs += [
    "-Duser.home=/home/zero"
]
```

NOTE   The WebSphere sMash Eclipse plugin does not use ZSO to launch applications. Instead, Eclipse launches the application JVM directly using a Run profile. So, you can pass JVM arguments as part of the Run profile in Eclipse.

Overriding Configuration Parameters

WebSphere sMash provides a number of ways to override configuration parameters. If you need to override a configuration parameter in a dependency, the easiest way is to set the parameter in your application's `zero.config`. As mentioned previously, the application's `zero.config` is processed first, and subsequent assignments to the same Global Context URI will be ignored.

There are times when you may want to override a configuration parameter in an application you are deploying, but you don't want to modify the application's `zero.config` file itself. For example, if the application is stored in your local repository as a packaged module, you can take advantage of WebSphere sMash's capability to update dependencies to retrieve updates to the application whenever they are available. In another scenario, you have unzipped an application into a local directory, and you want to isolate configuration changes from the application directory itself.

The first mechanism to override the configuration is to create a wrapper application. This procedure consists of creating a new application that includes the application you want to override as a dependency. You can name the new application whatever you'd like, but you should create it in a peer directory to the application you want to override. For example, if your apps are stored in a `myapps` directory, you can create an app called *wrapper* by executing the following from the CLI:

```
cd myapps
zero create wrapper linkto myorg:myapp
```

`linkto` is a special instruction that tells the `create` command to create a default application with the specified module as a dependency. If you look at `wrapper`'s `ivy.xml` file, you will see this dependency declaration:

```
<dependency name="myapp" org="myorg" rev="+"/>
```

Because we didn't specify a specific revision for the link, a + was inserted in the dependency. + means "the latest" in a dependency declaration.

The `create` command executes a resolve after the create completes. `myapp` could exist in the `myapps` directory as a peer to `wrapper`, in which case it would be found by the workspace resolver. If `myapp` were in the local repository, it would be found by the default local resolver. If `myapp` existed only in a remote repository, it would be found by a remote resolver.

Regardless of where `myapp` is found, you now have a wrapper application with which to work. You can edit `wrapper`'s `zero.config` file to override the desired parameters from `myapp`. Then, you can start the `wrapper` application, which will behave just like `myapp` only with your new configuration parameters. There is another benefit to this approach. Because `wrapper` is a full application with full virtual directory support across its dependencies, you can add things like HTML or CSS files to `wrapper` to override or enhance the original versions in `myapp`.

Another option for overriding configuration parameters is to specify pre- or post-configuration files as startup parameters for your application. Pre files are processed before any other `zero.config` files. Post files are processed after all other `zero.config` files. For example:

```
zero start -pre c:\test\before.config -post
    c:\test\after.config
```

Reverse Proxy Server Configuration

Every WebSphere sMash application runs on its own port. If you are running multiple WebSphere sMash applications in a production environment, you probably will want to present a single-port view of all your applications. You can do this by configuring a reverse proxy server in front of your WebSphere sMash applications.

We mentioned the `contextRoot` and `externalUriPrefix` configuration URIs in the previous section on Common Configuration URIs. Both of these parameters should be configured when using a reverse proxy server.

A full discussion of configuring a reverse proxy server is beyond the scope of this book. The WebSphere sMash Developers Guide contains an excellent description of how to set up a reverse proxy for WebSphere sMash on an Apache server using the `mod_proxy` module. We recommend that you refer to this documentation for more detail on this topic.

Conclusion

In this chapter, we introduced the primary ways to configure WebSphere sMash and WebSphere sMash applications. We discussed configuration of the CLI, Eclipse, and applications. We talked about dependency management and virtual directories. However, we purposefully deferred discussion of some configuration topics to later chapters where they are discussed in context to the topic being covered.

## CHAPTER 5

Global Context

The global context is a part of WebSphere sMash that provides unified access to environmental, application, and user-specific data. The global context consists of several zones, each forming a namespace that is rooted at "/". Each zone serves a particular purpose, providing data for the application that is applicable for a certain scope. In this chapter, we look at each of these zones in turn and then learn how to access these zones in Java, Groovy, and PHP.

Zones

The global context is divided into several zones by default. The standard set of zones includes the config, request, event, tmp, app, connection, user, and storage zones. These zones provide a wide range of scoped data and allow applications to add their own information. Zones come in two flavors: persistent and non-persistent. Persistent zones store their data in a data store, such as a database, so that it is available between restarts of the application. Non-persistent zones are not serialized to disk, so the data stored in these zones are available only for the lifetime of the application.

Non-Persistent Zones

There are five default non-persistent zones: config, request, event, tmp, and connection zones.

Config Zone (/config)

Data in the config zone is loaded from the application's configuration files. The config zone data is available for the entire lifetime of the application and is globally visible. The config zone data is modifiable, but changes are effective only for the lifetime of the application and will be reinitialized from the configuration files when the application is restarted. The config zone contains many useful variables including, but not limited to, the variables described in Table 5.1.

Table 5.1   Config Zone Variables

Config Variable	Description
/config/accessLogging	Contains a boolean value letting us know whether access logging is enabled
/config/appLogDir	Contains the file system path to the application's log directory
/config/contextRoot	Contains a string value that is the context root of the application. The application may define any context root it wants. If none is defined, the default is slash
/config/defaultContentType	Contains the default response data type to be used in responses
/config/http/port	Contains the port on which this application is configured and is often used when creating HTTP URLs to resources within the application
/config/https/port	Contains the port on which this application is configured and is often used when creating HTTPS URLs to resources within the application
/config/name	Contains the name of the application as configured
/config/root	Contains the file system path to the root directory of the application
/config/zeroHome	Contains the file system path to the zero home

In addition to the standard configuration variables, you may also store application variables in the config zone. Configuration variables can be set and modified through the zero.config file, which is in the config directory of your application.

Request Zone (/request)

All scripts in WebSphere sMash run in the context of an HTTP request. The request zone provides access to all HTTP request data. The request zone data is available only to the thread processing the HTTP request. This zone includes all incoming and outgoing data. Many of the request variables will be familiar to experienced web developers. The variables include, but are not limited to, those shown in Table 5.2.

Table 5.2 Request Zone Variables

Request Variable	Description
/request/locales	Contains a list of locales preferred by the client.
/request/cookies/in	Contains the list of cookies sent by the client.
/request/cookies/out	Contains the cookies to be sent to the client by the application.
/request/headers/in	Contains a list of headers sent by the client.
/request/method	Contains the HTTP method used by the client, such as GET or POST.
/request/protocol	Contains the HTTP request protocol.
/request/queryString	Contains the query string part of the URL passed to the application by the client.
/request/remoteAddress	Contains the IP address of the client that made the request to the application.
/request/remoteHost	Contains the host name of the client that made the request to the application.
/request/status	Contains the HTTP status code that is sent back to the client.
/request/params/<handlerName>Id	Contains the ID of a retrieve operation. For example, http://resources/person/1 would have "1" in the /request/params/personId location.
/request/params/<param name>	Contains the value of parameter from the query string.

Event Zone (/event)

The event zone is visible to any component that is subscribed to process an event. The data is available to the thread processing the event for the duration of the event. WebSphere sMash is an event-driven architecture in which handlers process events in a loosely coupled manner.

Custom event handlers give developers an extension point to WebSphere sMash. Custom event handlers are registered in the /config/handlers variable located in the config zone, specifically zero.config:

- **/event/_name**—Contains the name of the event that has fired.
- **/event/isAuthorized**—Contains a boolean value set during the secure event processing indicating if the user is considered authorized.

Tmp Zone (/tmp)

The tmp zone is a temporary zone that applications and system handlers can use to write temporary data (see Table 5.3). This zone is visible to the entire application and is cleared on restart of
the application. This zone is a good place to keep any scratch data you might use during the processing of requests. It's also not a bad place to keep caches because it is cleared on any restart of
WebSphere sMash. This includes restarts initiated by the Zero Socket Opener (ZSO), which is a
native nanny process that starts and stops the JVM as needed to free up system resources and
such. When your application is restarted, it can be configured using the zero.config file.

Table 5.3   Tmp Zone Variables

Tmp Variable	Description
/tmp/<mycache>	Contains some cache of data you have set up.
/tmp/<myvar>	Contains some volatile global variable that you need elsewhere in your application.

Connection Zone (/connection)

The connection zone is visible only to the thread that is using the Connection API to make and
process a connection. Each request has its own separate view of the connection zone, so there is
no data sharing among threads or requests. This zone is used only when implementing connection handlers and protocol extensions. The data in this zone is available only in the thread that is
using the Connection API (see Table 5.4).

Table 5.4   Connection Zone Variables

Connection Variable	Description
/connection/request/body	Contains the body of the connection request
/connection/request/headers	Contains the request headers for the connection

Persistent Zones

Persistent zones are serialized to a database or another data store. There are three default persistent zones: user, app, and storage. These zones are persistent across server recycles. There are two
serializers provided by WebSphere sMash: a Java serializer that serializes Java objects and a
JSON serializer that serializes JSON objects. The /config/zoneSerializers, defined in the
config zone, contains a hash table that maps zone prefixes to serializers. The three default persistent zones and their respective serializers are listed next.

User Zone (/user)

The user zone is available to all threads of the HTTP session. The HTTP session is identified by the zsessionid found at `/user/zsessionid`. By default, the HTTP session will timeout after 5 minutes of inactivity. Although the session may timeout, the serializable Java objects stored in this zone will persist between restarts of the application.

App Zone (/app)

The app zone data is visible to all threads of the application. This zone provides an open space that the application can use to store serializable Java objects. This zone is persistent across server recycles.

Storage Zone (/storage)

The storage zone data is visible to all threads of the application. This zone allows the application to store JSON objects. This zone is persistent across server recycles.

Accessing the Global Context

There are several operations that can be performed within the global context. Most often, we need to perform CRUD operations on the locations stored within the global context. Variables within the global context are created with `zput` and `zpost` operations. They are retrieved by `zget`, `zlist`, and `zlistAll`. They are updated using `zput` and `zpost`. Finally, they are deleted with `zdelete`. WebSphere sMash also has a few convenience methods designed to help the developer, as we see next.

There is a locking mechanism that allows the global context to enable concurrent access to the persistent zones. By default, the persistent zones are locked on write. One thread at a time holds the lock. The lock blocks all threads and processes until the lock is released. Locking is not support by the non-persistent zones.

For each language, we'll look at four data structures to be stored in the global context:

1. **Objects**—An object is any other serializable object that we might want to store, such as a string or integer.
2. **Lists**—A list is a simple list of values accessible by index.
3. **First element lists**—A first element list is a special list that allows access to the first element in the list without an index.
4. **Maps**—A map is a structure that consists of a list of key/value pairs.

Some of the information presented next is by necessity repetitive. We suggest that you skip to the section containing the language-specific API that you intend to use. The APIs are very similar, but each language-specific API is geared toward a developer familiar with that language.

Java APIs

Objects

zput Method

Objects are the most simple data type to add into the global context. We use the `zput` method to add a single variable into the global context:

```
boolean zput(String location, Object object);
```

The `zput` method places the object in the particular global context location (see Listing 5.1).

NOTE   `zpost` is not supported by objects.

Listing 5.1   The zput Method

```
GlobalContext.zput("/app/string", "string object");
GlobalContext.zput("/app/integer", new Integer(42));
```

In these two lines of code, we've created or replaced a string object and an integer object in the app zone so that we can use it at a later time; the app zone serializes these objects to a data store.

zputs Method

If we have several variables we'd like to place in the global context, we can use the `zputs` method:

```
Map zputs(String location, Map values);
```

This is a convenience method for placing several variables into the global context at once (see Listing 5.2).

Listing 5.2   The zputs Method

```
map.put("foo", "fooValue");
map.put("bar", "barValue");
GlobalContext.zputs("/app", map);
```

The `zputs` method places two variables with values into the app zone: `/app/foo` with a value of `fooValue` and `/app/bar` with a value of `barValue`.

zget Method

To retrieve variables placed in the global context, we use the `zget` method:

```
Object zget(String location [, Object defaultValue ]);
```

The `zget` method retrieves the object in the particular global context location (see Listing 5.3). Optionally, you can provide a default value for the object being retrieved. If a default is not provided and the location is not found, a null is returned.

Listing 5.3 The zget Method

```
String s = (String)GlobalContext.zget("/app/string", "default string");
Integer i = (Integer)GlobalContext.zget("/app/integer");
```

Here we are retrieving a string object with the default value of `"default string"` and an integer object that has no default value.

zdelete Method

To remove variable from the global context, we use `zdelete`:

```
boolean zdelete(String location [, boolean deleteChildren ]);
```

The `zdelete` method deletes the specified location, removing any values stored there.

In Listing 5.4, we are deleting both of the objects we've previously created and updated. The optional `deleteChildren` parameter enables you to delete the entire subtree of locations by specifying true for that parameter. By default, `zdelete` deletes only the specified location and not the entire namespace defined by the location.

Listing 5.4 The zdelete Method

```
GlobalContext.zdelete("/app/string");
GlobalContext.zdelete("/app/integer");
```

zcontains Method

Sometimes code requires that a particular variable be available before executing. We can test the availability of a variable by using the `zcontains` method.

```
boolean zcontains(String location);
```

The `zcontains` method returns a boolean value indicating if the particular variable is available in the global context (see Listing 5.5).

Listing 5.5 The zcontains Method

```
if(GlobalContext.zcontains("/app/string")
{
  //do something
}
```

The zcontains method can be used as a guard code and needs to have particular variables available.

zlist Method

Some applications may require retrieving a list of all available variables with a particular location prefix. To do this, we use the zlist method:

```
List<String> zlist(String locationPrefix [,boolean includePre-
    fix ]);
```

The zlist method returns a list of the variables with the specified prefix (see Listing 5.6).

Listing 5.6   The zlist Method

```
List list = GlobalContext.zlist("/app");
Iterator<String> i = list.iterator();
while(i.hasNext())
{
    String variable = i.next();
    //do something with the variable
}
```

The zlist method returns a list of strings that are currently stored as variables in the app zone. This returns only the top-level app zone variables, such as /app/foo but not /app/foo/bar, for instance. To retrieve all the variables, we use the zlistAll method:

> **NOTE**   The optional includePrefix parameter is true by default for Java.

```
List<String> zlistAll(String locationPrefix [,boolean include-
    Prefix ]);
```

The zlistAll method returns a deep list of all the variables defined by the prefix (see Listing 5.7).

Listing 5.7   The zlistAll Method

```
List list = GlobalContext.zlistAll("/app");
Iterator<String> i = list.iterator();
while(i.hasNext())
{
    String variable = i.next();
    //do something with the variable
}
```

The `zlistAll` method returns a complete list of the variables available in the app zone.

zdump Method

The last method we'll look at is the `zdump` method, which dumps all the variables starting with the location prefix `String`. This is a useful debug mechanism for developers when testing and debugging applications written with WebSphere sMash:

```
String zdump(String locationPrefix);
```

> **NOTE** The optional includePrefix parameter is true by default for Java.

The `zdump` method uses the `toString()` method of the stored objects to render the returned string (see Listing 5.8).

Listing 5.8 The zdump Method

```
GlobalContext.zput("/tmp/dumptest/string", "some string");
GlobalContext.zput("/tmp/dumptest/integer", new Integer(42));
String s = GlobalContext.zdump("/tmp/dumptest");
```

This code snippet places a couple of variables into the tmp zone and then dumps them to a string. You can then serialize this string to a log. This is a very valuable tool for debugging code.

Lists

zput Method

Lists are indexed list of objects. To place a single list variable into the global context, we use the `zput` method:

```
boolean zput(String location, List list);
```

The `zput` method places the object in the particular global context location (see Listing 5.9).

Listing 5.9 The zput Method

```
ArrayList list = new ArrayList();
list.add(new Integer(42));
list.add("string object");
GlobalContext.zput("/tmp/list", list);
```

With this code, we've created a list and then used `zput` to create or replace the list in the tmp zone, so that we can use it at a later time during the course of our application execution. We can replace single elements of our stored list by using #<key> to specify where to place the value:

```
GlobalContext.zput("/tmp/list#1", "new string");
```

This replaces `"string object"` with `"new string"` in our stored list. If we need to add to a list, we must use the `zpost` method.

zpost Method

To append to a list in the global context, we use the `zpost` method:

```
boolean zpost(String location, Object object);
```

The `zpost` method appends the object to the list stored at the given location (see Listing 5.10).

Listing 5.10   The zpost Method

```
ArrayList list = new ArrayList();
GlobalContext.zpost("/tmp/list", list);
GlobalContext.zpost("/tmp/list", "posted string object");
```

Here we've created an empty list and then posted a single element into the list. Notice that we can use the `zpost` method to create the list in the global context, as well as append to an existing list. This method can also be used to append a list to another list (see Listing 5.11).

Listing 5.11   More on the zpost Method

```
ArrayList list = new ArrayList();
GlobalContext.zpost("/tmp/list", list);
GlobalContext.zpost("/tmp/list", "posted string object");
list.add(new Integer(42));
list.add("string object");
GlobalContext.zpost("/tmp/list", list);
```

In this case, we've created an empty list and posted an element to the list stored in the tmp zone. Next, we add some elements to the Java list and then append them to the stored list using a `zpost`. If we have several lists that we'd like to place in the global context, we can use the `zputs` method just like we did with objects.

zputs Method

To place several lists in the global context, we use the `zputs` method:

```
Map zputs(String location, Map lists);
```

This is a convenience method to place several lists into the global context at once (see Listing 5.12).

Listing 5.12   The zputs Method

```
ArrayList slist = new ArrayList();
slist.add("string one");
slist.add("string two");
ArrayList ilist = new ArrayList();
ilist.add(new Integer(1));
ilist.add(new Integer(2));
Map map = new HashMap();
map.put("stringList", slist);
map.put("integerList", ilist);
GlobalContext.zputs("/app", map);
```

The `zputs` method places two variables containing the lists into the app zone: `/app/stringList` with the contents of `slist` and `/app/integerList` with the contents of `ilist`.

zget Method

To retrieve variables placed in the global context, we use the `zget` method:

```
Object zget(String location [, Object defaultValue ]);
```

The `zget` method retrieves the list in the particular global context location. Optionally, you can provide a default value for the list being retrieved. If a default is not provided and the location is not found, a null is returned (see Listing 5.13).

Listing 5.13   The zget Lists

```
List slist = (List)GlobalContext.zget("/app/stringList", new Array-
List());
List ilist = (List)GlobalContext.zget("/app/integerList");
```

Here we are retrieving our string list with a default empty `ArrayList` and our integer list with no default. We can also retrieve individual elements from our list by again using the #<key> notation (see Listing 5.14).

Listing 5.14   The zget Element in a List

```
String s = (String)GlobalContext.zget("/app/stringList#0");
Integer i = (Integer)GlobalContext.zget("/app/integerList#0");
```

This code retrieves the first element of each list.

zdelete Method

To remove a list from the global context, we use `zdelete`:

```
boolean zdelete(String location [, boolean deleteChildren ]);
```

The `zdelete` method deletes the specified location, removing any values stored there (see Listing 5.15).

Listing 5.15   zdelete a List

```
GlobalContext.zdelete("/app/stringList");
GlobalContext.zdelete("/app/integerList");
```

Here we delete both of the lists we've previously created and updated. The optional `deleteChildren` parameter works the same as the object usage of this method. As with `zput`, we can delete single elements from our list by specifying the #<key> in the location (see Listing 5.16).

Listing 5.16   zdelete a List Element

```
GlobalContext.zdelete("/app/stringList#0");
GlobalContext.zdelete("/app/integerList#1");
```

The first `zdelete` removes the first element of the string list, and the second `zdelete` removes the second element of the integer list. Sometimes code requires that a particular list be available before executing. We can test the availability of a list by using the `zcontains` method, the same way we do for objects.

zcontains Method

To test if a list is in the global context, we use the `zcontains` method:

```
boolean zcontains(String location);
```

The `zcontains` method returns a boolean value, indicating whether the particular list is available in the global context (see Listing 5.17).

Listing 5.17   The zcontains Method for a List

```
if(GlobalContext.zcontains("/app/stringList")
{
  //do something
}
```

The `zcontains` method can be used as a guard code that must have particular lists available. Like other list operations, the `zcontains` method can access particular elements of a list by using the #<key> notation (see Listing 5.18).

Listing 5.18 The zcontains Method for a List Element

```
if(GlobalContext.zcontains("/app/stringList#0")
{
  //do something
}
```

This code tests to be sure that the first element in the string list exists before executing some code. The rest of the global context methods (`zlist`, `zlistAll`, and `zdump`) work the same as they do with objects.

FirstElementLists

`FirstElementLists` work very much the same as lists in many cases. However, the first element is operated on by default. The general idea is that these lists operate like stacks. You would normally be operating only on the head of the list, which with a first element list is found at "`<zone or locationPrefix>/list`" instead of at "`<zone or locationPrefix>/list#0`" with a normal list.

zput Method

To put a `FirstElementList` into the global context, we use the `zput` method:

```
boolean zput(String location, List list);
```

The `zput` method places the `FirstElementList` in the particular global context location (see Listing 5.19).

Listing 5.19 Creating a FirstElementArrayList

```
FirstElementArrayList list = new FirstElementArrayList<String>();
list.add("some string");
list.add("string object");
GlobalContext.zput("/tmp/list#*", list);
```

The `FirstElementArrayList` is available in the zero.util package. With this code, we've created a list and then used `zput` to create or replace the list in the tmp zone so that we can use it later during the course of our application execution. Notice that with `FirstElementLists`, we must use the `#*` notation to indicate that we'd like to use a `FirstElementList`. We can replace single elements of our stored list by using `#<key>` to specify where to put the value:

```
GlobalContext.zput("/tmp/list#1", "new string");
```

This replaces "`string object`" with "`new string`" in our stored list. To replace the first item in the list, we don't need to use the `#<key>`. We simply need to use the location:

```
GlobalContext.zput("/tmp/list", "new first item");
```

This replaces the first item in the list. If we need to add to a list, we must use the `zpost` method.

zpost Method

To append to a `FirstElementList` in the global context, we use the `zpost` method:

```
boolean zpost(String location, Object object);
```

The `zpost` method appends the `FirstElementList` to the list stored at the given location (see Listing 5.20).

Listing 5.20   Using zpost to Append to a FirstElementList

```
FirstElementArrayList list = new FirstElementArrayList ();
GlobalContext.zpost("/tmp/list#*", list);
GlobalContext.zpost("/tmp/list", "posted string object");
```

Here we've created an empty list and then posted a single element into the list. This method can also be used to append a list to another list (see Listing 5.21).

Listing 5.21   Using zpost to Append a List to a FirstElementList

```
FirstElementArrayList list = new FirstElementArrayList ();
GlobalContext.zput("/tmp/list/#*", list);
GlobalContext.zpost("/tmp/list", "posted string object");
list.add("string object");
GlobalContext.zpost("/tmp/list#*", list);
```

In this case, we've created an empty list and posted an element to the list stored in the tmp zone. Next, we add some elements to the Java list and then append them to the stored list using a `zpost`. If we have several lists that we'd like to place in the global context, we can use the `zputs` method just like we did with objects.

zputs Method

To append to a `FirstElementList` in the global context, we use the `zpost` method:

```
Map zputs(String location, Map lists);
```

This is another convenient method to place several lists into the global context at once (see Listing 5.22).

Listing 5.22   Using zputs to Put Multiple Lists into the Global Context

```
FirstElementArrayList slist = new ArrayList();
slist.add("string one");
slist.add("string two");
```

```
FirstElementArrayList ilist = new ArrayList();
ilist.add(new Integer(1));
ilist.add(new Integer(2));
Map map = new HashMap();
map.put("stringList#*", slist);
map.put("integerList#*", ilist);
GlobalContext.zputs("/app", map);
```

The `zputs` method places two variables containing the lists into the app zone: `/app/stringList` with the contents of `slist` and `/app/integerList` with the contents of `ilist`.

zget Method

To retrieve variables placed in the global context, we use the `zget` method:

```
Object zget(String location [, Object defaultValue ]);
```

The `zget` method retrieves the list in the particular global context location. Optionally, you can provide a default value for the list being retrieved. If a default is not provided and the location is not found, a null is returned (see Listing 5.23).

Listing 5.23   zget of a FirstElementList

```
List slist = GlobalContext.zget("/app/stringList#*", new ArrayList());
List ilist = GlobalContext.zget("/app/integerList#*");
```

Here we are retrieving our string list with a default empty `ArrayList` and our integer list with no default. We can also retrieve individual elements from our list by again using the #<key> notation (see Listing 5.24).

Listing 5.24   zget of the First Element of a FirstElementList

```
String s = GlobalContext.zget("/app/stringList");
Integer i = GlobalContext.zget("/app/integerList");
```

This code retrieves the first element of each list. It is possible to retrieve the Nth item in the list as well, using the #<key> notation (see Listing 5.25).

Listing 5.25   zget of an Element from a FirstElementList

```
String s = GlobalContext.zget("/app/stringList#1");
Integer i = GlobalContext.zget("/app/integerList#2");
```

This code retrieves the second item in the string list and the third item in the integer list.

zdelete Method

To remove a list from the global context, we use `zdelete`:

```
boolean zdelete(String location [, boolean deleteChildren ]);
```

The `zdelete` method deletes the specified location, removing any values stored there (see Listing 5.26).

Listing 5.26   zdelete of a FirstElementList

```
GlobalContext.zdelete("/app/stringList#*");
GlobalContext.zdelete("/app/integerList#*");
```

Here we delete both of the lists we've previously created and updated. The optional `deleteChildren` parameter works the same as the object usage of this method. As with `zput`, we can delete single elements from our list by specifying the `#<key>` in the location (see Listing 5.27).

Listing 5.27   zdelete of an Element of a FirstElementList

```
GlobalContext.zdelete("/app/stringList");
GlobalContext.zdelete("/app/integerList#1");
```

The first `zdelete` removes the first element of the string list, and the second `zdelete` removes the second element of the integer list. Sometimes code requires that a particular list be available before executing. We can test the availability of a list by using the `zcontains` method, the same way we do for objects.

zcontains Method

To test if a list is in the global context, we use the `zcontains` method:

```
boolean zcontains(String location);
```

The `zcontains` method returns a boolean value indicating whether the particular list is available in the global context (see Listing 5.28).

Listing 5.28   zcontains of a FirstElementList

```
if(GlobalContext.zcontains("/app/stringList#*")
{
  //do something
}
```

The `zcontains` method can be used as a guard code that must have particular lists available. With `FirstElementLists`, we can test the first existence of the first by directly accessing the variable (see Listing 5.29).

Listing 5.29 zcontains of the First Element of a FirstElementList

```
if(GlobalContext.zcontains("/app/stringList")
{
  //do something
}
```

This code tests to verify that the first element in the list exists before executing code. We can test other elements in the list using the #<key> notation (see Listing 5.30).

Listing 5.30 zcontains of an Element from a FirstElementList

```
if(GlobalContext.zcontains("/app/stringList#1")
{
  //do something
}
```

This code tests to see whether the second element in the list exists. The rest of the global context methods (zlist, zlistAll, and zdump) work the same as they do with lists and objects.

Maps

Maps are lists of key/value pairs. To put a single map into the global context, we use the zput method.

zput Method

To put a map into the global context, we use the zput method:

```
boolean zput(String location, Map map);
```

The zput method places the object in the particular global context location (see Listing 5.31).

Listing 5.31 zput of a Map

```
HashMap map = new HashMap();
map.put("integer",new Integer(42));
map.put("string", "string object");
GlobalContext.zput("/tmp/map", map);
```

With this code, we've created a map and then used zput to create or replace the map in the tmp zone. This way, we can use it at a later time during the course of our application execution. We can replace single elements of our stored map by using #<key> to specify where to put the value:

```
GlobalContext.zput("/tmp/map#string", "new string");
```

This replaces `"string object"` with `"new string"` in our stored map. We can also use `zput` to add to a map:

```
GlobalContext.zput("/tmp/map#foo", "added foo");
```

zpost Method

If we need to merge two maps, we must use the `zpost` method:

```
boolean zpost(String location, Map map);
```

The `zpost` method appends the object to the map stored at the given location (see Listing 5.32).

Listing 5.32   zpost an Append to a Map

```
HashMap map = new HashMap();
map.put("foo", "foo value");
GlobalContext.zpost("/tmp/map", map);
map = new HashMap();
map.put("bar", "bar value");
GlobalContext.zpost("/tmp/map", map);
```

Here we create a map and place a single key/value pair into it. Then we create another new map with another key/value pair. Finally, we use `zpost` to merge the maps in the tmp zone. If we have several maps that we'd like to place in the global context, we can use the `zputs` method just like we did in the "Lists" section.

zputs Method

To put several maps into the global context, we use the `zputs` method:

```
Map zputs(String location, Map maps);
```

This is another convenient method to place several maps into the global context at once (see Listing 5.33).

Listing 5.33   zputs Several Maps into the Global Context

```
HashMap smap = new HashMap();
smap.add("one", "string one");
smap.add("two", "string two");
HashMap imap = new HashMap();
imap.add("one", new Integer(1));
imap.add("two", new Integer(2));
HashMap map = new HashMap();
map.put("stringMap", smap);
map.put("integerMap", imap);
GlobalContext.zputs("/app", map);
```

The `zputs` method places two variables containing the maps into the app zone: `/app/stringMap` with the contents of `smap` and `/app/integerMap` with the contents of `imap`.

zget Method

To retrieve variables placed in the global context, we use the `zget` method:

```
Object zget(String location [, Object defaultValue ]);
```

The `zget` method retrieves the map in the particular global context location. Optionally, you can provide a default value for the map being retrieved. If a default is not provided and the location is not found, a null is returned (see Listing 5.34).

Listing 5.34   zget a Map

```
Map smap = GlobalContext.zget("/app/stringMap", new HashMap());
Map imap = GlobalContext.zget("/app/integerMap");
```

Here we are retrieving our string map with a default empty `HashMap` and our integer map with no default. We can also retrieve individual elements from our map by again using the `#<key>` notation (see Listing 5.35).

Listing 5.35   zget a Map Value

```
String s = GlobalContext.zget("/app/stringMap#foo");
Integer i = GlobalContext.zget("/app/integerMap#one");
```

This code retrieves the specified value element of each map that corresponds to the given key. To remove a map from the global context, we use `zdelete`.

zdelete Method

To remove a map the global context, we use the `zdelete` method:

```
boolean zdelete(String location [, boolean deleteChildren ]);
```

The `zdelete` method deletes the specified location, removing any values stored there (see Listing 5.36).

Listing 5.36   zdelete a Map

```
GlobalContext.zdelete("/app/stringMap");
GlobalContext.zdelete("/app/integerMap");
```

Here we delete both of the maps we've previously created and updated. The optional `deleteChildren` parameter works the same as the object usage of this method. As with `zput`, we can delete single elements from our map by specifying the `#<key>` in the location (see Listing 5.37).

Listing 5.37   zdelete a Map Value

```
GlobalContext.zdelete("/app/stringMap#foo");
GlobalContext.zdelete("/app/integerMap#one");
```

The first `zdelete` removes the element with the `"foo"` key from the string map, and the second `zdelete` removes the element with the `"one"` key from the integer map. Sometimes code requires that a particular map be available before executing. We can test the availability of a map by again using the `zcontains` method, the same way we do for objects.

zcontains Method

To test if a map is in the global context, we use the `zcontains` method:

```
boolean zcontains(String location);
```

The `zcontains` method returns a boolean value indicating if the particular map is available in the global context (see Listing 5.38).

Listing 5.38   zcontains a Map

```
if(GlobalContext.zcontains("/app/stringMap")
{
  //do something
}
```

The `zcontains` method can be used as a guard code that needs to have particular maps available. Like other map operations, the `zcontains` method can access particular elements of a map by using the #<key> notation (see Listing 5.39).

Listing 5.39   zcontains a Map Value

```
if(GlobalContext.zcontains("/app/stringMap#foo")
{
  //do something
}
```

This code tests to be sure that the `"foo"` element in the map exists before executing code. The rest of the global context methods (`zlist`, `zlistAll`, and `zdump`) work as they do with objects.

Groovy APIs

To access the global context in Groovy, you can use the same APIs as presented in the Java section, but there are shortcuts in Groovy to aid access. In this section, we show you these shortcuts. Please refer to the previous Java API section for complete explanations of the Java APIs.

Objects

zput Method

The Java `zput` method places objects into the global context:

```
boolean zput(String location, Object object);
```

The Groovy version of this API is simply an assignment to the location for the particular context. In other words, you can address the global context directly in Groovy as if it were a variable in your Groovy script (see Listing 5.40).

Listing 5.40 Placing Groovy Variables into the Global Context

```
app.string =  "string object"
app.integer = 42
```

In these two lines of code, we've created or replaced a string object and an integer object in the app zone so that we can use it at a later time. To retrieve variables placed in the global context, we use the `zget` method in Java.

zget Method

The `zget` method retrieves the object in the particular global context location. In Groovy, we use the following to directly retrieve objects in the global context (see Listing 5.41).

Listing 5.41 Retrieving Variables from the Global Context with Groovy

```
var s = app.string[]
var i = app.integer[]
```

Here we are retrieving a string object and an integer object.

zdelete Method

To remove variables from the global context, we use `zdelete` in Groovy just like we do in Java. Please refer to the previous section on Java.

zcontains Method

In Java, to test if a variable exists in the global context, we'd use the `zcontains` method. However, because we access the global context directly in Groovy, we can test the availability of a variable in a natural way (see Listing 5.42).

Listing 5.42   Testing if the Global Context Contains a Particular Variable

```
if(app.string[])
{
  //do something
}
```

Like `zcontains`, this can be used as a guard code that needs to have particular variables available. In Groovy, there are no shortcuts for other Java methods, so we would just use the Java version in Groovy.

Lists

Just like Java, in Groovy, lists are indexed lists of objects. To put a single list variable into the global context in Java, we use the `zput` method.

zput Method

To put a list into the global context, we use the `zput` method:

```
boolean zput(String location, List list);
```

In Groovy, we can simply make a direct assignment:

```
tmp.list = [42, "string object"]
```

With this code, we've created a list and directly created or replaced the list in the tmp zone. We can replace single elements of our stored list by using array style indexes to specify where to put the value:

```
tmp.list[1] = "new string"
```

This replaces `"string object"` with `"new string"` in our stored list.

zpost Method

To append to a list in the global context, we use `zpost` in Groovy just like we do in Java. Please refer to the previous section on Java.

zget Method

In Java, to retrieve lists placed in the global context, we use the `zget` method:

```
Object zget(String location [, Object defaultValue ]);
```

In Groovy, we can access lists in the global context directly (see Listing 5.43).

Listing 5.43   Retrieving Lists from the Global Context with Groovy

```
var slist = app.stringList[]
var ilist = app.integerList[]
```

Here we are retrieving our string and integer lists and assigning them to a Groovy variable directly. We can also retrieve individual elements from our list by again using the array style indexing notation (see Listing 5.44).

Listing 5.44   Retrieving an Element from a List

```
var s = app.stringList[0]
var i = app.integerList[0]
```

This code retrieves the first element of each list.

zdelete Method

To remove a list from the global context, we use `zdelete` in Groovy just like we do in Java. Please refer to the previous section on Java.

zcontains Method

In Java, to test if a variable exists in the global context, we'd use the `zcontains` method. However, because we access the global context directly in Groovy, we can test the availability of a variable in a natural way (see Listing 5.45).

Listing 5.45   Testing if the Global Context Contains a Particular List

```
if(app.stringList[])
{
  //do something
}
```

This code tests to see if the list itself exists. If we want to test for a particular element in the list, we can do that directly as well. Like other list operations, we can access particular elements of a list by using the array style notation (see Listing 5.46).

Listing 5.46   Testing if the Global Context Contains a Particular Element from a List

```
if(app.stringList[0])
{
  //do something
}
```

This code tests to be sure that the first element in the string list exists before executing some code. The rest of the global context methods (`zlist`, `zlistAll`, and `zdump`) don't have any shortcuts in Groovy. Please refer to the section on the Java API for these methods.

FirstElementLists

As explained previously, `FirstElementLists` work in the same way as lists do in many cases. In Java, we'd create a new list using `zput`.

zput Method

To put a `FirstElementList` into the global context, we use the `zput` method:

```
boolean zput(String location, List list);
```

In Groovy, again we have direct access to these lists:

```
tmp.list['*'] = ["some string", "string object"]
```

With this code, we've created a list and then used `zput` to create or replace the list in the tmp zone so that we can use it at a later time during the course of our application execution. Notice that with `FirstElementList`, we must use the * index to indicate that we'd like to use a `FirstElementList`. We can replace single elements of our stored list by using an array style index to specify where to put the value:

```
tmp.list[1] =  "new string"
```

This replaces `"string object"` with `"new string"` in our stored list. To replace the first item in the list, we don't need to use the array style indexing. We simply need to use the location:

```
tmp.list = "new first item"
```

zpost Method

To append to a list in the global context, we use `zpost` in Groovy just like we do in Java. Please refer to the previous section on Java.

zget Method

To retrieve variables placed in the global context, we use the `zget` method in Java.

```
Object zget(String location [, Object defaultValue ]);
```

In Groovy, we have direct access to these variables, which enables us to access them in a more natural way (see Listing 5.47).

Listing 5.47   Retrieving a FirstElementList

```
var slist = app.stringList['*']
var ilist = app.integerList['*']
```

Here we are retrieving our string and integer list and assigning them directly to Groovy variables. We can retrieve the first element of our lists by directly accessing the variable (see Listing 5.48).

Listing 5.48 Retrieving the First Element from a FirstElementList

```
s = app.stringList
i = app.integerList
```

This code retrieves the first element of each list. It is possible to retrieve the Nth item in the list as well, using the array style notation (see Listing 5.49).

Listing 5.49 Retrieving an Element from a FirstElementList

```
var s = app.stringList[1]
var i = app.integerList[2]
```

This code retrieves the second item in the string list and the third item in the integer list.

zdelete Method

To remove a list from the global context, we use `zdelete` in Groovy just like we do in Java. Please refer to the previous section on Java.

zcontains Method

In Java, we test the availability of a list by using the `zcontains` method:

```
boolean zcontains(String location);
```

In Groovy, we can do this by directly accessing the variables (see Listing 5.50).

Listing 5.50 Testing if the Global Context Contains a FirstElementList

```
if(app.stringList['*'])
{
  //do something
}
```

This code tests to see if the list is available in the global context. We can test to see if the first element is available by accessing the variable directly (see Listing 5.51).

Listing 5.51 Testing if the Global Context Contains the First Element of a FirstElementList

```
if(app.stringList)
{
  //do something
}
```

This code tests to be sure that the first element in the list exists before executing some code. We can test to see if specific elements in the list exist by again using the array style notation (see Listing 5.52).

Listing 5.52   Testing if the Global Context Contains an Element of a FirstElementList

```
if(app.stringList[1])
{
  //do something
}
```

This code tests to see if the second element in the list exists. The rest of the global context methods (`zlist`, `zlistAll`, and `zdump`) work the same as they do with lists and objects. Please refer to the section on the Java API for these methods.

Maps

Maps are lists of key/value pairs. In Java, to put a single map into the global context, we use the `zput` method.

zput Method

To put a map into the global context, we use the `zput` method:

```
boolean zput(String location, Map map);
```

In Groovy, we can directly access the global context variable, which makes it much easier to create maps:

```
tmp.map = ["integer":42, "string": "string object"]
```

With this code, we've created a map and directly created or replaced the map in the tmp zone. We can replace single elements of our stored map by using associative array style syntax:

```
tmp.map['string'] = "new string"
```

This replaces `"string object"` with `"new string"` in our stored map. We can also use the associative array style syntax to add or replace individual elements of the map:

```
tmp.map['foo'] = "added foo"
```

zpost Method

To merge two maps, we use `zpost` in Groovy just like we do in Java. Please refer to the previous section on Java.

zget Method

In Java, to retrieve maps placed in the global context, we use the `zget` method:

```
Object zget(String location [, Object defaultValue ]);
```

However, in Groovy, we can access maps in a more natural and direct way (see Listing 5.53).

Listing 5.53   Retrieving a Map from the Global Context

```
var smap = app.stringMap[]
var imap = app.integerMap[]
```

In Listing 5.54, we are retrieving our string and integer map directly. We can also retrieve individual elements from our map by again using the associative array notation.

Listing 5.54   Retrieving an Element from a Map

```
var s = app.stringMap['foo']
var i = app.integerMap['one']
```

This code retrieves the specified value element of each map that corresponds to the given key.

zdelete Method

To remove a map from the global context, we use `zdelete` in Groovy just like we do in Java. Please refer to the previous section on Java.

zcontains Method

In Java, we test the availability of a map by using the `zcontains` method:

```
boolean zcontains(String location);
```

In Groovy, we directly access the global context variables (see Listing 5.55).

Listing 5.55   Testing if the Global Context Contains a Map

```
if(app.stringMap)
{
  //do something
}
```

This code tests to see if the map exists before executing the block. We test to see if particular elements of a map exist by again using the associative array notation (see Listing 5.56).

Listing 5.56   Testing if the Global Context Contains a Value from a Map

```
if(app.stringMap['foo'])
{
  //do something
}
```

This code tests to be sure that the `"foo"` element in the map exists before executing some code. The rest of the global context methods (zlist, zlistAll, and zdump) work the same as they do with Lists. Please refer to the section on the Java API for these methods.

PHP APIs

The PHP APIs are nearly identical to the Java APIs, but utilize PHP idioms. In other words, the PHP APIs are geared toward PHP developers, using familiar naming schemes and so forth.

Objects

Objects are the most simple data type to put into the global context.

zput Method

To put a single variable into the global context, we use the `zput` method (see Listing 5.57).

Listing 5.57   zput to Put an Object into the Global Context

```
zput("/app/string", "string object");
zput("/app/integer", 42);
```

In these two lines of code, we've created or replaced a string object and an integer object in the app zone.

zget Method

To retrieve variables placed in the global context, we use the `zget` method:

```
Object zget(String location [, Object defaultValue ]);
```

The `zget` method retrieves the object in the particular global context location. Optionally, you can provide a default value for the object being retrieved. If a default is not provided and the location is not found, a null is returned (see Listing 5.58).

Listing 5.58   zget to Get an Object from the Global Context

```
$s = zget("/app/string", "default string");
$i = zget("/app/integer");
```

Here we are retrieving a string object with a default and an integer object with no default.

zdelete Method

To remove variables from the global context, we use `zdelete`:

```
boolean zdelete(String location [, boolean deleteChildren ]);
```

The `zdelete` method deletes the specified location, removing any values stored there (see Listing 5.59).

Listing 5.59   zdelete to Delete an Object from the Global Context

```
zdelete("/app/string");
zdelete("/app/integer");
```

Here we delete both of the objects we've previously created and updated. The optional `deleteChildren` parameter enables you to delete the entire sub-tree of locations by specifying true for that parameter. By default, `zdelete` deletes only the specified location and not the entire namespace defined by the location. Sometimes code requires that a particular variable be available before executing. We can test the availability of a variable by using the `zcontains` method.

zcontains Method

To test if an object is in the global context, we use the `zcontains` method:

```
boolean zcontains(String location);
```

The `zcontains` method returns a boolean value indicating if the particular variable is available in the global context (see Listing 5.60).

Listing 5.60   zcontains Test if an Object Is in the Global Context

```
if(zcontains("/app/string")
{
  //do something
}
```

The `zcontains` method can be used as a guard code that needs to have particular variables available. Some applications may require retrieving a list of all available variables with a particular location prefix. To do this, we use the `zlist` method.

zlist Method

To get a list of variables from the global context, we use the `zlist` method:

```
array zlist(String locationPrefix [,boolean includePrefix
  ]);
```

The `zlist` method returns a list of the variables with a particular prefix (see Listing 5.61).

Listing 5.61   zlist to Get a Dump of All the Variables in the App Zone

```
$list = zlist("/app", true);
var_dump($list)
```

The zlist method returns a list of strings that are the currently stored variables in the app zone. This returns only the top-level app zone variables such as /app/foo but not /app/foo/bar. To retrieve all the variables, we use the zlistAll method. Note that the includePrefix parameter is false by default in PHP. The zlistAll method is actually zlist_all in PHP.

zlist_all Method

To get a list of all the variables in the global context, we use the zlist_all method:

```
array zlist_all(String locationPrefix [,boolean includePrefix ]);
```

The zlist_all method returns a deep list of all the variables defined by the prefix (see Listing 5.62).

Listing 5.62   zlist_all to Get a Deep Dump of All the Variables in the App Zone

```
$list = zlist_all("/app");
var_dump($list)
```

The zlist_all method returns a complete list of the variables available in the app zone. The last method to look at is the zdump method, which dumps all the variables starting with the location prefix as a string. This is a useful debug mechanism for developers when testing and debugging applications written with WebSphere sMash.

zdump Method

To dump the contents of the global context to a string, we use the zdump method:

```
String zdump(String locationPrefix);
```

The zdump method uses the toString() method of the stored objects to render the returned string (see Listing 5.63).

Listing 5.63   zdump to Dump All the Objects Stored in a Particular Prefix to a String

```
zput("/tmp/dumptest/string", "some string");
zput("/tmp/dumptest/integer", 42);
$s = zdump("/tmp/dumptest");
```

This code snippet places a couple of variables into the tmp zone and then dumps them to a string. This is a very valuable tool for debugging code.

Lists

When we say "lists," we are referring to indexed lists of objects. To put a single list variable into the global context, we use the zput method.

zput Method

To put a list into the global context, we use the `zput` method:

```
boolean zput(String location, array list);
```

The `zput` method places the object in the particular global context location (see Listing 5.64).

Listing 5.64   zpt to Put a List into the Global Context

```
$list = array(42, "string object");
zput("/tmp/list", $list);
```

With this code, we've created a list and then used `zput` to create or replace the list in the tmp zone so that we can use it at a later time during the course of our application execution. We can replace single elements of our stored list by using #<key> to specify where to put the value:

```
zput("/tmp/list#1", "new string");
```

This replaces `"string object"` with `"new string"` in our stored list. If we need to add to a list, we must use the `zpost` method. At the time of this writing, we are unable to create lists in PHP, but we can manipulate those that have already been created. We're including what we believe the syntax for list creation will be once this oversight is rectified.

zpost Method

To append to a list in the global context, we use the `zpost` method:

```
boolean zpost(String location, Object object);
```

The `zpost` method appends the object to the list stored at the given location (see Listing 5.65).

Listing 5.65   zpost to Append to a List

```
$list = array();
zpost("/tmp/list", $list);
zpost("/tmp/list", "posted string object");
```

Here we've created an empty list and then posted a single element into the list. Notice that we can use the `zpost` method to create the list in the global context, as well as append to an existing list. This method can also be used to append a list to another a list (see Listing 5.66).

Listing 5.66   zpost to Append a List to a List Stored in the Global Context

```
$list = array();
zpost("/tmp/list", $list);
zpost("/tmp/list", "posted string object");
zpost("/tmp/list", array(13, "from a posted list"));
```

In this case, we've created an empty list and posted an element to the list stored in the tmp zone. Next, we append a new list to the stored list using a zget.

zget Method

To retrieve variables placed in the global context, we use the zget method:

```
Object zget(String location [, Object defaultValue ]);
```

The zget method retrieves the list in the particular global context location. Optionally, you can provide a default value for the list being retrieved. If a default is not provided and the location is not found, a null is returned (see Listing 5.67).

Listing 5.67   zget to Retrieve a List from the Global Context

```
$slist = zget("/app/stringList", array());
$ilist = zget("/app/integerList");
```

Here we are retrieving our string list with a default empty ArrayList and our integer list with no default. We can also retrieve individual elements from our list by again using the #<key> notation (see Listing 5.68).

Listing 5.68   zget to Retrieve an Element from a List in the Global Context

```
$s = zget("/app/stringList#0");
$i = zget("/app/integerList#0");
```

This code retrieves the first element of each list.

zdelete Method

To remove a list from the global context, we use zdelete:

```
boolean zdelete(String location [, boolean deleteChildren ]);
```

The zdelete method deletes the specified location, removing any values stored there (see Listing 5.69).

Listing 5.69   zdelete to Delete a List from the Global Context

```
zdelete("/app/stringList");
zdelete("/app/integerList");
```

Here we delete both of the lists we've previously created and updated. The optional deleteChildren parameter works the same as the object usage of this method. As with zput, we can delete single elements from our list by specifying the #<key> in the location (see Listing 5.70).

Listing 5.70   zdelete to Retrieve an Element from a List in the Global Context

```
zdelete("/app/stringList#0");
zdelete("/app/integerList#1");
```

The first `zdelete` removes the first element of the string list, and the second `zdelete` removes the second element of the integer list. Sometimes code requires that a particular list be available before executing. We can test the availability of a list by using the `zcontains` method, the same way we do for objects.

zcontains Method

To test if a list exists in the global context, we use the `zcontains` method:

```
boolean zcontains(String location);
```

The `zcontains` method returns a boolean value indicating if the particular list is available in the global context (see Listing 5.71).

Listing 5.71   zcontain to Test if a List Exists in the Global Context

```
if(zcontains("/app/stringList")
{
  //do something
}
```

The `zcontains` method can be used as a guard code that needs to have particular lists available. Like other list operations, the `zcontains` method can access particular elements of a list by using the #<key> notation (see Listing 5.72).

Listing 5.72   zcontain to Test if an Element in a List Exists in the Global Context

```
if(zcontains("/app/stringList#0")
{
  //do something
}
```

This code tests to be sure that the first element in the string list exists before executing some code. The rest of the global context methods (`zlist`, `zlist_all`, and `zdump`) work the same as they do with objects.

FirstElementLists

`FirstElementLists` are similar to lists in many cases. The main difference is that with a `FirstElementList`, the first element is what is operated on by default. The idea is that these lists operate like stacks. Normally you would be operating only on the head of the list, which would be found at `"<zone or locationPrefix>/list"` instead of at `"<zone or locationPrefix>/list#0"` with a normal list. At the time of this writing, we were unable to create `FirstElementLists` in PHP. What follows is how we believe they will work once this oversight is corrected.

zput Method

To put a `FirstElementList` into the global context, we use the `zput` method:

```
boolean zput(String location, array list);
```

The `zput` method places the object in the particular global context location (see Listing 5.73).

Listing 5.73 zput to Create a FirstElementList in the Global Context

```
$list = array("string");
array_push($list, "some string");
array_push($list, "string object");
zput("/tmp/list#*", $list);
```

With this code, we've created a list and then used `zput` to create or replace the list in the tmp zone so that we can use it at a later time during the course of our application execution. Notice that with `FirstElementLists`, we must use the `#*` notation to indicate we'd like to use a `FirstElementList`. We can replace single elements of our stored list by using #<key> to specify where to put the value.

```
zput("/tmp/list#1", "new string");
```

This replaces `"string object"` with `"new string"` in our stored list. To replace the first item in the list, we don't need to use the #<key>. We simply need to use the location.

```
zput("/tmp/list", "new first item");
```

This replaces the first item in the list. If we need to add to a list, we must use the `zpost` method.

zpost Method

To append to a `FirstElementList` in the global context, we use the `zpost` method:

```
boolean zpost(String location, Object object);
```

The `zpost` method appends the object to the list stored at the given location (see Listing 5.74).

Listing 5.74 zpost to Append to a FirstElementList in the Global Context

```
$list = array();
zpost("/tmp/list#*", $list);
zpost("/tmp/list", "posted string object");
```

Here we've created an empty list and then posted a single element into the list. This method can also be used to append a list to another list (see Listing 5.75).

Listing 5.75 zpost to Append a List to a FirstElementList in the Global Context

```
$list = array();
zput("/tmp/list/#*", $list);
zpost("/tmp/list", "posted string object");
array_push($list, "string object");
zpost("/tmp/list#*", $list);
```

In this case, we've created an empty list and posted an element to the list stored in the tmp zone. Next, we add some elements to the array and then append them to the stored list using a zpost.

zget Method

To retrieve variables placed in the global context, we use the zget method:

```
Object zget(String location [, Object defaultValue ]);
```

The zget method retrieves the list in the particular global context location. Optionally, you can provide a default value for the list being retrieved. If a default is not provided and the location is not found, a null is returned (see Listing 5.76).

Listing 5.76 zget to Retrieve a FirstElementList in the Global Context

```
$slist = zget("/app/stringList#*", array());
$ilist = zget("/app/integerList#*");
```

Here we are retrieving our string list with a default empty array and our integer list with no default. We can also retrieve individual elements from our list by again using the #<key> notation (see Listing 5.77).

Listing 5.77 zget to Retrieve the First Element from a FirstElementList in the Global Context

```
$s = zget("/app/stringList");
$i = zget("/app/integerList");
```

This code retrieves the first element of each list. It is possible to retrieve the Nth item in the list as well, using the #<key> notation (see Listing 5.78).

Listing 5.78 zget to Retrieve an Element from a FirstElementList in the Global Context

```
$s = zget("/app/stringList#1");
$i = zget("/app/integerList#2");
```

This code retrieves the second item in the string list and the third item in the integer list.

zdelete Method

To remove a list from the global context, we use `zdelete`:

```
boolean zdelete(String location [, boolean deleteChildren ]);
```

The `zdelete` method deletes the specified location, removing any values stored there (see Listing 5.79).

Listing 5.79   `zdelete` to Delete a FirstElementList

```
zdelete("/app/stringList#*");
zdelete("/app/integerList#*");
```

Here we delete both of the lists we've previously created and updated. The optional `deleteChildren` parameter works the same as the object usage of this method. As with `zput`, we can delete single elements from our list by specifying the `#<key>` in the location (see Listing 5.80).

Listing 5.80   zdelete to Delete the First Element from a FirstElementList

```
zdelete("/app/stringList");
zdelete("/app/integerList#1");
```

The first `zdelete` removes the first element of the string list, and the second `zdelete` removes the second element of the integer list. Sometimes code requires that a particular list be available before executing. We can test the availability of a list by using the `zcontains` method, the same way we do for objects.

zcontains Method

To test if a `FirstElementList` exists in the global context, we use the `zcontains` method:

```
boolean zcontains(String location);
```

The `zcontains` method returns a boolean value indicating if the particular list is available in the global context (see Listing 5.81).

Listing 5.81   zcontains to Test if the Global Context Contains a FirstElementList

```
if(zcontains("/app/stringList#*")
{
  //do something
}
```

The `zcontains` method can be used as a guard code that needs to have particular lists available. With `FirstElementLists`, we can test the existence of the first by directly accessing the variable (see Listing 5.82).

Listing 5.82   zcontains to Test if the Global Context Contains the First Element of a FirstElementList

```
if(zcontains("/app/stringList")
{
  //do something
}
```

This code tests to be sure that the first element in the list exists before executing some code. We can test other elements in the list using the `#<key>` notation (see Listing 5.83).

Listing 5.83   zcontains to Test if the Global Context Contains an Element of a FirstElementList

```
if(zcontains("/app/stringList#1")
{
  //do something
}
```

This code tests to see if the second element in the list exists. The rest of the global context methods (`zlist`, `zlist_all`, and `zdump`) work as they do with lists and objects.

Maps

When this book was written, maps could not be created in PHP; they could only be manipulated. However, this oversight should be corrected by the time you are reading this. So, we present here what we believe the API will be. Maps are lists of key/value pairs. To put a single map into the global context, we use the `zput` method.

zput Method

To put a map into the global context, we use the `zput` method:

```
boolean zput(String location, array map);
```

The `zput` method places the object in the particular global context location (see Listing 5.84).

Listing 5.84   zput to Create a Map in the Global Context

```
$map = array();
$map["integer"] = 42;
$map["string"] = "string object";
zput("/tmp/map", $map);
```

With this code, we've created a map and then used `zput` to create or replace the map in the tmp zone so that we can use it at a later time during the course of our application execution. We can replace single elements of our stored map by using #<key> to specify where to put the value.

```
zput("/tmp/map#string", "new string");
```

This replaces `"string object"` with `"new string"` in our stored map. We can also use `zput` to add to a map.

```
zput("/tmp/map#foo", "added foo");
```

If we need to merge two maps, we must use the `zpost` method.

zpost Method

To append to a map in the global context, we use the `zpost` method:

```
boolean zpost(String location, array map);
```

The `zpost` method appends the object to the map stored at the given location (see Listing 5.85).

Listing 5.85   zpost to Append to a Map in the Global Context

```
$map = array();
map["foo"] = "foo value";
zpost("/tmp/map", $map);
$map = array();
map["bar"] = "bar value";
zpost("/tmp/map", $map);
```

Here we create a map and place a single key/value pair into it. Then we create another new map with another key/value pair. Finally, we use `zpost` to merge the maps in the tmp zone.

zget Method

To retrieve variables placed in the global context, we use the `zget` method:

```
Object zget(String location [, Object defaultValue ]);
```

The `zget` method retrieves the map in the particular global context location. Optionally, you can provide a default value for the map being retrieved. If a default is not provided and the location is not found, a null is returned (see Listing 5.86).

Listing 5.86   zget to Retrieve a Map in the Global Context

```
$smap = zget("/app/stringMap", array());
$imap = zget("/app/integerMap");
```

Here we are retrieving our string map with a default empty `HashMap` and our integer map with no default. We can also retrieve individual elements from our map by again using the `#<key>` notation (see Listing 5.87).

Listing 5.87   zget to Retrieve an Element from a Map in the Global Context

```
$s = zget("/app/stringMap#foo");
$i = zget("/app/integerMap#one");
```

This code retrieves the specified value element of each map that corresponds to the given key.

zdelete Method

To remove a map from the global context, we use `zdelete`:

```
boolean zdelete(String location [, boolean deleteChildren ]);
```

The `zdelete` method deletes the specified location, removing any values stored there (see Listing 5.88).

Listing 5.88   zdelete to Remove a Map from the Global Context

```
zdelete("/app/stringMap");
zdelete("/app/integerMap");
```

Here we delete both of the maps we've previously created and updated. The optional `deleteChildren` parameter works the same as the object usage of this method. As with `zput`, we can delete single elements from our map by specifying the `#<key>` in the location (see Listing 5.89).

Listing 5.89   zdelete to Remove an Element from a Map in the Global Context

```
zdelete("/app/stringMap#foo");
zdelete("/app/integerMap#one");
```

The first `zdelete` removes the element with the `"foo"` key from the string map, and the second `zdelete` removes the element with the `"one"` key from the integer map. Sometimes code requires that a particular map be available before executing. We can test the availability of a map by again using the `zcontains` method, the same way we do for objects.

zcontains Method

To test is a map exists in the global context, we use the `zcontains` method:

```
boolean zcontains(String location);
```

The `zcontains` method returns a boolean value indicating if the particular map is available in the global context (see Listing 5.90).

Listing 5.90   zcontains to Test if a Map Exists in the Global Context

```
if(zcontains("/app/stringMap")
{
  //do something
}
```

The `zcontains` method can be used as a guard code that must have particular maps available. Like other map operations, the `zcontains` method can access particular elements of a map by using the #<key> notation (see Listing 5.91).

Listing 5.91   zcontains to Test if an Element in a Map Exists

```
if(zcontains("/app/stringMap#foo")
{
  //do something
}
```

This code tests to be sure that the `"foo"` element in the map exists before executing code. The rest of the global context methods (`zlist`, `zlist_all`, and `zdump`) function as they do with objects.

Conclusion

In this chapter, we've run the gambit of what the global context is and what we can do with it. We learned about the different persistent and non-persistent zones. We examined the scope of each zone and what each zone should be used for. Finally, we learned how to access the global context in each of the three languages supported by WebSphere sMash.

## CHAPTER 6

Response Rendering

Every Conversation Requires a Response

There are many ways to respond to requests in WebSphere sMash. Essentially, there are two logical request models in a web application. The first is aimed to serve people in the form of rendered visual content, and the other is focused more on delivering data and other resources. The second form is typically referred to as REST and is covered in Chapter 7, "REST Programming." For now, we will focus on true visual response rendering and cover the different ways you can perform a classic interactive web browser experience in WebSphere sMash.

In a typical web experience, a user clicks a link in a browser and expects a new page in response. This is the classic browser page-by-page, request/response cycle. In the early days of the Internet, simple static pages were the only possible response type. This worked well but limited the potential of a dynamic web experience. It wasn't too long before CGI enabled site owners to provide simple dynamic content to their users. The CGI concept evolved into true application servers that were capable of advanced content generation using modern languages and programming APIs, such as Java Servlets, .Net, Ruby on Rails, PHP, and many others. The Java Servlet API and its derivatives and .Net, grew in both capability and complexity. It became the preferred enterprise solution for hosting web-based applications. On the other hand, Rails and PHP won the hearts and minds of developers outside of the big corporations but was dismissed as not secure and scalable enough to run real business applications.

WebSphere sMash works to the middle of these two worlds by providing the ease of development offered by the scripting world of PHP and providing the enterprise-ready environment of a Java-based solution. In doing so, we can go from a basic page-by-page static website, all the way up to a full-blown rich Internet application, which can transform the simple browser into a fully capable application platform.

Serving Static Files

The easiest way to start responding to URL requests is to place static files inside the project's /public directory. As the name implies, this is where all publicly accessible resources are located. Static files include HTML markup pages, CSS stylesheets, JavaScript files, images, and anything else that you would place on a plain old web server. Well, this isn't very exciting, is it? If your users wanted to see static content, they could go read a book. What we want is dynamic content that can react to specific input data and generate a custom response. That's what this Web 2.0 world is all about anyway, so let's give our users a truly interactive experience. Do not fret, static files—you still have an important role to serve. Even the richest of Internet applications requires a bootstrap HTML page to get things started, and images, style sheets, and, of course, Javascript to enable the browser as an application platform.

Remember, any files located within the public directory are directly accessible by the URL. This means that you must ensure that you secure sensitive data behind an authentication scheme and also not rely on simple page flow to control your application. An example might be an online quiz. After the student answers a question, he is forwarded to the answer page for further discussion. If your file and directory conventions are similar to /topic1/question.html and /topic1/answer.html, you might be surprised how well your students do when taking these tests! There are many ways to prevent such obvious URL hacking, but you must be aware of how files may be accessed inside the public directory.

Internationalizing Static Files

For performance reasons, support for serving internationalized files is disabled in WebSphere sMash. If you plan on offering pages in multiple languages for your application, you will want to enable this feature. Internationalization (i18n) uses content negotiation to determine the browser's preferred language. We'll discuss content negotiation in more detail in Chapter 7. To enable internationalization support in your application, add the lines shown in Listing 6.1 to your zero.config file.

Listing 6.1   Adding i18n Support in zero.config

```
# Set to true to enable internationalization support.
/config/fileserver/contentNegotiation=true


# Set this variable to override default locale
/config/fileserver/defaultLanguage="en"
```

When a request comes in with content negotiation enabled, WebSphere sMash will check the Accept header for preferred languages. It will then attempt to serve up the requested file with the first desired language code appended to the resource. Failing that, the next preferred language is attempted in the same manner. If all the preferred languages are exhausted without a hit, the application's default language, set in the configuration, is served.

An example is in order here to illustrate the point. First, I set the language preferences of my Firefox browser, as shown in Figure 6.1. In the application, I've added several files, as shown in Figure 6.2. Now, let's request a static file from our WebSphere sMash application. We request the /chap6/i18n.html file. Because our preferred language is fr-ca, WebSphere sMash will check for an i18n.html.fr files to server. Because that file is found, it is served back to our browser, as shown in Figure 6.3. Note that WebSphere sMash does not currently support locales, so even though our preferred language setting is fr-ca, only the fr suffix is searched.

Figure 6.1   Browser language settings

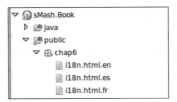

Figure 6.2   Internationalization project files

Figure 6.3   Internationalization browser response

This same file-naming schema applies to more than HTML files. Any static content can be served up in this manner. Therefore, you can have a custom banner image for each supported language. A sample banner image filename might be /public/images/banner.png.fr.

Supporting internationalization is easy within WebSphere sMash for serving static files, but there are a few items to address. First, only static files are supported. You cannot serve php, groovy, or groovy template files using the language suffix syntax. If you want to support i18n within dynamic files, you will have to use an implementation native to that language. Another thing to note is that when enabling internationalization, you cannot have a base version of the i18n files (for example, i18n.html) present, or it will take precedence over the language-specific files.

Internationalization can be a powerful addition to any web application, and potentially increase your audience exponentially. WebSphere sMash makes it easy to add a global view of your world. It won't, however, actually translate all those pages for you! That is an exercise for your friends in other countries.

Serving Dynamic Content

Serving up dynamic content is performed in a similar way as static files. The key difference is that the contents of the file are processed before rendering. Dynamic files also have the benefit of easily including external fragments of markup or other files into the response. This gives you the ability to create modular designs and to create consistent theme and structure elements into the response.

There are two basic types of dynamic file languages currently supported by WebSphere sMash. You can choose to use either the PHP or Groovy language. Native Java may also be used either in conjunction with Groovy or as its own language environment. For this discussion, we'll treat it as an extension to Groovy. Although it's certainly possible to use both PHP and Groovy in the same project, it is probably not a good idea. For this reason, let's discuss each language separately.

From a programmatic point of view, writing output to STDOUT will create a response. So whatever language you choose, just output text using either echo or println statements as appropriate for the language. PHP and Groovy templates treat everything outside of the scriptlet tags as direct output for rendering.

PHP Rendering

PHP files are identified with a .php suffix. PHP files can either work as a simple scripting environment or as a properly structured class file. Because PHP is considered an embedded scripting language, you can have standard HTML content within the file itself. Dynamic content is generated with the normal PHP script tags. Listing 6.2 shows a very basic PHP file that echoes the input parameters. It shows how you can seamlessly mix normal HTML markup and PHP logic.

Listing 6.2   args.php—Simple php Example

```
<h1>Arguments:</h1>
<ul>
<?php
$arr = zlist("/request/params", false);
```

```
foreach( $arr as $arg) {
    echo "<li>$arg = " . zget("/request/params/$arg") . "</li>";
}
?>
</ul>
```

In this example, we obtain a list of the incoming request parameters and iterate over each one obtaining the value of each in the loop. When we load this file in our browser, passing in a few arguments on the URL, we see those arguments listed on the response page, as shown in Figure 6.4.

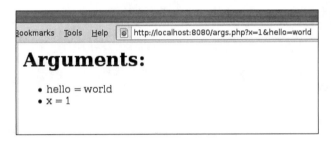

Figure 6.4   Argument echo response

Groovy Rendering

If you choose to use Groovy as your WebSphere sMash functional language, you have a few options for rendering. A normal groovy file is identified by a ".groovy" suffix. It can be structured as a simple script, or as a proper Groovy class file. There is also a Groovy Template file (.gt) that combines normal HTML markup and groovy code.

Placing normal ".groovy" script files in the public directory is a valid way to directly expose functionality on your application, but I personally do not like doing this. I can't provide a hard justification for not doing it, other than it just feels wrong to me to put a pure script in a location directly accessible via a URL. I would much rather use a groovy template file for direct rendering and have inline code, or better yet, make calls to external scripts for my business logic. Again, this is my opinion, and as you will see, using a Groovy template with inline scripting is directly equivalent to a groovy script. I guess it boils down to a matter of personal taste.

Let's try the same example we wrote in PHP using a Groovy script file. In Listing 6.3, we have a normal groovy script that extracts the parameters and lists them in the response. From a rendering perspective, groovy templates are a simple way to mix markup and logic together.

Listing 6.3   args.groovy—Simple Groovy Script Example

```
println("<h1>Arguments:</h1><ul>")
zlist("/request/params", false).each {
  println("<li>${it} = " + zget("/request/params/$it") + "</li>")
}
println("</ul>")
```

In Listing 6.4, we show the same code sample but use a groovy template instead. These two samples are semantically identical, and it's up to you to decide which version best fits your needs. You can see that the examples are very similar.

Listing 6.4   args.gt—Simple Groovy Template Example

```
<h1>Arguments:</h1>
<ul>
<% zlist("/request/params", false).each { %>
<li>${it} = <%= zget("/request/params/$it") %></li>
<% } %>
</ul>
```

The output of each of these groovy-based solutions is exactly the same as our PHP sample shown in Figure 6.1. Although these basic examples don't explore the full capabilities of PHP or Groovy, they're meant to show that it is easy to produce dynamic output using WebSphere sMash. We have only scratched the surface of how we can render content within WebSphere sMash. So, let's continue, explore the possibilities, and show how easy it is to create full-featured and modular applications within WebSphere sMash.

Serving Default Files

All web servers have a concept of default files to be served when the URL ends with a directory instead of a direct file reference. The file is universally known as the index file, and if it is present when a Directory URL is requested, it will be served up. When a directory request is made, WebSphere sMash will look for the following files in order—it will render the first one located as a response.

Default files for Groovy projects are as follows:

1. index.gt

2. index.groovy

3. index.html

An interesting anomaly is that if you have the PHP module included in your project, the search order for default files is rearranged somewhat, with the index.php being the most preferred as expected, but the groovy and gt files switch order. Thus, the new order becomes the following:

1. index.php

2. index.groovy

3. index.gt

4. index.html

This is really more of an academic exercise, as you should not have multiple index files and worry about which one will be picked up. I can't think of a valid reason you would ever have multiple index files in a directory, but you never know.

So, what happens if you request a directory, and there is not an index file to serve up? By default, WebSphere sMash will return a generic "404 Not Found" error. The exception to the 404 is the top-level directory. WebSphere will display a simple welcome message, as shown in Figure 6.5, to indicate that the application is up and running if you do not provide an index file. For this reason, you should always include a top-level index file for any application.

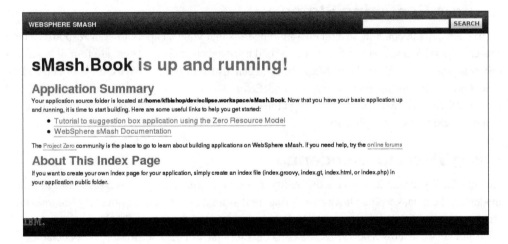

Figure 6.5   Default welcome page

Directory Browsing

There are times when you may want to simply show a directory listing instead of getting a 404 error on directories. To enable this feature, add the following lines to your `zero.config`, as shown in Listing 6.5.

Listing 6.5   zero.config—Enable Directory Browsing

```
# Setting this to true enables global directory browsing.
# Overridden by an index.* file, or the top level /public directory
/config/fileserver/directoryBrowsing = true

# Set this to override the default directory listing template
# Default is: /app/views/listing.gt (from zero.core)
# Hint: Use core's implementation as a guide
/config/fileserver/directoryView = "customDirectoryListing.gt"
```

I would typically recommend that you do not enable this feature on a production application unless you have a valid reason to do so. By allowing users to view and traverse directories, you are making it that much easier for hackers to probe your site for holes or access files that you might not intend for them to see. Conversely, if your application is primarily focused on providing files for users to download, you may want to have a simple way for users to see all the files in a directory. For those directories for which you want to have tighter control, either add an index file or set up access controls for particular trees.

Custom Rendering States

WebSphere sMash contains several custom renderers that you can apply to your response. These renderers provide a standard mechanism to send back data to a client. There are four defined renderers supplied with WebSphere sMash, but you can also define your own to suit your needs. Two renderers are for visual response: View and Error. The other two are for data responses and include JSON and XML formats. We'll go through each of these and explain how they can assist you in developing your applications.

Using Views for Rendering

Another facility available to you is the ability to use views for rendering your response. In even a modest application, keeping all your rendering logic stuffed into the public directory becomes cluttered and redundant. WebSphere sMash provides two virtual directories that help us separate our logic and view concerns. The `/app/scripts` directory provides a place to store proper classes and scripts for reuse. You can then make calls to these using the invokeScript and invokeMethod calls.

For reusable blocks of view logic, you can place static and dynamic rendering files into the `/app/views` directory and dynamically pull them into your response. This is a great way to include common blocks of output that can be used by multiple pages. The View files can be dynamic scripts, but a well-designed application would strive to limit their functionality to more of a templating language and leave the business logic in the `/app/scripts` directory.

To include a View file in Groovy, simply set the request.view to your desired file, relative to the /app/view directory itself, and call `render`, as shown in Listing 6.6. For a PHP-based application, the process is basically the same with only a slightly different syntax, as shown in Listing 6.7.

Listing 6.6 Groovy View Include Syntax

```
request.view="quiz/theme/header.gt"
render()
```

Listing 6.7 PHP View Include Syntax

```
<?php
zput("request/view", "quiz/theme/header.php");
render_view()
?>
```

Let's go through a sample application to illustrate the flow of a typical application that uses scripts and views. In this sample, we have an application that can serve several different quizzes to the user. We want each quiz to have a consistent look and navigation. First, we have our main index.gt file, as shown in Listing 6.8, which contains standard HTML visuals, and also includes several reusable view components.

Listing 6.8 index.gt—Quiz Application Home Page

```
<html>
<% request.view = "quiz/theme/head.html"; render() %>
<body>
<table width="100%" cellspacing="0'" cellpadding="0">
<tr><td colspan="2" class="banner">
<% request.view = "quiz/theme/header.html"; render() %>
</td></tr>
<tr><td class="nav">
<% request.view = "quiz/theme/nav.gt"; render() %>
</td>
<td class="content">

<!-- MAIN CONTENT -->
<h1>Quiz Home page</h1>
<h3>Welcome to the ACME Quiz Factory</h3>
<h4>To take a quiz, select it from the left navigation links</h4>
<!-- MAIN CONTENT --></td>
```

```
</td>
</tr>
<tr><td colspan="2" class="banner">
<% request.view = "quiz/theme/footer.html"; render() %>
</td></tr>
</table>
</body>
</html>
```

The only other file of interest here is the navigation block (nav.gt), which contains the links to each quiz. This file is shown in Listing 6.9. When we render our home page, shown in Figure 6.6, we see the beginnings of our quiz application. Each quiz in the application will have its own target file that is essentially an exact copy of the index.gt, with the exception of the main content. A graphical representation of this is shown in Figure 6.7.

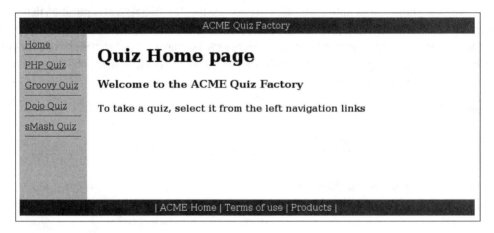

Figure 6.6   Quiz home page

Listing 6.9   /app/views/theme/nav.gt—Navigation View Block

```
<%
def links = [
   "Home"        : "home.gt",
   "PHP Quiz"    : "php.gt",
   "Groovy Quiz": "groovy.gt",
   "Dojo Quiz"   : "dojo.gt",
   "sMash Quiz"  : "smash.gt"
```

```
]
links.each() { label, page ->
  def uri = getRelativeUri( page )
%>
<a href="${uri}">${label}</a><br/><hr/>
<% } %>
```

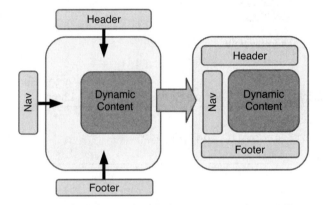

Figure 6.7 Basic assembly flow

You may be seeing the beginnings of some antipatterns here. There is a lot of redundancy in the boilerplate HTML; it's difficult to locate the actual content among the HTML, and there is business logic embedded in our view with the list of quizzes. Wouldn't it be nicer if we extracted out the business logic into a controller and had a theme view that could simply inject the desired content into itself? Let's move around some pieces and see if we can improve upon our application.

In the following example, we are going to define our desired content elements, pass them into our view on the request zone, and have our theme pull them in for us. This will save us from having to repeatedly build up our pages with common code fragments. First, let's move all of our code directly into a controller script. From a graphical viewpoint, our new design will look like Figure 6.8.

Our index script page now looks like Figure 6.8, which does nothing more than invoke our controller, as shown in Listing 6.10. We now have a business controller script called quiz.groovy located in our `/app/scripts` directory, as shown in Listing 6.11.

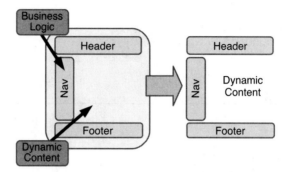

Figure 6.8   Updated assembly flow

Listing 6.10   /public/quiz/index.gt—Simple Redirect to Business Logic

```
<%
invokeMethod("quiz.groovy", "go", null)
%>
```

Listing 6.11   /app/scripts/quiz.groovy—Business Logic Controller

```
def go() {
  if ( request.params.quiz[] == null ) {
    request.params.page = "home"
  } else {
    request.params.page = "quiz"
    request.params.quiz = getQuizData()
  }
  // This would be pulled from DB or config file
  request.params.nav = [
    'home'   : 'Home',
    'php'    : 'PHP Quiz',
    'groovy' : 'Groovy Quiz',
    'dojo'   : 'Dojo Quiz',
    'smash'  : 'sMash Quiz'
  ]
  request.view = "quiz/theme/main.gt"
  render()
}
```

```
def getQuizData() {
  // Determine quiz, and get questions.
  return [
    'title': 'PHP Quiz',
    'questions': [
      [
        'q': 'A PHP script block looks like:',
        'a': [
                '<?php ... ?>',
                '<$php ... $>',
                '<php{ ... }>',
                '<%php ... %>'
              ]
      ],
      /*Other questions*/
      [:], [:], [:], [:]
    ]
  ]
}
```

As you can see, all of our controller and business logic is contained with the quiz.groovy script. We essentially set our target content page and push a view variable onto the request. Finally, we render our theme view template. I won't repeat the code for the theme, but it's essentially the page load of HTML and includes our header, footer, and navigation, which also had its business-specific content moved into our controller. The only difference now is we dynamically pull in our target content page, as shown in Listing 6.12. The nice thing here is that it would be trivial to modify this to handle either a single or multidimensional array of target pages to include, so we can have a simple mash-up environment.

Listing 6.12   /app/views/quiz/theme/main.gt (fragment)—Include Our Content Page

```
<td class="content">
<%
  request.view = 'quiz/' + request.params.page[] + '.gt'
  render()
%>
</td>
```

The last item we should look at is the new quiz.gt view file, shown in Listing 6.13. In our controller file, we defined a complex quiz data object that we put on the request. This allows our quiz view to be ignorant of the data contents and thus makes it highly reusable. The first page of our PHP quiz can now be seen in Figure 6.9. In a real application, we would enable the viewing and answering of other questions, but this should give you the basic foundation of a well-structured application using views.

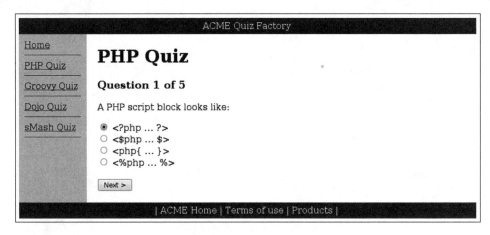

Figure 6.9   PHP quiz rendered from theme

Listing 6.13   /app/views/quiz/quiz.gt—Quiz View Page

```
<%
def quiz = request.params.quiz[]
def currentQuestion = 1 // get from req param
def question = quiz.questions[ currentQuestion-1 ]
%>
<h1>${quiz.title}</h1>
<h3>Question ${currentQuestion} of ${quiz.questions.size()}</h3>
<p>${question.q}</p>
<% question.a.each() { %>
<input type="radio" name="q${currentQuestion}"
/> ${zero.util.XMLEncoder.escapeXML(it)}<br/>
<% } %>
<br/>
<button>Next &gt;</button>
```

As a general rule, if an entity is accessed directly via URL, it belongs in /public; otherwise, you should probably think about moving it into /app/scripts and /app/views as appropriate.

Typically, what I do is use an index file in /public, which simply invokes the appropriate business logic in /app/scripts. The business logic then assembles the response as a collection of view pieces from /app/views into the response. Following this structure will provide your applications with a clean separation of concerns and aligns well to the standard Model-View-Controller design pattern.

Managing Errors

There is an old saying that says "stuff happens," or something like that. No matter how careful you are in developing your application, things will eventually go wrong. These may either be bugs in your code or other external influences that you did not account for. I have seen applications where the majority of the code is dedicated to nothing but trying to address every conceivable error condition that could arise, and the actual business logic is buried among all this exception handling code. Most Web 2.0 applications tend to eschew this gated and walled environment and take a more relaxed attitude toward errors. Basically, if something fails, so be it, and try again later. There have even been several papers and articles written that go so far as to question if error trapping and handling is even a worthwhile effort. I guess I sit somewhere in the middle. Again, this is dependent on your style and the nature of the application you are creating. If your application is managing financial transactions, error handling should probably be fully baked in. But a Twitter-monitoring application can probably be somewhat more relaxed in its error checking.

WebSphere sMash enables you to be as strict or casual in your error handling as you see fit. Both PHP and Groovy support the normal "try/catch" exception handling, so you can at a minimum trap expected or unreliable situations. You can then either choose to deal with error in an application-centric way, or simply bail out by setting an error code and letting WebSphere sMash deliver the bad news to the user. Often, this is actually the easiest and most pragmatic way to deal with truly exceptional conditions. Here is an example that we can walk through to see how we can deal with errors and also promote them for WebSphere sMash to deal with.

In our example, we have a request that comes in, and we need to extract some data from a notoriously unreliable legacy system. Let's first create a Groovy template file to act as our view controller, as shown in Listing 6.14.

Listing 6.14   legacy1.gt—Get Some Data from "That" System

```
<%
def getLegacyData( ask ) {
  if ( ask == "please" ) {
    return "My pleasure. Your data has been sent."
  }
  throw new Exception("You should really ask nicely!");
}
```

```
try {
    def answer = getLegacyData( request.params.ask[] )
%>
<h1>Legacy Data</h1>
<h2>Answer: ${answer}</h2>
<%
} catch( Exception e ) {
    request.view = "error"
    request.status = HttpURLConnection.HTTP_SERVER_ERROR
    //request.error.view = "errorLegacy.gt"
    request.error.message = "This system never works: " + e.message
    render()
}
%>
```

Let's go through this sample and see how it works. When a request comes into legacy.gt, we make a call to our legacy system, passing in the "ask" parameter. Our legacy system is rather testy and does not always properly respond to our requests. If we ask nicely by saying "please," we get our expected data returned. Otherwise, it throws an exception. In our catch block, we set our request view to "error," which is a special reserved view renderer type in WebSphere sMash. We then set our status to a general error value of 500 (HTML_SERVER_ERROR), to which Web-Sphere sMash will automatically define our error view page to error500.* upon rendering. We discuss these status codes more thoroughly in Chapter 7. Instead of setting the error status code, we could also just directly set the error view page. Next, we provide an error message and tell WebSphere sMash to render the error. As you can see in Figure 6.10, we get a standard error page informing us of the situation.

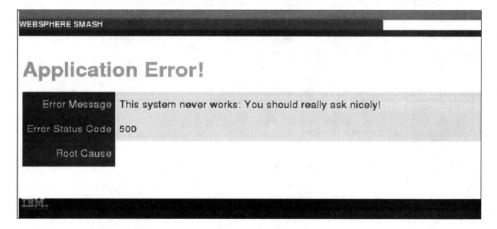

Figure 6.10   Application error

So, what's happening behind the scene here? When you set the request.view to "error" and call render, WebSphere sMash looks in the "/app/errors" virtual directory for an error document matching the error status number, which in our example is "error500.*" for a SYSTEM FAILURE. If that document is not found, a default "error.*" is used. Because we haven't yet defined any of these error documents in our application, a default one is used. There is a lot we can do to improve on our current design, so let's refactor things a little and let WebSphere sMash help us out here.

First, let's play fast and loose and get rid of all our error checking in our application. Listing 6.15 shows our new legacy2.gt file.

Listing 6.15   /public/legacy2.gt—Nothing But Application Code

```
<%
answer = invokeMethod("legacySystem", "getData", request.params.ask[] )
%>
<h1>Legacy Data</h1>
<h2>Answer: ${answer}</h2>
```

Well, that's certainly a lot cleaner. We've extracted out the getLegacyData method into a reusable script and blissfully ignored any exceptions that may get thrown. We are now left with nothing but application logic and presentation. We can't ask for much more than that. So, how do we cleanly deal with those exceptions that are sure to crop up? It's simple: Let's put our error handling into an error document, as shown in Listing 6.16.

Listing 6.16   /app/errors/error.gt—Errors Is as Errors Do

```
<style>
.banner {
    background-color:#00f; color:#fff;
    width:100%; text-align:center;
}
.error { color:#f00; }
</style>
<h2 class='banner'>ACME Quiz Factory</h2>
<h1 class='error'>${request.error.message[]}:
${request.error.exception[].message}</h1>
<h2 class='banner'> </h2>
```

Now when we call the legacy application and don't provide the proper etiquette—make that parameter—we get an amazingly stylized error message in response, as shown in Figure 6.11. A real application may want to be a little more aware of error conditions than we show here, but you should be able to see how WebSphere sMash provides a clean separation of concerns with application logic and error handling.

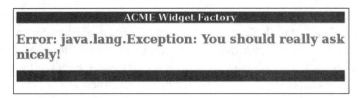

Figure 6.11 Custom error page

Data Rendering

Rendering data for RESTful requests is a fundamental process within WebSphere sMash. There are two default data renderers available within WebSphere sMash to aid you in servicing REST requests: JSON, which stands for JavaScript Object Notation, and XML. The process to respond with one of these data formats is essentially the same. First, you set your view to the desired response type. Then you set your output with the data to be returned, and finally render the output. Under the covers, WebSphere sMash will automatically convert the data from the native internal structure to the desired type. Be aware that WebSphere sMash uses introspection to perform this data conversion, and complex types may cause a performance hit. Although the primary use of data rendering is within REST services, we'll cover the data aspects of it here and expose its proper use when discussing REST in Chapter 7.

There are no hard and fast rules for deciding which data format you should support in your application. As a rough guide, if you have a well-defined, browser-based client server application, JSON might be the right solution. If you have potentially nonbrowser clients and other undefined consumers of your data, XML is probably a better solution due to its universal acceptance as a data interchange format. Specific purpose-defined schemas are also available for XML. One such schema is ATOM, which is the standard for read/write syndication of news feeds. The bottom line is to do some research and choose one or more data formats to suit the widest audience possible. You will see that WebSphere sMash makes it easy to support multiple response types.

JSON Data Rendering

Disregarding the acronym, JavaScript Object Notation (JSON) is a de-facto standard for data interchange with AJAX client application. AJAX, which stands for Asynchronous JavaScript and XML, was initially designed to integrate XML data streams with browsers. Due to performance efficiencies and ease of use, JSON soon became the dominant data structure for AJAX requests because it's a native object type in JavaScript. Details on the JSON syntax can be found at json.org, along with an API for just about every language conceivable.

There is a single configuration option that affects the rendering of JSON data. It is a Pretty Print option. By default, WebSphere sMash will render JSON data into a single line of text. With Pretty Print enabled, the data is expanded out to nicely show the structure of the data. This makes it easier for humans to read the data, but computers don't care. There is a slight bandwidth increase by enabling this setting, but that is basically negated whenever the wire compression is enabled. The configuration option is shown in Listing 6.17.

Listing 6.17 Enable Pretty Print for JSON Data

```
#-- Turn on nice formatting of JSON data
/config/json/prettyPrint = true

#-- If set, you should also enable over the wire compression
/config/compressResponse = true
```

To render JSON data, you set the request view to the string 'JSON' and then supply the native object to be rendered to the request.json.output slot (see Listing 6.18). When you render the output, the data object is automatically encoded (see zero.json.Json.encode). As you can see in Listing 6.19, the response has been Pretty Print formatted, and is very similar, but not exact, to the groovy data object created in the getQuizData function shown earlier in this chapter.

Listing 6.18 JSON Rendering with Groovy

```
def quiz = invokeMethod('quiz.groovy', 'getQuizData', null)
request.view = 'JSON'
request.json.output = quiz
render()
```

Listing 6.19 Resulting JSON Object

```
{
    "title": "PHP Quiz",
    "questions": [
        {
            "q": "A PHP script block looks like:",
            "a": [
                "<?php ... ?>",
                "<$php ... $>",
                "<php{ ... }>",
                "<%php ... %>"
            ]
        },
        {
        },
        {
        },
        {
        },
        {
        }
    ]
}
```

We can also produce the same results using PHP, as shown in Listing 6.20. Assume that we reproduced our quiz.groovy script located at /app/scripts/ in PHP in the following example. The JSON output is exactly the same as in the Groovy example.

Listing 6.20   JSON Rendering with PHP

```php
//-------------------------------------------------------
// From: /app/scripts/quiz.php
// Shown for Reference
//-------------------------------------------------------
<?php
function getQuizData() {
  // Determine quiz, and get questions.
  return array(
    "title" => "PHP Quiz",
    "questions" => array(
      array(
        "q" => "A PHP script block looks like:",
        "a" => array('<?php ... ?>', '<$php ... $>',
                     '<php{ ... }>', '<%php ... %>')
      ), array(), array(), array(), array()
    )
  );
}
?>


//-------------------------------------------------------
// From: /public/dumpQuizPhp.php
//-------------------------------------------------------
<h1>Dump Quiz Data in PHP:</h1>
<div style='font:12px monospace; background-color:#ccc; margin:10px'>
<?php
include "quiz.php";
$quiz = getQuizData();
echo json_encode( $quiz )
?>
</div>
```

```
//---------------------------------------------------------
// From: /app/resources/quizJson.php
// If servicing as a rest resource
//---------------------------------------------------------
<?php
include "quiz.php";
$quiz = getQuizData();
zput('/request/view', 'JSON');
zput('/request/json/output', $quiz);
render_view();
?>
```

XML Rendering

The most commonly used data interchange format has to be XML. Although it's overly verbose, and cumbersome to process and manipulate, it's well understood by everyone. The process to produce XML output is very similar to JSON rendering, with the exception of a few more options. Because every well-defined XML document has a root element, we need to supply that to the encoding process. We also have the option to supply ID references, which will insert a unique ID attribute value to each generated node. Listings 6.21 and 6.22 show our quiz data being encoded in XML for both Groovy and PHP. Figure 6.12 shows the results of our quiz rendered in XML.

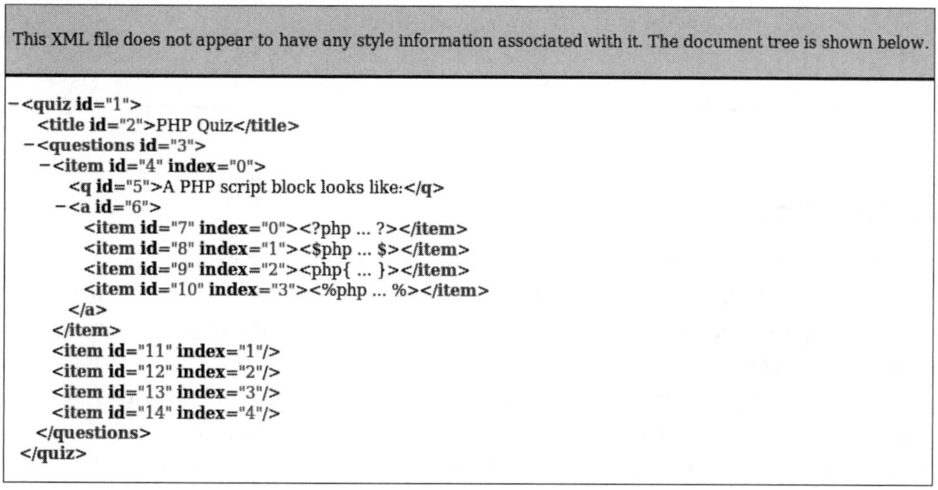

```
This XML file does not appear to have any style information associated with it. The document tree is shown below.

- <quiz id="1">
    <title id="2">PHP Quiz</title>
  - <questions id="3">
    - <item id="4" index="0">
        <q id="5">A PHP script block looks like:</q>
      - <a id="6">
          <item id="7" index="0"><?php ... ?></item>
          <item id="8" index="1"><$php ... $></item>
          <item id="9" index="2"><php{ ... }></item>
          <item id="10" index="3"><%php ... %></item>
        </a>
      </item>
      <item id="11" index="1"/>
      <item id="12" index="2"/>
      <item id="13" index="3"/>
      <item id="14" index="4"/>
    </questions>
  </quiz>
```

Figure 6.12   Results of XML rendering

Listing 6.21   XML Rendering with Groovy

```
//-----------------------------------------------------------
// From: /app/resources/quiz.groovy
//-----------------------------------------------------------
def quiz = invokeMethod('quiz.groovy', 'getQuizData', null)
request.view = 'XML'
request.xml.output = quiz
// Always set root element name. Default is 'linkedHashMap'
request.xml.rootElement = 'quiz'
request.xml.idRefs = true
render()
```

Listing 6.22   XML Rendering with PHP

```
//-----------------------------------------------------------
// From: /app/resources/quizXml.php
//-----------------------------------------------------------
<?php
include "quiz.php";
$quiz = getQuizData();
zput('/request/view', 'XML');
zput('/request/xml/output', $quiz);
zput('/request/xml/rootElement', 'quiz');
zput('/request/xml/idRefs', true);
render_view();
?>
```

Conclusion

This chapter has provided a variety of different ways to respond to incoming requests. The type of response is always dependent on the type of request and how you should render your output. Humans making a direct browser request will typically want an HTML page in response, whereas a remote computer or AJAX response will generally want a native data format, such as JSON or XML, in response. WebSphere sMash provides the tools to enable you to properly respond to any of these requests. The next chapter delves deeper into dealing with REST-based requests and helps you dynamically respond to these requests based on content negotiations.

CHAPTER 7

REST Programming

REST as a technology certainly has caused a stir in the web development space. There is a lot of detractors that dismiss REST for not being as robust as a classic SOAP-based SOA solution. And basically, they are right, but that's the point. REST is based on the HTTP protocol, which is well understood and easy to adopt without changing your existing web infrastructure. This simplicity allows for an easy-to-implement solution, while allowing for the existing web standards for authentication and security to maintain a trusted operating environment.

Before we delve into REST programming with WebSphere sMash, let's do a quick debriefing on HTTP and REST. Having a base understanding of these principals will greatly enhance your ability to create robust RESTful applications. This is by no means a complete description of REST principals, and I may play a little loose with some of the specifics, but forgive these transgressions, and maybe you'll walk away with a newfound understanding of how REST and the web work.

What Is REST?

The term REST stands for Representational State Transfer, which boils down to the concept of accessing remote resources using a URL pattern and HTTP-specific methods. OK, so that's a little bit oversimplified, but it's a good starting point for our discussion. Let's build up and confirm our knowledge of how the web works. In doing so, we'll be describing that REST is the fundamental layer we are utilizing when browsing.

The most basic concept when browsing is typing a URL into the browser address bar and clicking Go. The browser connects to a remote server and is returned a page of content. But what's really going on here? Let's dissect this simple activity and examine the details. First, we have a sample URL like this: http://my.host.com:80/customers.jsp?status=gold&active=true.

The first part is http://, which represents the protocol to be used. Fairly obvious, right? REST is built upon the HTTP protocol, and it is central to properly defining how resources are managed. The server from which we are requesting data is defined next in our URL as my.host.com, at a given network port :80. Port 80 is the default port for HTTP requests, so this part is optional. After this, we have a direct resource request for customers.jsp. The actual resource could be any content, such as an html page, JSP/ASP dynamic page, image, text, XML, or literally anything else. Finally, we pass in a couple of arguments indicated by the ? delimiter. Each argument is represented as a name=value pair, with an & separating the arguments.

This is all well and good, and I'm sure you already know all this. Why bother with this little review of accessing a web page? What this is doing is creating a GET request to the resource defined by the URL. The GET method is used to access read-only resources without any side effects. Because a GET request (including the URL and arguments) uniquely identifies a resource on the web, it is cacheable and bookmarkable. When a resource is requested, several HTTP headers are also sent along with the request. We will look into these headers when we discuss content negotiations. For now, just accept that we are making GET (read) requests via URL addressing for a resources.

REST supports other methods that allow for altering resources as well. These are POST, PUT, and DELETE, as shown in Table 7.1. With these simple actions, you can perform all the classic data-related Create, Read, Update, and Delete (CRUD) actions. This is the power and simplicity of REST.

Table 7.1   REST Methods

REST Verb	Action	Description
GET	Read	Read a remote resource. There are no side effects, and the request is easily cacheable and may be bookmarked.
HEAD	Read	This method is similar to GET but only returns headers and does not include the actual response content. Although this is valid as an HTTP verb, it's not particularly applicable to our discussion here.
POST	Create	Perform a Create action to a remote server. The content of the entity to be created is sent as part of the POST action. POST actions are not cacheable or bookmarkable.
PUT	Update	Perform an update of an existing resource. PUT actions are not cacheable or bookmarkable.
DELETE	Delete	Perform a delete of the resource defined by the URL.

From a REST point of view, web browsers have historically only supported GET and POST operations. A GET could be performed either from a direct URL request from a link or address bar, and through the `action="get"` attribute of a form. POSTs were also performed from the action attribute of forms. By looking at Table 7.1, it becomes apparent that you cannot perform all the actions supported by REST, and also that form POSTs are really misused. Due to this, HTML is not a fully functional client for REST programming. This is where the JavaScript XMLHttpRequest object (also known as AJAX) comes in to fully realize the power of REST. XMLHttpRequests are capable of sending any of the defined REST methods to a remote resource. This gives us incredible power to easily take advantage of RESTful designs to access and alter remote resources from a web application with a minimum of overhead required of the server.

Response Codes

When an HTTP request is made to a remote service, a response is expected. Depending on the method used, there may or may not be content returned. The HTTP protocol defines a series of response codes that indicate if the request was successful or not. We are all familiar with the classic 404 error code that indicates a resource was not found. Although we won't show all the defined error codes, we'll show the codes commonly used in REST programming. If you want to view a full listing and description of all defined response codes, see Section 10 of the W3 HTTP specification at www.w3.org/Protocols/rfc2616/rfc2616-sec10.html.

We also show the constant value for each response code from the Java SE API class java.net.HttpURLConnection at http://java.sun.com/j2se/1.4.2/docs/api/java/net/HttpURLConnection.html. We'll be using some of the following HTTP codes in our code samples later in the chapter.

- **2xx: Successful response code class.** All response codes in the 200 range are considered success.

- **200: [HTTP_OK].** The request was received and processed successfully. On GET requests, the response body contains the requested resource. For a POST, the response will either contain the created artifact, or some other descriptive information, such as the generated artifact ID or something similar, although a 201 is typically more appropriate.

- **201: [HTTP_CREATED].** The POST request has resulted in the creation of the supplied entity. The response body should contain a URI that points to the new entity. If the entity cannot be created immediately, a 202 can be sent back.

- **202: [HTTP_ACCEPTED].** The request has been accepted but processing has not completed. There is no indication of actual success or failure with the response. It is up to the client to make a future request to confirm that the processing actually completed. The response body should contain information that will enable the client to check the status of the processing.

- **4xx: Client-level errors.** Any response codes in the 400 range indicate an improper request by the client. For any of these errors, you should include a descriptive error message within the response body.

- **400: [HTTP_BAD_REQUEST].** This is a generic error that indicates the server can't figure out the request. This could be for bad parameters, parameter values, request content issues, or anything else that just doesn't compute. You may want to send back informational instructions on proper usage to your service.

- **401: [HTTP_UNAUTHORIZED].** This indicates that required authorization credentials are not present. This could be the lack of the proper WWW-Authenticate header or similar missing login refusal. This is typically caused by not logging in properly or a session timeout. The client should either ensure the required credentials are defined prior to making a request, or by prompting for login authorization upon receiving a 401 error.

- **403: [HTTP_FORBIDDEN].** This error indicates that although the user credentials appear valid, other restrictions prevent the server from completing the request. This would normally indicate an access control layer (ACL) violation. If the resource is highly sensitive in nature and you don't want to encourage snooping, it is valid to respond with a 404 error instead of a 403.

- **404: [HTTP_NOT_FOUND].** This error is so common, it has entered into the normal daily lexicon of many geeks. Obviously, this error indicates that a resource is simply not found. It could also be used as a general nonspecific error response to user access style restrictions where you don't want to provide too much information to the remote resource.

- **405: [HTTP_BAD_METHOD].** This error should be returned when a method is requested that is not valid for the requested resource. If this error is returned, a list of valid methods should be returned in an Allow header of the response. Of course, its also OK to return a simple 404 in this situation as well.

- **406: [HTTP_NOT_ACCEPTABLE].**This error is the result of the client requesting a response format that is not supported by the server. As an example, a client might request a response formatted as "application/json," but the server only supports XML-encoded responses; this error should be returned. The server should include in the response body a list of acceptable content types.

- **5xx: Server-related failures.** This class of errors should be returned upon some logic or resource failure on the server.

- **500: [HTTP_SERVER_ERROR].** Typically, this indicates that some unrecoverable and exceptional situation has occurred on the server. The client may want to retry the action. This also typically indicates that the server-side application logic is not appropriately capturing and handling exceptions! There is never a "valid" reason to respond with a 500 error, and this is typically a last resort of the server container.

- **503: [HTTP_UNAVAILABLE].** This error indicates that the server is not able to handle requests at this time. This could be due to maintenance, backups, upgrades, or being outside of a valid service window or similar "planned" downtime. If known and appropriate, the time when the service will be up again can be placed in the Retry-After header.

Request Accept Headers

When a request is made to a resource, the client may optionally stipulate how the response should be rendered. This can be done in a few different ways. One that is unfortunately used too often is sending arguments on the URL that dictate how the response data should be formatted. Although this works, it clutters up the URL and forces an arbitrary naming and style convention to the server. For file-based resources, the file's extension often defines the formatting, such as an .xml file. A much better approach uses HTTP Accept headers, as defined in Chapter 14 of the W3 specification at www.w3.org/Protocols/rfc2616/rfc2616-sec14.html.

The Request Accept headers are an easy way to inform the server of how the response data should be returned. There are several different Accept headers, each having its own special function (see Table 7.2).

Table 7.2   Request Headers

Header	Description
Accept	Defines the media types acceptable as a response. The format consists of a base type, followed by a specific implementation of that type. A generic "*/*" entry indicates that any media type is acceptable. Multiple types may be sent as a comma-separated list. The order should be least specific to most specific. If the server cannot accommodate the requested media type, a 406 (Not Acceptable) should be returned. Example: text/html,application/xhtml+xml
Accept-Encoding	Defines the acceptable encoding on the response. This is typically used to inform the server that the client accepts compressed response data. Example: gzip,deflate
Accept-Language	Defines the acceptable languages supported by the client. The format is a comma-separated list of acceptable languages, in descending order of preference. Example: en-us, en, fr
Accept-Charset	Defines what character sets are acceptable on the response. The format is a list of encodings that range from least preferred to most preferred. Note: WebSphere sMash currently only supports UTF-8. Example: ISO-8859-1,utf-8

By adding these Accept headers to your requests, you can potentially affect the response to suit your needs. The server is under no particular obligation to honor these specific requests, but at least you are dealing with a consistent pattern.

Response Headers

As with the Request Accept headers, the response can also send back a set of meta-data describing what is being returned. Many of the Response headers deal with caching issues that we will not address here. What we are interested in now are headers that deal with the actual content for REST communications (see Table 7.3). If you want to view a full listing and description of the W3C-defined Request and Response headers, see Section 14 of the W3 HTTP specification at www.w3.org/Protocols/rfc2616/rfc2616-sec14.html.

Table 7.3   Response Headers

Header	Description
Allow	Defines the valid methods allowed for future requests. This is a required header when a 405 (method not found) is returned. Example: GET, POST
Content-Encoding	Defines any special encoding applied to the response. Typically, this is some form of compression. This header and the actual encoding is managed by the server and is not managed by the application itself. Note: WebSphere sMash does not compress responses by default. To enable compression on the response, set the following config variable in `zero.config`: **/config/compressResponse=true**. The client browser must still send this Accept-Encoding header to allow compression. Example: gzip
Content-Language	Defines the language(s) returned in the response. Example: en, fr
Content-Type	Describes the type of response being returned. Size of the response body. Note: WebSphere sMash supports only UTF-8. Example: text/html; charset=UTF-8

We show you how these Response headers are set using WebSphere sMash in a moment. You now have enough knowledge of HTTP to successfully and comprehensively create a REST-based services application. Done correctly, and with a little forethought, these services you create are not limited for your target application, but for any consumer within your enterprise or the broader Internet in general.

REST Handling Within WebSphere sMash

Now that we know the essential basics about REST and HTTP, we are ready to create the server-side logic to handle these requests. This is handled by creating resource event handlers in a WebSphere sMash project.

WebSphere sMash has a very straightforward and effective approach to servicing REST requests. Each resource—think Noun—to be made available is contained within a Groovy script or PHP entity. Within these files are several methods, each handling a specific type of REST method—think Verb. WebSphere sMash uses a convention of putting all RESTful resources under the `/app/resources` directory. These are addressed by the URL as `/resources/{entity}/{identifier}`. Table 7.4 shows each REST method and the event method that is fired within the Groovy class. As you can see, there is a distinction between dealing with a list of resources versus a single entity.

Table 7.4   Event to Method Mapping

Event Method	REST Method	Description
onList()	GET (collection)	This method will return a collection of resources defined by the URL. Filters, in the form of request parameters, may be applied to limit the result set. Example: /resources/car
onRetrieve()	GET (singleton)	This method will return a single resource entity defined by the URL, or which a specific identifier is requested. Example: /resources/car/54
onCreate()	POST (collection)	Create a new entity within the resource defined by the URL. The details of the new entity are presented as part of the request data stream. Its possible to perform several creates at once (batch), based on the incoming data, but this is not a common pattern. Example: /resources/car
onPostMember()	POST (singleton)	Create or update an entity. The server must determine if the ID'd entity currently exists. If so, perform an update; otherwise, perform a create using the supplied ID. The details of the replacement entity are presented as part of the request data stream. Example: /resources/car/1

Table 7.4   Event to Method Mapping

Event Method	REST Method	Description
onUpdate()	PUT (singleton)	Update an existing entity within the resource defined by the URL. The details of the entity to be updated are supplied in the request data stream. It is valid to treat this as a create action if the resource does not currently exist. In this case, the response status should be 201 (CREATED); otherwise, a 200 (OK) is appropriate. Example: /resources/car/54
onPutCollection()	PUT (collection)	Updates a full collection of entities in a single call. Based upon strict adherence, this would imply that you are replacing the entire collection, with the new collection on the request. You can see where this could have devastating consequences, so you should be careful in how you actually implement this method. Example: /resources/car
onDelete()	DELETE (singleton)	Deletes an entity within the resource defined by the URL. The only data is supplied as a unique identifier on the URL. Example: /resources/car/88
onDeleteCollection()	DELETE (collection)	Delete a full collection of entities in a single call. Care should be used with allowing this method, as in theory, you could essentially delete your entire car collection with a single DELETE call. Example: /resources/car

It is your decision if you want to name the resources with a plural reference, such as "cars," or a singular reference of "car." This is a personal preference and has no logical bearing on how the data is processed. For GET collection calls, it does sound better to request "/resources/cars" instead of "/resources/car," but this stumbles slightly when requesting a single entity such as "/resources/cars/88." This is the same argument database administrators have argued for years when naming tables. I personally prefer to use a singular noun-based reference for resources, but you do what's best for your situation.

Creating a Groovy Resource Handler

Let's go through an example REST resource handler written in Groovy. Resource handlers are located within the `/app/resources/` virtual directory. The groovy filename must match the resource it represents. Because we are representing cars, our groovy file will be called `car.groovy` in Listing 7.1.

Listing 7.1   /app/resources/car.groovy—Car Resource Handler

```
// GET (Collection)
def onList() {
  logger.INFO {"List starting"}
  // Extract all cars from storage and return
  def result = getCars() // Assume this method exists
  request.headers.out."Content-Type" = "application/json"
  request.view="JSON"
  request.json.output = result
  render()
}


// GET (Singleton)
def onRetrieve() {
  // Get the ID of car to get, this param is fixed
  def carId = request.params.carId[]
  // Alternative accessor method: zget("/request/params/carId")
  def result = getCar( carId ) // Assume this method exists
  request.headers.out."Content-Type" = "application/json"
  request.view="JSON"
  request.json.output = result
  render()
}


// POST (Add)
def onCreate() {
  // The new data for the record with could be in any param
  def carData = request.params.carData[]
  logger.INFO {"Create starting"}
  // Insert a new car into storage.
  def carId = addCar( carData ) // Assume this method exists
  request.headers.out."Content-Type" = "application/json"
  request.status = HttpURLConnection.HTTP_CREATED
  request.view="JSON"
  request.json.output = carId
  render()
}
```

```
// PUT (Update)
def onUpdate() {
  // Get the ID of car to update, this param is fixed
  def carId = request.params.carId[]
  logger.INFO {"Update starting for: ${carId}"}
  // The data to update the record with could be in any param
  def carData = request.params.someData[]
  // Update data for existing car
  updateCar( carData ) // Assume this method exists

  // We don't need to return anything on this update.
request.status = HttpURLConnection.HTTP_NO_CONTENT
}

// DELETE
def onDelete() {
 // Get the ID of car to delete, this param is fixed
  def carId = request.params.carId[]
  logger.INFO {"Delete attempted for: ${carId}"}
  // Lets not allow deletion of Cars
  request.status = HttpURLConnection.HTTP_BAD_METHOD
}
```

As you can see, this is easy to grasp. Each REST method that your resource supports is directly mapped to one of these methods. For methods that expect a specific identifier, such as onRetrieve, you can see that WebSphere sMash has the convention of using the entity name appended with Id—in our example, each specific reference is found in the request parameters as carId. This will become more important when we discuss binding resources later in the chapter.

Creating a PHP Resource Handler

Creating a PHP handler is similar to the Groovy handler. It's a matter of placing a php file within the /app/resources/ virtual directory, where the filename is directly mapped to the resource it represents. The contents of the PHP resource files can be defined in two different ways, depending on your preference.

In Listing 7.2, we have a basic PHP script that represents the same car resource as we defined in Groovy. One issue to observe is that the same GET request is used for list and singleton reads. You need to test the /event/_name variable to determine the proper intent of the request as shown in the listing.

Listing 7.2   /app/resources/car.php—Car Resource Handler in PHP

```php
<?php
$method = zget('/request/method');
switch($method) {
  // GET (Singleton and Collection)
  case 'GET':
    if (zget('/event/_name') == 'list') {
      echo "GET List starting";
      // Perform a list-specific operation on the collection

    } else { // /event/_name = "retrieve"
      $carId = zget("/request/params/carId");
      echo "GET Retrieve starting for: ".$carId;
      // Retrieve the resource
      zput('/request/view', 'JSON');
      zput('/request/json/output', $employeeRecords);
    }
    break;
  case 'POST':
    echo "POST starting";
    break;
  case 'PUT':
    $carId = zget("/request/params/carId");
    echo "PUT starting for: ".$carId;
    break;
  case 'DELETE':
    $carId = zget("/request/params/carId");
    echo "DELETE starting for: ".$carId;
    break;
}
?>
```

The second way to create PHP handlers is to create a proper PHP class that has the same name as the resource and file. This can be seen in Listing 7.3.

Listing 7.3   /app/resources/car.php—Alternate Car Resource Handler in php

```php
<?php
class Car {
  function onList() {
    // GET (Collection)
```

```
    echo "GET List starting";
    zput('/request/view', 'JSON');
    zput('/request/json/output', $employeeRecords);
    render_view();

  }
  function onRetrieve() {
    // GET (Singleton)
    $carId = zget("/request/params/carId");
    echo "GET Retrieve starting for: ".$carId;
  }
  function onCreate() {
    echo "POST starting";
  }
  function onUpdate() {
    $carId = zget("/request/params/carId");
    echo "PUT update starting for: ".$carId;
  }
  function onDelete() {
    $carId = zget("/request/params/carId");
    echo "DELETE attempted for: ".$carId;
    zput("/request/status", 405);
  }
}
?>
```

Content Negotiation

In many real-world applications, there often becomes a need to provide different responses based on client requests. An example of this is that the consumer of a service may want to receive the data in a preferred language. Another example is that one consumer may want to receive the data in JSON format, but another may want to deal with only XML data. As a service provider, you may choose to allow these custom response types. How you deal with these special requests—or more properly stated as "content negotiation" within WebSphere sMash—is the topic of this section.

As stated earlier, you have several choices when dealing with content negotiation. You can simply allow custom parameters on the request, such as `format=xml&language=fr`, but this is problematic. You need to define and agree upon these parameter names and values between the client and server, and how you publish these values to unknown consumers. The complexity of doing this can rapidly reach beyond a manageable solution. A much better approach is to use the definitions already provided by the HTTP protocol to support just this situation. Of course, I'm talking about the request headers.

Checking for and taking action on request headers is easy in WebSphere sMash. Each request header is located within the `/request/headers/in/*` global context variables. The header values are returned as a single string, and because each is set as a comma-separated list of preferred values, they need to be parsed to work with each discreet value. In the following Groovy code block, we have a wrapper method that takes the name of a request header and returns an array of values for you to work with (see Listing 7.4). This script is located at /app/scripts/rest/ headers.groovy in the downloadable code.

Listing 7.4   /app/scripts/rest/headers.groovy—Process Request Headers

```groovy
/**
 * @return array of header values, ordered by preference
 * Breaks out request headers into a usable list for processing.
 */
def getRequestHeaderValues( headerName ) {
  def rawHeader = zget("/request/headers/in/${headerName}")
  logger.FINER {"Raw Header value for ${headerName}: ${rawHeader}" }
  def headers = []
  if ( rawHeader ) {
    for ( value in rawHeader.split(",") ) {
      // Strip off quality and variable settings, and add to list
      headers << new String( value.split(";")[0] ).trim()
    }
  }
  return headers
}


/**
 * @return map of headers and their values
 * Breaks out all request headers into a usable map for processing.
 */
def getRequestHeaderMap() {
  return [
    "Accept"          : getRequestHeaderValues("Accept"),
    "Accept-Encoding": getRequestHeaderValues("Accept-Encoding"),
    "Accept-Language": getRequestHeaderValues("Accept-Language"),
    "Accept-CharSet" : getRequestHeaderValues("Accept-Charset"),
    "Authorization"  : getRequestHeaderValues("Authorization"),
  ]
}
```

Now we can make a quick call to this convenience method and take appropriate action based on our desired values. Let's update our `onRetrieve` method to allow for a specific request for an XML response instead of the default JSON. We test the Accept header for `text/xml` and if found, we alter our response appropriately. First, let's take a look at our new `onRetrieve` method for our "car" resource. You can see that we obtain an array of our Accept header values using the script shown previously. Then we check to see if the client wants an XML response. If so, we alter our response to send XML instead of the default JSON (see Listing 7.5).

Listing 7.5   /app/resources/car.groovy—Dynamic Content Negotiation

```groovy
// File: /app/resources/car.groovy
def onRetrieve() {
  // Get the ID of car to get, this param is fixed
  def carId = request.params.carId[]
  // Extract all cars from storage and return
  def content = invokeMethod('rest/get', 'json', "/public/data/car-
      ${carId}.json")
  def accept = invokeMethod('rest/headers', 'getRequestHeaderValues',
      "Accept")
  if ( accept.contains("text/xml") ) {
    invokeMethod('rest/send', 'xml', content, "car")
  } else {
    invokeMethod('rest/send', 'json', content)
  }
}
```

Again, we are using several convenience methods to render our response. There is nothing particularly interesting going on in these methods, but they do save us a fair amount of boilerplate code. The two rendering methods are shown in Listing 7.6.

Listing 7.6   /app/scripts/rest/send.groovy—Response Data Helper Functions

```groovy
// File: /app/scripts/rest/send.groovy
/**
 * Render our response as JSON.
 * @input result String (Json formatted), or Json/Groovy object to be
rendered
 */
def json(result) {
  logger.FINEST {"sending json data: ${result}"};
  request.headers.out."Content-Type" = "application/json"
  request.view="JSON"
```

```
  if (result instanceof java.lang.String ) {
    request.json.output = Json.decode(result)
  } else {
    request.json.output = result
  }
  render()
}


/**
 * Render our response as XML.
 * @input result String (Json formatted), or actual Json/Groovy object
to be rendered
 * @input root   String (optional). name of root element. Default is
"hashmap"
 */
def xml(result, root) {
  logger.FINEST {"sending XML data: ${result}"};
  request.headers.out."Content-Type" = "text/xml"
  request.view="XML"
  if (result instanceof java.lang.String ) {
    request.xml.output = Json.decode(result)
  } else {
    request.xml.output = result
  }
  if ( root ) {
    request.xml.rootElement=root
  }
  render()
}
```

As you can see, it is a simple task to support full content negotiation for your REST services using WebSphere sMash. This leaves your request parameters for more important business domain-level values, such as response filtering based on certain values, or other things that don't have anything to do with the actual response payload itself.

Bonding Resources Together

The way WebSphere sMash deals with REST resources is fairly flat. Unfortunately, the world is round. Wait, wrong concept. Data in this round world is often hierarchical. WebSphere sMash can handle this stacked view of data by using bonding files. A bonding file creates a relationship between two or more resources. An example is in order here.

Let's assume that we are providing resources for an automobile race. Some resources that we may want to represent include cars, teams, and race. Each of these resources can exist as a stand-alone resource. However, let's assume you want to know which cars were used by a specific team at a specific race. In REST parlance, this could be represented as follows:

```
/resources/race/{raceId}/team/{teamId}/car
```

This is fairly easy to read, but the key is that we need to link each of these resources together to get a comprehensive response from our WebSphere sMash resources. To define a bonding, you create a file with the same name as the primary resource you want to extend, with a .bnd extension. This file resides in the same /app/resources directory as your event handlers. Because we are ultimately looking for cars as our primary resource, our bonding file will be called car.bnd. Listing 7.7 shows how we can bond together these resources in WebSphere sMash.

Listing 7.7   /app/resources/car.bnd—Bonding File for Car Resources

```
car
team/car
race/team/car
```

From this bonding definition, we can now access car data using three different entry paths. The first one is assumed and not needed, but I like to list it for completeness. It says that we can access car data directly using a URL like /resources/car. The second line defines a relationship between a particular team and a car. Although not explicitly stated in the bonding, a team ID is required to access the car data, so our URL would look like /resources/team/Ferrari/car, where Ferrari is the unique identifier for the team. The final example extends our constraint to a particular race. Again, a uniquely identifying race ID is required in the URL.

Now that we have our bonding defined, we still need to modify our event handlers to account for the potentially new IDs coming into the methods. Using the WebSphere sMash conventions, we already know what our ID variables on the parameters will be, as shown in Listing 7.8.

Listing 7.8   /app/resources/car.groovy—Filtered Car Resources Selection

```
// /app/resources/car.groovy
// GET (Singleton), with possible bonding extensions.
def onRetrieve() {
  // Get the ID of car to get, this param is fixed
  def carId  = request.params.carId[]
  def teamId = request.params.teamId[]
  def raceId = request.params.raceId[]
```

```
if( raceId ) {
  logger.INFO {"Retrieve RACE/TEAM specific car data for: " +
    "${raceId} / ${teamId} / ${carId}" }
} else if ( teamId ) {
  logger.INFO {"Retrieve TEAM specific car data for: " +
    "${teamId} / ${carId}" }
} else {
  // Extract car from storage and return data
  logger.INFO {"Retrieve normal car data for: ${carId}" }
}
}
```

As you can see, we have now defined a multilayered approach to accessing car data, without resorting to using obscure parameters to define filters for the data. Be careful when using this layered approach to modifier methods. Although it's certainly possible and realistic to create a new race/team/car combination, application-specific details need to ensure that you account for the extra constraints being applied and that they are applicable. For instance, you probably wouldn't want to create a new instance of the actual car entity through the /race/team/car path. It would likely be a better approach to create a /team/car entity and then decide to add that team/car combination to a race. The final use case would then be, "The team creates a new car, and then, the team enters the car into a race."

Error Handling and Response Codes

As we discussed earlier in this chapter on response codes, there are several well-defined status codes that should be returned based on specific conditions. By default, WebSphere sMash resources will return a 200 (HTTP_OK) response to any request that has a matching method and does not incur any uncaught runtime exceptions. Any uncaught exceptions will throw an expected 500 (HTTP_SERVER_ERROR) response. Although this is fine for a basic use, we should think about implementing a broader range of response codes that will provide a robust and well-architected REST application.

Setting the response status code is simply a matter of assigning an appropriate value to the "request.status" to the desired value. It is a best practice to use the constants defined in the java.net.HttpUrlConnection class, with the values shown in the Response Codes section of this chapter, rather than simply using the less-descriptive numeric value. For maintenance purposes, it is easier to read HTTP_BAD_METHOD than to figure out what a 405 status means.

As an example, if your service doesn't support a particular method, you can simply not define it, in which case, WebSphere sMash will automatically return a 405 (Method Not Found) status code and log any attempts at that method as an error in the logs. If you want to maintain this functionality but also perform some other actions, you can just as easily define the method and manually set the request status, as shown in Listing 7.9. It's much easier to comprehend and is obviously in better form. We'll address status codes and error handling in a moment.

Listing 7.9   Sample Error Handling Example

```
// DELETE
def onDelete() {
  // We don't support deleting of cars,
  // but want to take some action here.
  request.status = java.net.HttpURLConnection.HTTP_BAD_METHOD
}
```

As discussed in Chapter 6, "Response Rendering," you can force custom error pages to be rendered for any of these error responses. For browser clients, this is fine, but typically, the consumers of our REST services are other programs either running as AJAX on a browser, or some other system that wants to process our data. In this environment, you typically do not want to send back a nicely formatted HTML document describing the error. It's best to simply set the status code and then put in the response body information that conforms to the expected result content-type format, such as JSON or XML.

The final word on error handling for REST services is to treat errors as you would any other response processing. Set your response code, apply your appropriate content—even if it is an error message—and render your view.

Enabling SSL Communication Handlers

Most enterprise environments require strict security measures when handling sensitive data. WebSphere sMash can be easily set up to handle SSL (https://) communications for all REST requests. To enable SSL support for your application session listeners, define the following variables in your /config/zero.config file (see Table 7.5).

Table 7.5   Communication Configuration

Config Value	Description
/config/http/port	This setting controls the normal (non-SSL) port listener. To completely disable the non-SSL listener, set this value to '0'.
/config/https/port	This is the port to listen on for requests. The browser standard default SSL port is 443, but you must define it here to enable SSL. A value of '0' will disable the SSL listener. This setting is mandatory to enable SSL support.

Table 7.5   Communication Configuration

Config Value	Description
/config/https/ipAddress	This will bind your listener port to a specific IP address. The default is to listen on any IP address exposed by the server.
/config/https/sslconfig#keyStore	The file location of the store that contains the keys and certificates to manage the encryption of the data. This is a required field to support SSL.
	Note: By including the WebDeveloper module in your application, a dummy keystore will be defined. This is good for development, but very dangerous in a production environment.
/config/https/sslconfig#keyStorePassword	This is the password used to seed the SSL key. This field is required. The actual value is XOR encoded, which helps to keep honest people honest. To generate an XOR-encoded version of the password, run the following command, and paste the resulting value onto this variable:
	$ zero encode mySecretPassword
/config/https/sslconfig#keyStoreType	This is the actual type of keystore file used. Currently, the two defined values for store types are: JKS (Java JEE Keystore), and PKCS12 (Personal Information Exchange Syntax Standard). For most Java-based installations, the value should be set to JKS.
/config/https/sslconfig#trustStore	The file location of the trust store that contains the public SSL keys and certificates. If not defined, no truststore will be used.
/config/https/sslconfig#trustStorePassword	This is the XOR-encoded password used to access the truststore. This field is required if the truststore is defined. Use zero encode as shown previously to generate the XOR version of the password.
/config/https/sslconfig#trustStoreType	The type of file used for the truest store. Valid values are JKS and PKCS12. Required if truststore is defined.
/config/https/sslconfig#clientAuthentication	Do we require client authentication for an SSL connection? Valid values are true or false. The default is false.

Let's show these settings in a real-world setting (see Listing 7.10). In our secure application, we need to secure all REST resources. Here are the relevant contents of our `zero.config` file. In this case, we are completely disabling the non-SSL listener and defining our SSL-specific settings.

Listing 7.10   /config/zero.config—SSL-Only Configuration Sample

```
/config/http/port  = 0
/config/https/port = 443
/config/https/sslconfig = {
        "keyStore": "./config/key.jks",
        "keyStorePassword": "<xor>JTotMC8+LCw=",
        "keyStoreType": "JKS"
}
```

Refer to Chapter 9, "Security Model," for more information on setting up your actual keystore and truststore values, as these are specific to your Java environment.

For more information on setting up SSL, refer to the following resources. For IBM Java key management using the ikeyman tool, see http://download.boulder.ibm.com/ibmdl/pub/software/dw/jdk/security/50/GSK7c_SSL_IKM_Guide.pdf. For Sun's keytool utility, refer to http://java.sun.com/j2se/1.5.0/docs/guide/security/jsse/JSSERefGuide.html#CreateKeystore. For another good resource for defining a secure environment using keystores, see the "Using the Java Secure Socket Extension in WebSphere Application Server" article from the *IBM WebSphere Developer Technical Journal* by Messaoud Benantar at http://www.ibm.com/developerworks/websphere/techjournal/0502_benantar/0502_benantar.html. Although we are providing references to more information on SSL, see the following articles for IBM at http://www.ibm.com/developerworks/java/jdk/security/50/secguides/jsse2Docs/JSSE2RefGuide.html, and from Sun at http://java.sun.com/j2se/1.5.0/docs/guide/security/jsse/JSSERefGuide.html.

If you are not ready to purchase a valid certificate from a recognized certificate authority, you can still move forward in your development using a local dummy keystore. Simply include the zero.core.webtools dependency, and a dummy keystore is automatically available for use. Please refer to Chapter 9 for more details.

Testing and Documentation

After you have written all of your REST services, you now have the daunting task of creating a test environment to validate all your resources and the methods supported with each. Sure, any competent programmer can create a Dojo application to test each use case and display the results and response codes. You could even use external tools such as the Poster plugin for Firefox or similar utilities.

Now that you've gotten the tools to test your services, you need to document each service resource and its methods. Nobody likes documentation, but you know it needs to be done, and more important, it needs to remain accurate and current to the actual code. The only thing worse than no documentation is wrong documentation!

Wouldn't it be nice if WebSphere sMash provided a tool that could examine our resources and create a test environment for us? Or maybe it could even generate our documentation, too? I guess you know where I'm heading with this. All we need to do is supply some annotation comments directly in the code, where it's much more likely to stay current and accurate, and the RESTDoc module available in WebSphere sMash will create both clean documentation and a basic test environment for us. Maybe we can take Friday off after all!

To begin using the RESTDoc tool, add the latest available version of the zero.restdoc. webtools module as a dependency to your project. If you have not previously downloaded the RESTDoc tool into your repository, follow these steps to pull it down. This will need to be done only once.

Under the Eclipse environment, open the /config/ivy.xml file and click Add. For App-Builder, click on the Dependencies tab:

1. Click the Manage Repositories button to open the module management window.

2. In the top right, search for the zero:zero.restdoc.webtools module, as shown in Figure 7.1.

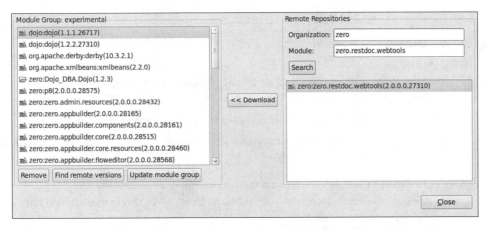

Figure 7.1 Adding RESTDoc tooling

3. After the search is complete and you see the desired module, click the Download button to bring it into your local repository.

4. When the download completes, close the module management window.

5. Back at the Dependency Selection window, locate and select the zero:zero.restdoc. webtools module, as shown in Figure 7.2.

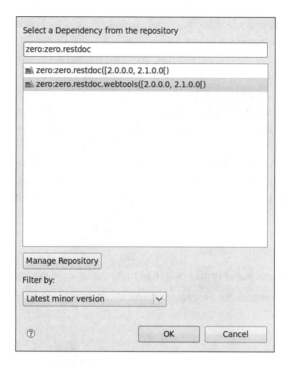

Figure 7.2   Dependency selection

Note that there may also be a zero:zero.restdoc module shown in your repository. You do NOT need to add this particular module because it's used by the CLI, as we'll see later.

6.   Verify that the new restdoc module is shown in your dependency list.

7.   For Eclipse, save and close your ivy.xml file. For AppBuilder, simply switch back to your File Editor view.

Our next step is to annotate each event method within our resources. Table 7.6 shows the annotations that can be used to document your services. Descriptive text can be applied after any annotation to aid in your documentation.

Table 7.6   Documentation Annotations

Annotation	Description	Example
@success	The status code returned upon successful completion of the service. There can be 0+ success codes defined. 200 is the default.	@success 200 @success 201
@error	The status code returned when an error condition occurs. There can be 0+ error codes defined.	@error 500 @error 503

Table 7.6   Documentation Annotations

Annotation	Description	Example
@format	Defines the Content-Types that will be returned on a GET operation, or the expected data format to be received on a POST action. Standard mime type should be used, but any value is acceptable.	@format text/xml

@example	Displays a sample of the expected response data (GET), or incoming request data (POST/PUT). This is informational only and you can show data in any freeform format.	@example
		[
		  {
		    id: 1,
		    name: "joe"
		  },
		  ...
		]

Let's add some RESTDoc annotations to our sample car resource and see how it is processed. In Listing 7.11, we document our updates to the `onRetrieve` method of our car resource.

Listing 7.11   /app/resources/car.groovy - RESTDoc Annotations

```
/**
 * /app/resources/car.groovy
 * GET (Singleton), with possible binding extensions.
 *
 * @success 200 Returns car specific data for a given ID
 * @failure 503 System is down for maintenance
 * @format application/json
 * @example
 * {
 *     id: id,
 *     make: String,
 *     model: String,
 *     year: YYYY,
 *     number: XX,
 *     driver: {
 *         // Driver object
 *     },
 *     team: {
 *         // Team object
```

```
*         }
*  }
*
*/
def onRetrieve() {
    //...
}
```

One item that may seem overly obvious, but can easily trip you up, is to not use block-level comments (/* ... */) within the example section of the RESTDoc. This will corrupt the overall comment block and cause all sorts of problems. It's fine to use a regular inline comment, however, as shown in the preceding example.

At this point, we have all the pieces necessary to view our service documentation and perform basic unit test of the services themselves. Start (or restart) the application, and open your browser to http://localhost:8080/resources/restdoc; you should see a list of all available resources in your application, similar to Figure 7.3.

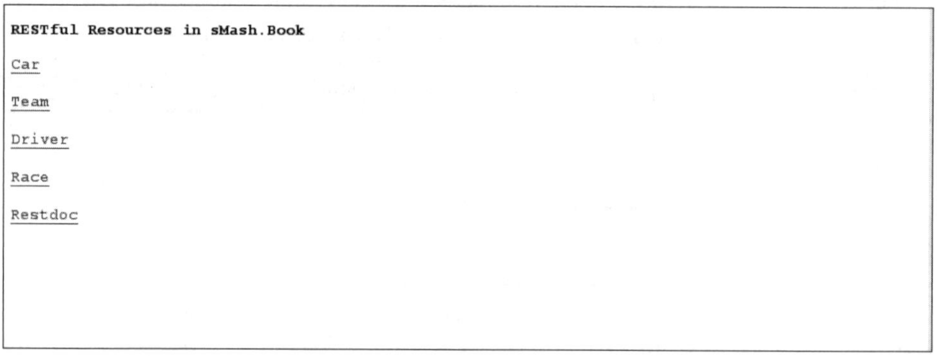

```
RESTful Resources in sMash.Book

Car

Team

Driver

Race

Restdoc
```

Figure 7.3   RESTDoc view of resources

When you click on one of the resources, you will see all the REST methods supported by this service. In Figure 7.4, you can see that we support all the methods. For each method, you can see the URL pattern, support response format(s), and expected success code.

Clicking on a URI for a method enables you to perform an interactive test of that method.

When testing a method, you will be prompted for any required arguments, such as the ID for singleton requests. You have the option to add custom headers for services that support content negotiation. In Figure 7.5, we clicked on the single retrieve GET method and have entered an ID to pass into the service. After we submit the request, the response is shown, as in Figure 7.6.

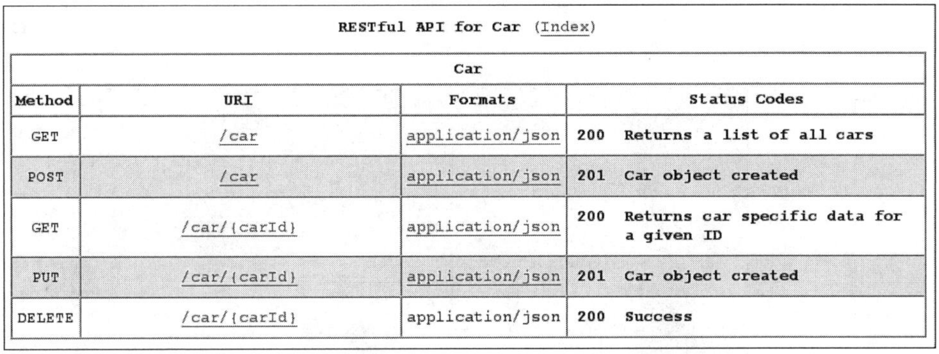

RESTful API for Car (Index)			
Car			
Method	**URI**	**Formats**	**Status Codes**
GET	/car	application/json	200 Returns a list of all cars
POST	/car	application/json	201 Car object created
GET	/car/{carId}	application/json	200 Returns car specific data for a given ID
PUT	/car/{carId}	application/json	201 Car object created
DELETE	/car/{carId}	application/json	200 Success

Figure 7.4 RESTDoc list of methods

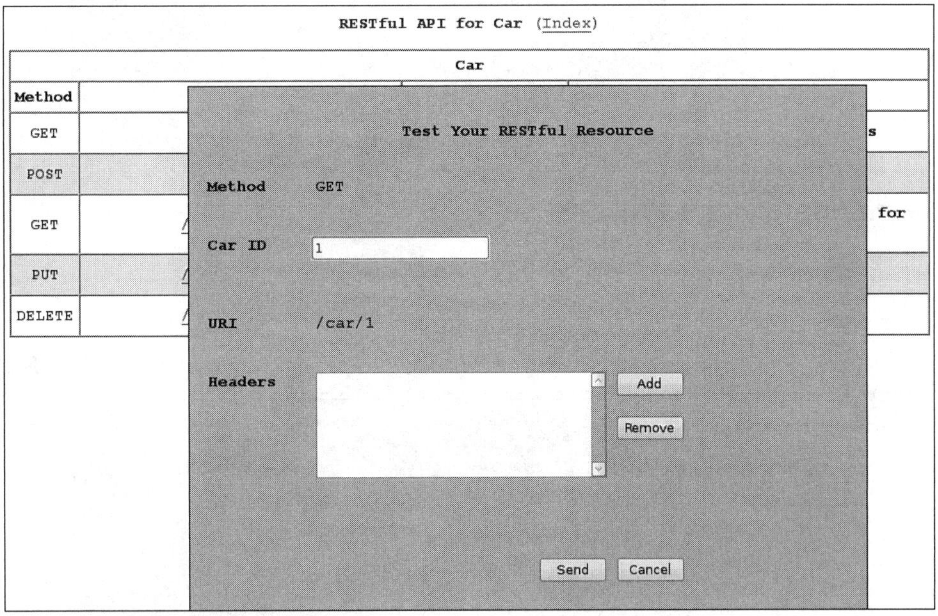

Figure 7.5 Test resource GET method

In the final test case, we want to see an error condition. Because we don't actually want to allow DELETE actions, we send back a 405 (BAD_METHOD) error status, as shown in Figure 7.7.

If we click on the format for a method, the examples we specified will be displayed, as shown in Figure 7.8.

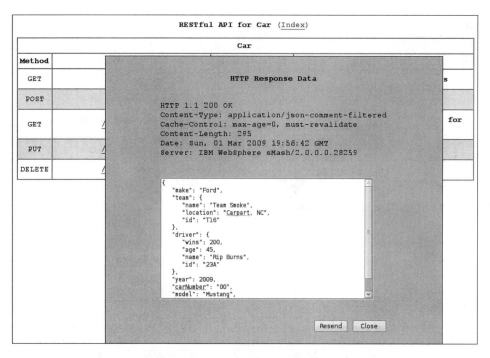

Figure 7.6   GET method response

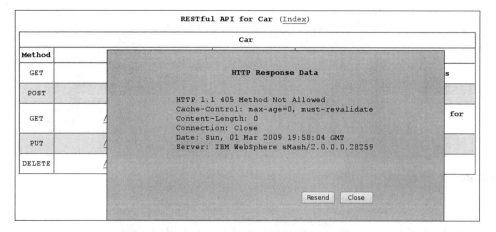

Figure 7.7   Resource response to the DELETE method

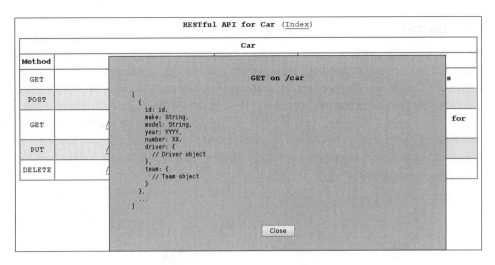

Figure 7.8 Format for the GET method

Before we close out our discussion of RESTDoc, there are few things worth mentioning. First, if you don't want to include the webtools version of RESTDoc that allows a real-time introspection of the services and methods, you can use the version that's available from the command line. Just run `zero restdoc` from your project directory. This creates a static version of the resources into a newly created `/public/docs` directory. This will still allow interactive testing of the services in your project but will not show any changes made unless you rerun the `restdoc` command from the CLI.

The most important thing to remember about RESTDoc is the power it gives a web user. It is critical that you protect either the `/resources/restdoc` or the `/docs` directory depending on what you go into production with to prevent normal users to access these tools. It's simply way too easy to make irrevocable and potentially disastrous changes to your data with RESTDoc. You must weigh the advantages of being able to quickly test and examine your resources with the potential for destruction in deciding if you should include the RESTDoc resource in your application.

The RESTDoc modules do not cover complex scenarios and currently do not properly deal with compound resources defined through bonding files. However, it's still a useful utility that you should keep in your WebSphere sMash toolkit. Using the RESTDoc tool provides both a clean way to document your services, and a nice, easy, and consistent interactive test environment.

Conclusion

We've spent a good deal of time going over REST, from both a standard protocol scenario and in its use within WebSphere sMash. REST is quickly becoming the preferred protocol for use in rich client applications and also as an accepted alternative for the more complex Service-Oriented Architecture (SOA) implementations, such as SOAP Web Services and Remote Procedure Calls (RPC). WebSphere sMash is perfectly positioned to act as the RIA server environment and also as a standalone REST service layer. Having a solid understanding of REST concepts and how the WebSphere sMash resource events support REST will give you an upper hand in creating applications for today's requirements.

Database Access

Introduction

There is no doubt about it—the most common and critical part of any application is quick and efficient access to relational data. The relational database model has endured all the object-oriented thinking of the past couple decades and is as strong as ever. From the small company, all the way up to the largest enterprises, virtually everyone uses relational databases to persist company data. In this chapter, we cover how to utilize the tools available within WebSphere sMash to work with this data.

For simple applications, WebSphere sMash provides a deceptively simple data access layer called the Zero Resource Model (ZRM) that automatically handles the management of tables, and the resources to access and modify these tables using RESTful access patterns. For more involved applications, in which you need to provide complex selection and modifier statements, WebSphere sMash provides the pureQuery layer that sits on top of the standard JDBC API. With PureQuery, WebSphere sMash manages your connections and other resource handlers for you. All you need to be concerned with is defining your statements and working with the data. Finally, for the ugly applications, in which you need to carefully control your database connections and other resources, you can always fall back to traditional JDBC access.

WebSphere sMash makes working with relation databases a breeze. Be forewarned, however—when you start using WebSphere sMash to access your databases, you'll never want to go back to any other platform! Let's learn how to juggle data like a crazed chainsaw-wielding clown in a two-bit traveling circus. Ignore those nightmare-inducing images you may be visualizing right about now. Hmmm.... Maybe that's what happens to those grumpy old database administrators.

Databases Supported in WebSphere sMash

Before we begin, we need to cover the database vendors supported in WebSphere sMash. Vendors not listed will probably work as long as they support JDBC, and you can acquire the necessary driver files required to connect to the database server. The database vendors that are supported and known to work with WebSphere sMash are as follows:

- Apache Derby
- MySQL
- IBM® DB2®
- Informix
- Microsoft® SQL Server®
- Oracle

Configuration Settings

As with most things in WebSphere sMash, we need to start by configuring our application dependencies. To use database accesses in the application, you need to first add the zero.data dependency, as shown here:

```
<dependency name="zero.data" org="zero"
  rev="[2.0.0.0,3.0.0.0["/>
```

The next step is to define the database connections. There are only a couple items to be concerned about here, such as defining the database driver, and the connection details. If you are impatient, skip ahead to the ZRM discussion, because WebSphere sMash will work automatically with the embedded Apache Derby database with no configuration requirements.

All database connection information is placed inside /config/db stanzas in the /config/zero.config file. For each database connection configuration, there needs to be a named database section that is used to access the manager associated with that connection. The name should be symbolic of the data accessed more than any particular connection specifics. For the samples used in this chapter, we use the name bookmark, because we'll be accessing a database of URL references that may be shared among several users.

Within the configuration stanza, a driver name must be defined that indicates the actual JDBC class to be used to access the data. It is preferred to use a normal JDBC Type 4 driver. These are pure Java solutions and do not require any special operating system configuration. Just place the appropriate JAR file inside the environment CLASSPATH or preferably add it to the application's /lib directory. Non-Type 4 drivers can be used, but you must supply any external configuration settings to make them operational.

Listing 8.1 shows a generic database connection configuration. We cover specific configurations needed for each database type, but this should give you an idea of the information required.

Listing 8.1   Generic Database Connection Configuration

```
/config/db/employee {
  "class"        : "{Java driver name}",
  "serverName"   : "{host.domain.com}",
  "portNumber"   : {portNumber},
  "databaseName" : "{Database name}",
  "username"     : "{User name}",
  "password"     : "<xor>Lz4sLCgwLTs="
}
```

As noted previously, it is preferred to obfuscate any configuration password field using XOR encoding. It won't stop a bad guy from figuring out the real password, but it will keep honest people honest. And besides, why are you allowing bad guys to look at your configuration files anyway? Use the smash command line and run `zero encode mypassword` to encode a password, as shown in Figure 8.1. Use the XOR'd results in place of the real password.

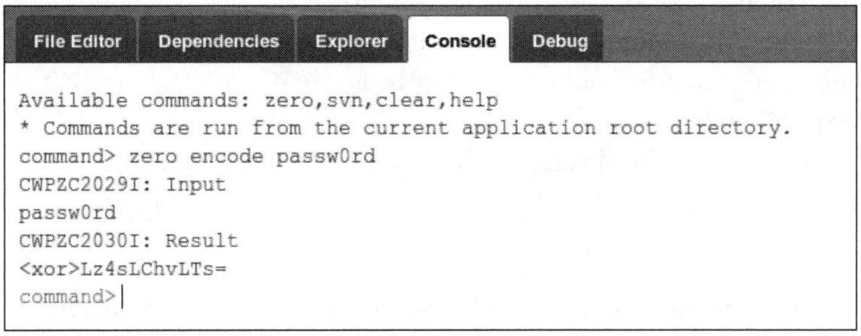

```
 File Editor    Dependencies    Explorer    Console    Debug

Available commands: zero,svn,clear,help
* Commands are run from the current application root directory.
command> zero encode passw0rd
CWPZC2029I: Input
passw0rd
CWPZC2030I: Result
<xor>Lz4sLChvLTs=
command>|
```

Figure 8.1   Zero encode command to hide passwords

In the following sections are configuration settings for common database servers. Every installation is different, and it is up to you and your favorite database administrator to determine the exact settings required to connect to your database server.

Apache Derby

Apache Derby is an embedded database solution used for WebSphere sMash. The nice thing about using Derby is that the drivers are automatically included, and you do not need any special environment to start using the embedded database. This is the default database used if not explicitly defined in the application's configuration.

To use a local "embedded" Derby database, add the following module dependency into your application:

```
<dependency name="derby" org="org.apache.derby"
   rev="[10.3.0.0, 10.4.0.0["/>
```

By default, just adding this dependency to your application will enable automatic use of a default Derby instance created within the application structure created in the /db directory. If you want to define an alternative location to create or use an existing Derby database instance, create a custom derby configuration stanza similar to that shown in Listing 8.2.

Listing 8.2   Embedded Derby Database Configuration

```
#-- Derby Embedded
/config/db/bookmark = {
  "class"           : "org.apache.derby.jdbc.EmbeddedDataSource",
  "databaseName"    : "db/smashdb",
  "createDatabase"  : "create"
}
```

Tables are created or used underneath the defined `databaseName` attribute. This value is relative to the smash application. The embedded version of Derby has a unique attribute called `"createDatabase"`, as shown in Listing 8.2, which automatically creates a database upon first access if it does not already exist. This enables you to create new databases on-the-fly but can cause confusion if the `databaseName` path changes and new tables are created, when you expect them to be read from an alternative location. Just be aware of the database path and ensure that it's what you expect it to be.

If you are using a networked version of Derby, use the client module instead:

```
<dependency name="derbyclient" org="org.apache.derby"
  rev="[10.3.0.0, 10.4.0.0["/>
```

Note: The version numbers may be different than that shown here, so adjust to match your installation.

Although the embedded version of Derby requires no configuration stanza, the networked version does need some extra information for WebSphere sMash to know where to locate the server. Listing 8.3 shows a sample networked Derby database configuration statement.

Listing 8.3   Networked Derby Database Configuration

```
#-- Derby Networked
/config/db/bookmark = {
  "class"           : "org.apache.derby.jdbc.ClientDataSource",
  "serverName"      : "dbs.mycompany.com",
  "portNumber"      : 1527,
  "databaseName"    : "db/smashdb",
  "user"            : "root",
  "password"        : "passw0rd",
}
```

By default, WebSphere sMash uses an embedded Apache Derby database. Derby is fine for a small application, but for anything serious, you will want to define and use a more robust relation database, such as IBM's DB2, Oracle, or MySQL.

IBM DB2

IBM's DB2 family of databases ranges from the freely available "community" edition, all the way up to large enterprise UDB editions used to drive some of the largest business in the world. To use DB2 with WebSphere sMash, use the DB2 JCC drivers, ensuring that the driver version matches the version of the DB2 instance to which you will be connecting.

A sample DB configuration is shown in Listing 8.4. These settings should be familiar to anyone who's worked with DB2 in the past. If you don't know the proper values for any of these settings, drop by your DBA's desk with a hot coffee as an offering, and you'll walk away with the right settings.

Listing 8.4 DB2 Database Configuration

```
#-- DB2
/config/db/bookmark = {
   "class"         : "com.ibm.db2.jcc.DB2SimpleDataSource",
   "driverType"    : 4,
   "serverName"    : "db.mycompany.com",
   "portNumber"    : 50000,
   "databaseName"  : "SMASHDB",
   "user"          : "db2inst1",
   "password"      : "passw0rd"
}
```

For more information on the DB2 DataSource Connection details, refer to the following URL: http://publib.boulder.ibm.com/infocenter/db2luw/v9/index.jsp?topic=/com.ibm.db2.udb. apdv. java.doc/doc/tjvdsdep.htm.

The drivers needed to connect to a DB2 server are normally available as part of the installation. If needed, you can also acquire DB2 connection drivers from the following URL:

DB2: ftp://ftp.software.ibm.com/ps/products/db2/fixes2/english-us/

DB2 "Community" edition: http://www.ibm.com/db2/express/download.html?S_CMP= ECDDWW01&S_TACT=projectzero.

MySQL

MySQL is a popular open source relational database. To use MySQL in your WebSphere sMash application, you must have previously installed and configured MySQL, and then define the MySqlDataSource driver. Listing 8.5 shows a sample MySQL configuration.

Listing 8.5   MySQL Database Configuration

```
#-- MySQL
/config/db/bookmark = {
  "class"          : "com.mysql.jdbc.jdbc2.optional.MysqlDataSource",
  "serverName"     : "db.mycompany.com",
  "portNumber"     : 3306,
  "databaseName"   : "SMASHDB",
  "password"       : "<xor>Lz4sLCgwLTs="
}
```

WebSphere sMash comes with a predefined dependency for MySQL, so you do not need to go out and locate the required driver. Just search for and add the following dependency to your application, as shown in Listing 8.6. The actual version number will likely be different than that shown:

```
<dependency org="mysql" name="mysql-connector-java"
  rev="5.0.3"/>
```

If this doesn't work for you, or you have specific driver requirements, you can manually download and add a MySQL driver. To download the MySQL JDBC driver, go to http://dev.mysql.com/downloads/connector/j/ and select the proper archive file based on your platform. Follow the prompts. You will be asked to optionally register, but you can go directly to the download.

Oracle

The following sample shows how to configure an Oracle JDBC connection within WebSphere sMash. Oracle drivers can be downloaded from http://www.oracle.com/technology/software/ tech/java/sqlj_jdbc/index.html.

Listing 8.6   Oracle Database Configuration

```
#-- Oracle
/config/db/bookmark = {
  "class"          : "oracle.jdbc.pool.OracleDataSource",
  "serverName"     : "db.mycompany.com",
  "portNumber"     : 1521,
  "driverType"     : "thin",
  "databaseName"   : "SMASHDB",
  "user"           : "mydbuser",
  "password"       : "<xor>Lz4sLCgwLTs="
}
```

Microsoft SQL Server

Microsoft's SQL Server database can be accessed using normal JDBC type 4 drivers available directly from the Microsoft MSDN website located at http://msdn.microsoft.com/en-us/data/ aa937724.aspx.

A sample configuration stanza for a SQL Server connection is shown in Listing 8.7. Specific details for server and port number should be available from your DBA.

Listing 8.7   MS SQL Database Configuration

```
#-- MS SQL-Server
/config/db/mydb = {
  "class"        : "com.microsoft.sqlserver.jdbc.SQLServerDataSource",
  "serverName"   : "db.mycompany.com",
  "portNumber"   : 1433,
  "databaseName" : "MYDBNAME",
  "user"         : "mydbuser",
  "password"     : "<xor>Lz4sLCgwLTs="
}
```

Zero Resource Model

WebSphere sMash provides a nice way to persist and present relational data without the normal issues of defining the actual tables, fields, constraints, and the common boilerplate code to expose that data within an application and as referenceable services. In this section, we discuss WebSphere sMash's Zero Resource Model (ZRM) and how you can utilize this subsystem to rapidly create interactive data-driven applications. Although it is possible to define the configuration files necessary to use ZRM within the Eclipse development environment, there is currently no tooling defined to assist in the creation of the data definition files. The AppBuilder tool is the recommended way to create the files used in ZRM-backed applications. When defined, you may then transfer the files to an Eclipse project if you want.

Establishing a New ZRM Application

Start by opening the AppBuilder and creating a new WebSphere sMash application called Book.DB.ZRM. If you want to connect to a specific database, you need to add the appropriate database driver information discussed earlier. Otherwise, let WebSphere sMash create and use the Derby database automatically. If using a custom database configuration for the ZRM, you need to define it to the system by placing the following statement in the zero.config file:

```
/config/resource/dbKey = "bookmark"
```

This would point back to the name used to define the database connection. Only one database connection can be used for ZRM-backed resources.

Creating a Zero Resource Model

Enter the application, and select New File > Zero Resource Model using the Wizard link. On the first view of the wizard shown in Figure 8.2, you are asked to enter a resource name. We'll be creating a bookmarking application in this example, so enter "bookmark" as the resource to define. You can leave the other inputs at their defaults and click next to go to the second step of the wizard.

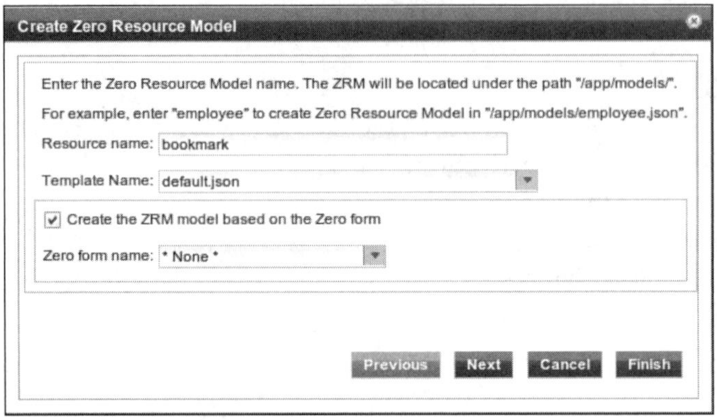

Figure 8.2   Create ZRM from Wizard—step 1

Next, select the check box to have a resource stub automatically created for access to the bookmarks data, as shown in Figure 8.3. The created stub simply defers all REST calls directly to the ZRM manager for processing, so there is a lot of repetitive code that is now taken care of for us. Select your preferred programming language, as long as that's either Groovy or PHP (this is Groovy for our sample), and click Next to proceed to step three of the ZRM wizard.

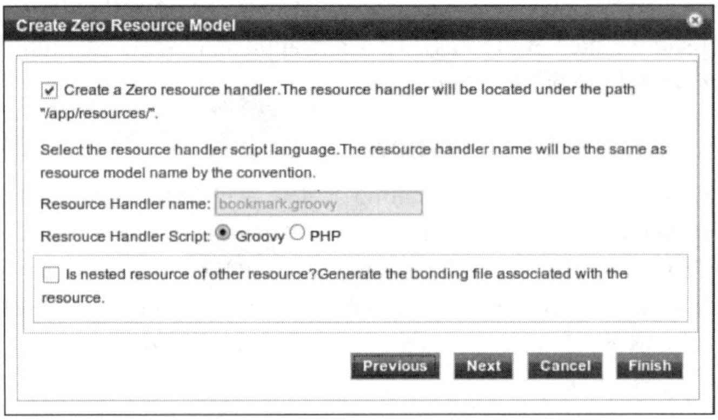

Figure 8.3   Create ZRM Wizard—step 2

The final wizard view is shown in Figure 8.4. Here, we are offered some more convenient file creation options. Select both options and click Finished to complete the ZRM Wizard. You may be asked if you want to include a resource dependency; click yes to add the new module.

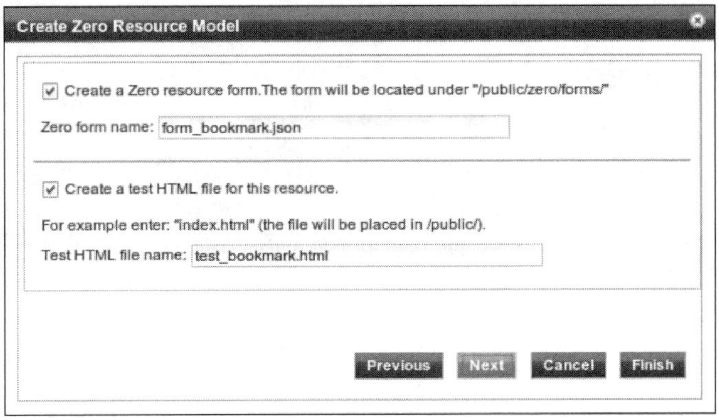

Figure 8.4   Create ZRM Wizard—step 3

At this point, WebSphere sMash has created the base files required to define a ZRM for our bookmark's database table. An empty table definition is opened. We need to define the fields that will go into this table. For our application, we need the following fields shown in Table 8.1. For each field shown, click the button that corresponds to the Field Type column. A new field type is added to the table. You can either edit the field in the table, or (what I find to be easier) click the properties icon—the second-to-last icon in each row—and enter the definitions that way. Note that some of the settings may reside under the Advanced tab. When completed, your table fields should look like Figure 8.5. Although the table definition builder makes creating ZRM tables easy, you can also use an editor to create the definition in JSON. Click on the Source tab to see the table definition represented in JSON.

Table 8.1   ZRM Fields

Field Type	Name	Label	Required	Other Properties
String	url	Site Url	Checked	Maximum Length: 1024
String	description	Description		Maximum Length: 1024
Date	created	Created		Default Value: 1/1/1900 Automatically set initial value: checked

Table 8.1   ZRM Fields

Field Type	Name	Label	Required	Other Properties
Date	last_visited	Last Visited		Default Value: 1/1/1900
				Automatically set initial value: checked
				Automatically update: checked
Integer	visits	Visited Count		Default Value: 0
String	tags	Tags		Maximum Length: 1024

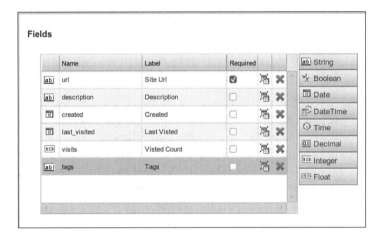

Figure 8.5   ZRM table fields GUI

You are now ready to create the new bookmark table in our database.

To push our table definition into the defined database, you need to access the command line and run `zero model sync`. Just click the console tab and run this command, as shown in Figure 8.6. You should not see any errors in the output. Should you see a message that states that the "model" task cannot be found, or if you do not get an output similar to that shown in the figure, try running a `zero resolve` first. If the table is being created for the first time, you will notice that ZRM automatically adds two other fields, called `id` and `updated`. These are for referential integrity, and you do not need to be concerned by them. It is important that you are fairly satisfied with your table definition prior to running the sync command. Although you can add new fields at any time, you may not change field names or types without exporting your data, dropping the table, re-syncing (creating) the table, and then importing the data back into the table.

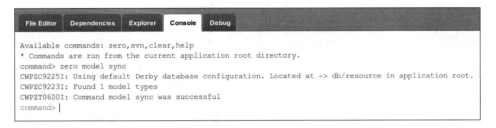

Figure 8.6   Zero model sync command

Making ZRM Data Available as a Service

Now that you have defined your data model, you need to make it available for consumption as REST services. We discussed how to do this previously in the REST chapter by creating a service class under /app/resources and then adding in the accessor and modifier functions to be exposed as the REST verbs: GET, POST, PUT, and DELETE. Within each of these functions, there is the code to parse the input parameters, obtain a database connection, make a parametrized SQL call, process the results, and return them to the client. Wouldn't it be nice if the ZRM subsystem would help us out here. Well, you know where this is going, don't you. ZRM provides a simple abstraction for all this—essentially boilerplate—code that exposes our data as REST services.

In the spirit of the ZRM philosophy of keeping things simple, we need to define a delegate service handler for our ZRM model. If you selected to have the ZRM create a resource handler in step 2 of the ZRM Wizard, this has already been done for you. Otherwise, create a new REST handler file named /app/resources/bookmark.groovy, or /app/resources/bookmark.php, depending on your preferred scripting language. Within the resource file, add the appropriate code, as shown in Listings 8.8 and 8.9. As you can see, we just hand over the responsibility of REST services handling over to the ZRM subsystem. If your needs require you to have custom handling of REST calls, you can always supply your own REST handler functions.

Listing 8.8   /app/resources/bookmark.groovy

```
ZRM.delegate()
```

Listing 8.9   /app/resources/bookmark.php

```
<?php
zrm_delegate();
?>
```

The ZRM delegate handles all the normal RESTful verbs. The resources listed in Table 8.2 are available immediately.

Table 8.2   RESTful Verbs

REST Verb	Overridden Method	Sample URL
GET (Collection)	onList()	/resources/bookmark
GET (Singleton)	onRetrieve()	/resources/bookmark/123
POST (Singleton)	onCreate()	/resources/bookmark
PUT (Singleton)	onUpdate()	/resources/bookmark/123
PUT (Collection)	onPutCollection()	/resources/bookmark
DELETE (Singleton)	onDelete()	/resources/bookmark/123

By using the ZRM delegate, you can potentially save yourself hundreds of lines of boiler-plate code per resource. That's a huge savings in terms of development time and maintenance costs. ZRM is the best junior developer your team has ever had, without all that clowning around.

Adding Data to a Zero Resource Model

A database-backed resource without data is like a circus without dancing poodles—not much to look at. Let's fix that situation by adding data records to our bookmark table. This can be done in a couple different ways. If you have a large block of data to load, it's best to format it into a special fixed format used by WebSphere sMash and bulk load it into the table. Alternately, you can use the predefined sample page to manually add records one by one. Obviously this is not an ideal solution if there is a lot of data to load, so spend the effort to swizzle your data and perform the bulk load. Most databases also provide a native means to bulk load data into tables as well, but that's not within the spirit of sMashing things, so let's create a sample loader file instead.

To perform a bulk data load, you need to create a JSON data file in the `/app/model/fixtures` directory of the project. In AppBuilder, with the Book.DB.ZRM project open, select New File > Other File. In the dialog box, type the full filename of `/app/models/fixtures/load.json` and click Create. You may use any filename you want, but `load.json` keeps things obvious. The structure of the load file allows for defining data for multiple tables at once, as set by the `"type"` value. An empty editor will be displayed, where you can paste in your JSON-formatted data. The contents are a JSON array of objects, with a type member, which is a string that maps to the ZRM model name, and a fields object, which contains a direct mapping of our data fields. Only fields defined as required must be present in the JSON. Because several of our fields will be automatically generated by our database, we don't need to reference them at all in the load file. A sample of bookmark data is shown in Listing 8.10.

Listing 8.10 Sample Bookmark Data

```
[
    {
        "type": "bookmark",
        "fields": {
            "url": "http://www.projectzero.org",
            "description": "Project Zero",
            "tags" : "zero,smash,groovy,php,java,dojo"
        }
    },
    {
        "type": "bookmark",
        "fields": {
            "url": "http://dojotoolkit.org",
            "description" : "Dojo Toolkit",
            "tags": "dojo"
        }
    },
    ...
]
```

To load this JSON data file into the table, go back to the Console tab of the AppBuilder and run the command `zero model loaddata load.json`, as shown in Figure 8.7. Match the filename to the one you used as a loader file. Assuming that everything goes OK, your data will be loaded and ready to go. If there are problems, you should check your file for syntax errors using the AppBuilder editor or by using a site such as jsonlint.com to validate your file structure.

There is a special file called `/app/models/fixtures/initial_data.json` that can be defined that will automatically load anytime there is a model sync command run. This can save you the extra `loaddata` step and can be useful during development of new ZRM models. The structure of this file is the same as any other load file. The `model sync` command will simply look for this specially named file and load it for you automatically.

Loading Data Using a ZRM Test Page

If you recall from earlier when running the ZRM Wizard, on step 3 there was an option to create a test page for the model. You can use this to view and manually enter or modify records in the database. The sample page requires the Dojo toolkit, which is not currently added to the project during the wizard process. So, before we can start the application and load the test page, you need to go to the project's Dependencies tab and add the `zero:zero.dojo` dependency. You need the zero version of Dojo to pull in some widgets provided by Zero and not available under the standard Dojo build. If this module does not show up in your list of available modules, click Manage

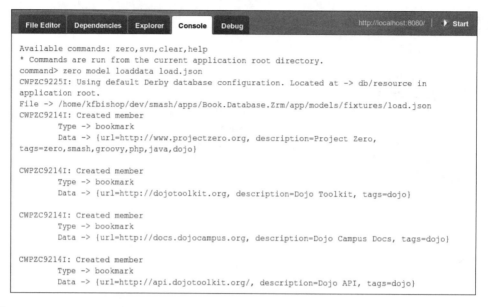

```
   File Editor   Dependencies   Explorer   Console   Debug                    http://localhost:8080/  | ▶ Start

Available commands: zero,svn,clear,help
* Commands are run from the current application root directory.
command> zero model loaddata load.json
CWPZC9225I: Using default Derby database configuration. Located at -> db/resource in
application root.
File -> /home/kfbishop/dev/smash/apps/Book.Database.Zrm/app/models/fixtures/load.json
CWPZC9214I: Created member
        Type -> bookmark
        Data -> {url=http://www.projectzero.org, description=Project Zero,
tags=zero,smash,groovy,php,java,dojo}

CWPZC9214I: Created member
        Type -> bookmark
        Data -> {url=http://dojotoolkit.org, description=Dojo Toolkit, tags=dojo}

CWPZC9214I: Created member
        Type -> bookmark
        Data -> {url=http://docs.dojocampus.org, description=Dojo Campus Docs, tags=dojo}

CWPZC9214I: Created member
        Type -> bookmark
        Data -> {url=http://api.dojotoolkit.org/, description=Dojo API, tags=dojo}
```

Figure 8.7   Results of the **zero model loaddata** command

Repository, enter the search filters as shown in Figure 8.8, and add the latest version located. Now you can start the application and load the test page in your browser.

Go to http://localhost:8080/test_bookmark.html. Assuming that things are all in order, you should see a page similar to that in Figure 8.9. Not too shabby! Go ahead and explore both the UI and the source code to the test page located under the /public folder of the application. This test page enables you to add, edit, and delete records. To edit a field, just double-click, and the field will become editable. Don't forget to click the Save button when you've made some edits. If you are using Firefox and have the Firebug debugger installed you can see the REST calls being made with each action.

A word of caution is in order here. DO NOT (guess that makes two words) leave this test page around on a production application! That is, unless you don't mind having your company's inventory being manipulated by some vengeful clown. I know this is obvious, but still, it has to be said.

Iterative Zero Resource Model Design

During development, you will frequently find yourself creating and modifying models as new requirements arise. Zero helps in this effort. For newly created models, you can simply run the `zero model sync` command, and these models will be processed to create the new tables. Existing models that have been modified get just a bit trickier. For these, we need to export the current data (assuming that you want to keep it, of course), reset the model, and then reload the exported data. If needed, you can edit the exported data to include new data for the modified fields, or as long as they are not required fields, simply reload the original data into the new model.

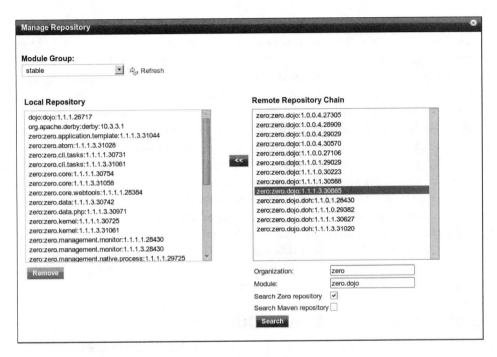

Figure 8.8   Adding the `zero:zero.dojo` dependency

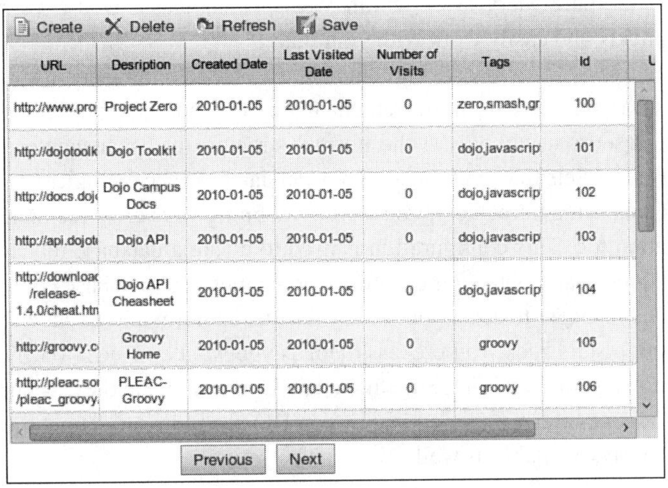

Figure 8.9   Test ZRM page

The `zero model dumpdata <filename>` command exports all ZRM data to the specified file. The filename is defined relative to the project's home directory. So, assuming you want to export the data to the fixtures directory, use the command `zero model dumpdata app/models/` `fixtures/export.json`. If you remember what was said a moment ago, you could export the data to the `app/models/fixtures/initial_data.json` file so that the same data will be automatically loaded when you re-sync the models. This command is also a good way to make quick data backups and works well in daily administration scripts.

The next step is to use the `zero model reset` command to drop any existing tables and re-create them based on the new model definitions. This is a nonrecoverable step, so be sure you have exported any data you want to retain. Otherwise, you will be sticking your head in a hungry lion's mouth. The model and tables will now be in sync, and you can reload the exported data using the `zero model loaddata <filename>` command. Be sure that any field name changes in the model are reflected in the data to be reloaded, or load errors will occur.

WebSphere sMash's Zero Resource Model enables ridiculously easy and iterative development of database-driven applications. It takes the best practices of model-driven table design and convention-driven RESTful access of data and even provides a simple, yet useful, test page to verify and modify data. It doesn't get much easier than that. So, with all that time you've saved, sit back and watch the rest of the circus that is your traditional development environments.

Database Access with pureQuery

The Zero Resource Model is a wonderful way to quickly define and access relational data. However, it does have limitations in how you can manipulate the data, and how to query data using complex joins. If your application outgrows the capabilities provided by the ZRM, you need to step up to using the pureQuery layer within WebSphere sMash. Don't worry—this is still a simple way to quickly and easily work with your data.

WebSphere sMash provide an implementation of the pureQuery database access layer defined by the IBM Information Management team. The pureQuery's API provides for easy access to JDBC resources without all the normal structure and management of Connections, Statements, and ResultSets that are typical of normal database access logic.

To access data using pureQuery, you start by defining your database manager in the application configuration file. This configuration is used to create a database manager handle that is used to perform queries and obtain other information about your database connection. It's then a matter of using the manager to access or modify data using normal SQL statements. For queries, when you get your results back, you process them as you want and move on. There is no need to track and close down your ResultSet, Statement, and Connection handles, as pureQuery will take care of all that messiness for you. Of course, if you DO need to worry about these things, classic JDBC access is always available as well.

Working with pureQuery

In its simplest form, pureQuery consists of obtaining a handle to the database manager as defined in the configuration, passing in the SQL and parameters to the appropriate query or modifier function, and then processing the results. You don't need to worry about tracking or closing handles.

To set up the following scenario, we used the ZRM steps described earlier in this chapter to create a bookmark database using a MySQL instance. We used ZRM just as a quick-and-dirty way to define and populate the bookmark database. Later in this chapter, we cover how you can use the Zero command line to process table creation and modification statements, inserts, and other administration-level commands. Listing 8.11 shows the configuration for the MySQL-based bookmark connection.

Listing 8.11   MySQL Bookmark Connection Configuration

```
/config/db/bookmark = {
   "class"         : "com.mysql.jdbc.jdbc2.optional.MysqlDataSource",
   "serverName"    : "localhost",
   "portNumber"    : 3306,
   "databaseName"  : "bookmark",
   "user"          : "root",
   "password"      : "<xor>Lz4sLChvLTs="
}
```

Because we have ZRM manage the data access through a bookmark resource using the `zrm.delegate()` statement, we created a new resource file called `/app/resources/link.groovy` to use for the examples in this section. Listing 8.12 displays a rather typical flow of performing a query of a database within WebSphere sMash. The first task is to obtain a reference to the Database driver. This is done using the `Manager.create()` statement. The manager object provides all the required information on the connection to perform queries or update statements to the associated database defined in the configuration. The manager is then used to execute the query, which returns our data records. After we have our data, this sample sets the response type to JSON and returns the results. The response sent back to the browser in this case is a JSON structure of all our links in the bookmark table. Notice that we didn't use the word ResultSet, because the returned data is automatically coerced into an easy-to-process object or list structure based on the type of query that is used.

Listing 8.12   Typical sMash Query Flow

```
def onList() {
    def mgr = zero.data.Manager.create('bookmark')
    def result = mgr.queryList('SELECT * FROM bookmark')
    logger.INFO{"Query Links Results size: " + result.size() }
    request.headers.out."Content-Type" = "application/json-comment-
        filtered"
    request.view="JSON"
```

```
request.json.output = result
render()
}
```

If you are merging legacy application code, or for some reason have not defined your data-base in the configuration file, you may also instantiate a Manager instance by passing in a javax.jdbc.Datasource or javax.jdbc.Connection object. Under normal circumstances, you should follow convention and place database connection information inside your config file.

Simple Query Methods

For queries where we either know we will get only a single item back, such as when specifying something by ID, or you want only the first of potentially multiple results, use the queryFirst function, and the results will be a simple object. Other times, when you know you'll be getting multiple records, or are unsure if you'll get one or more records, the queryList command is more appropriate, as it will return a list of items as the result.

In the preceding example, we used the mgr.queryList() method passing in a simple select query. The logging statement shows that for our example we retrieved 18 links from our database, as shown in Listing 8.13. Make a REST GET call using your browser to localhost:8080/resources/links, and you should receive a JSON array of links.

Listing 8.13   Query Log Output

```
2010-02-23 20:20:57 app.resources.link.groovy::onList Thread-12
        INFO [ Query Links Results size: 18 ]
```

There are other times when you may want to query for a link specifically by ID or some other specific query where you know we will obtain a single result. This can be done using the mgr.queryFirst() method, as shown in Listing 8.14. The results of this type query returns a single object represented in JSON.

Listing 8.14   Single Link Request

```
def onRetrieve() {
    def id = request.params.linkId[]
    def mgr = zero.data.Manager.create('bookmark')
    def result = mgr.queryFirst("select * from bookmark where id =
      ${id}")
    logger.INFO{"Link URL Result for ID: " + id + " = " + result.url}
    request.headers.out."Content-Type" = "application/json-comment-
      filtered"
    request.view="JSON"
```

```
request.json.output = result
render()
}
```

When we make a singular REST call to our link resource (http://localhost:8080/resources/link/3), we get back the record identified by ID = 3. In the database, this is storing our favorite Dojo documentation site, as shown in the console output in Listing 8.15. Of course, the whole record is also returned to your browser for examination as well.

Listing 8.15   Log Output Of Single Link Request

```
2010-02-23 20:29:30 app.resources.link.groovy::onRetrieve Thread-11
            INFO [ Link URL Result for ID: 3 = http://docs.dojocampus.org ]
```

You are not limited to retrieving complex maps or lists of maps in pureQuery. If your query requests a single field, you may request the result type as the second argument of the call, and the resulting data will be coerced into that type. Logically, a list of the scoped type is returned if there are multiple results matching your query. To showcase this, let's assume that I only wanted to retrieve a list of the URLs as type String in the bookmark table tagged with "Dojo". The SQL query would look like that shown in Listing 8.16: "select url from bookmark where tags like '%Dojo%'". The results returned when called with the mgr.queryList call would be a list of strings.

Listing 8.16   Custom Query for Dojo URLs as Strings

```
def result = mgr.queryList("SELECT url FROM bookmark where tags like
'%Dojo%'", String)
```

The results when returned as JSON to the browser should resemble Listing 8.17.

Listing 8.17   Results of Dojo URLs Query

```
["http://www.projectzero.org","http://dojotoolkit.org","http://docs.d
ojocam-pus.org","http://api.dojotoolkit.org/","http://dojodocs.
uxebu.com/"," http://download.dojotoolkit.org/release-1.4.0/cheat.html",
"http://www.sitepen.com/"]
```

Retrieving JavaBeans or GroovyBeans is done the exact same way. Just supply the wanted Bean class as the second argument to the queryXXX() method. The result will then be the requested bean type or a list of beans as appropriate. Assume we have a GroovyBean called Link, as shown in Listing 8.18. We then make a DB query, as shown in Listing 8.19. The result list contains Link bean instances. The bean's `toString()` method is then iterated to display our results, as shown in Listing 8.20.

Listing 8.18   Link Class: /app/scripts/Link.groovy

```
class Link {
    // properties
    Integer id
    String url
    String description

    String toString() {
      return this.id + ":" + this.url + " = " + this.description
    }

}
```

Listing 8.19   Selecting Data into a List of Beans

```
def links = mgr.queryList("SELECT * FROM bookmark where tags like
'%dojo%'", Link)
links.each{ link -> logger.INFO{ "Link: " + link } }
```

Listing 8.20   Results of Iterating the Bean List

```
2010-02-23 21:32:50 app.resources.link.groovy::onList Thread-11
    INFO [ Link: 1:http://www.projectzero.org = Project Zero ]
2010-02-23 21:32:50 app.resources.link.groovy::onList Thread-11
    INFO [ Link: 2:http://dojotoolkit.org = Dojo Toolkit ]
2010-02-23 21:32:50 app.resources.link.groovy::onList Thread-11
    INFO [ Link: 3:http://docs.dojocampus.org = Dojo Campus Docs ]
```

The Manager class provides a convenience method called `eachRow` that allows you to mix a `queryList` with an `each` call on the results. Listing 8.19 could be rewritten as shown in Listing 8.21.

Listing 8.21   Selecting Data into a List of Beans

```
mgr.eachRow("SELECT * FROM bookmark where tags like '%dojo%'", Link)
{
    link -> logger.INFO{ "Link: " + link }
}
```

Data Manipulation Statements

You are not limited to making read-only queries into your data. You may also perform the other classic CRUD operations: essentially Create, Read, Update, and Delete. Because we have covered the Read action, let's focus on using statements that alter data. There is nothing different here, other than instead of obtaining results back in the form of an object, or list of objects, we get a simple integer that indicates how many rows were affected by the modification statement. You can test this value to verify the operation performed as expected. Getting a zero back would typically indicate that something is amiss, unless the filtering of the statement excluded all records. Also, if the SQL were poorly formed, the statement would throw a `com.ibm.pdq.runtime.exception.DataRuntimeException` that you can trap and recover from appropriately. Let's briefly cover each of the modifier statements. If you need more information, consult the documentation for your database of choice.

Let's walk through a few data manipulation statements. The only unique thing to notice is when dealing with auto-generated keys during an insert statement. You need to inform the meta manager of the keys that will be auto-generated. This is done by passing in an array of keys that are auto-generated by the database. In the case of our first sample in Listing 8.22, we have a single `'id'` field that is auto-generated. Passing this in as the second argument ensures that this field is managed properly. Other parameter values are passed after the auto-gen fields array. The other statements for updates and deletes operate as you would expect.

Listing 8.22   Sample Data Manipulation Calls

```
//-- Create a manager reference
def manager = zero.data.groovy.Manager.create('bookmark')

//-- Perform an Insert, using mapped parameters
def map = [
    'url'          : 'http://www.w3schools.com/sql/default.asp',
    'description' : 'W3Schools SQL tutorial',
    'tags'         : 'sql'
]

def sql = """INSERT INTO bookmark (url, description, tags)
          VALUES (${map.url}, ${map.description}, ${map.tags} )"""
//-- Notice how we need to tell the manager our auto-gen fields below
def result = manager.insert( sql, ['id'] )
logger.INFO{"Rows inserted: "+ result}



//-- An Update (Reset all visited counts to zero.)
sql = "UPDATE bookmark SET visited=0;"
```

```
def updatedRows = manager.update( sql )
logger.INFO{"Rows updated: " + updatedRows)

//-- A Delete action, because we have to clean out any bad stuff
sql = "DELETE FROM bookmark WHERE tags like ?";

def deletedRows = manager.update( sql, ["%asp%"] )
logger.INFO{"Rows deleted: " + deletedRows}
```

Prepared Statements

Creating queries by assembling SQL statements from strings fragments has many disadvantages. First, it is prone to errors in SQL syntax, especially for quote mismatches. The other major issue with dynamically built SQL statements based on input parameters is the classic SQL injection attack. Discussing the vagaries of SQL injection attacks is out of our scope, but properly crafted user input destined for an SQL parameter value can be used to obtain unlimited information about your database. If only there were an easy way to prevent the bad guys from hacking our queries, stealing our data, and generally causing us a lot of pain! Well, luckily, prepared statements can save the day.

WebSphere sMash provides several methods to define prepared statements for queries, which allow dynamic SQL queries based on input parameters, but with the safety of fixed string queries. Prepared statements use tokens to define where custom data elements should be inserted into the query statement. These tokens can be replaced with variable data, named elements of a map, or positional indexes from a list. Listing 8.23 shows how to use a query with a simple ordinal parameter replacement. The second argument to the queryFirst—or any of the other query statements—is a string, list, or map of values to be used as replacements in the query string.

Listing 8.23   Prepared Statement Using Request Parameter

```
def id = request.params.id[]
def result = mgr.queryFirst("select * from bookmark where id = ?",
?", id)
```

A more descriptive way to process parameters in an SQL statement is to use named parameters common in GroovyStrings. Listing 8.24 shows how we can make our SQL a little more descriptive by using a named parameter instead of the ambiguous question mark.

Listing 8.24 Prepared Statement Using Named Variable

```
def id = request.params.id[]
def result = mgr.queryFirst("select * from bookmark where id =
${id}")
```

That's a bit better, and its benefits are more dramatic when you have several parameters to replace. This also enables you to use a map to plug in several values at once using a map object in the form of ${obj.field}.

List expansion works just as well using this syntax. Listing 8.25 shows how a list of values can be inserted into a SQL statement.

Listing 8.25 Prepared Statement Using Positional List Parameters

```
def ids = [101, 102, 105]
def result = mgr.queryList("select * from bookmark where id in
(${ids[0]},${ids[1], ${ids[2]})")
```

The official WebSphere sMash documentation states that you can apply an entire list directly into a SQL statement, as shown in Listing 8.26, but this seems to always produce an error, no matter how we tried to make it work. It's preferred to use named parameters anyway, so don't feel too stressed about not being able to plop in a list of values, but we can easily envision when this would be useful in certain circumstances.

Listing 8.26 Prepared Statement Using Single List Argument

```
def ids = [101, 102, 105]
def result = mgr.queryList("select * from bookmark where id in
${ids}")
```

The SQL like clause is a common area where we want to perform fuzzy searches of data. WebSphere sMash handles this easily, as shown in Listing 8.27. Here we grab our search key from the request and wrap it with percent signs, which are wildcards in SQL parlance. I've also placed the tag value inside a map to show an alternative way of calling named parameters.

Listing 8.27 Prepared Statement Using Fuzzy Search

```
def args = ['tag': '%' + request.params.tag[] + '%' ]
def result = mgr.queryList("select * from bookmark where tags like
:tag", args)
```

There are a few more permutations of complex positional parameters that can be used in query statements, but using ordinal parameters or named parameters should cover most of your needs.

Externalizing SQL Statements

WebSphere sMash enables you to externalize your SQL statements into the configuration file and then reference these statements in the code. Some developers like to keep their SQL statements with the code that processes the data. Others tend to prefer to consolidate all SQL statements together and reference them within the code. We've seen previously how to directly define and use SQL statements within your data access code. The primary benefit to externalizing SQL statements is that it makes it easier for a DBA to examine and optimize all the statements used for an entire application in a single location without having to scan through the code. The disadvantage of this setup is that you tend to lose the strong natural binding between the SQL and the processing of the result data. I personally prefer to keep my SQL near the code, so that it's obvious what fields are being processed in the code. As is typical, it comes down to personal preference on how you manage your SQL statements.

To utilize externalized SQL statements, you need to add the statements to the associated database stanza in the configuration. An example of this is shown in Listing 8.28.

Listing 8.28   External SQL Statements

```
/config/db/bookmark/statements = {
    "GET_ALL"    : "select * from bookmark",
    "GET_BY_TAG" : "select * from bookmark where tags in :tag",
    "ADD"        : "insert into bookmark (url, description) values
(?,?)"
}
```

To use these named statements, just make a standard query*() request, passing the named SQL variable instead of a query string. sMash automatically substitutes the statement key with the proper query and make any defined parameter substitutions as well. An example can be seen in Listing 8.29.

Listing 8.29   SQL Using External SQL Statement

```
def args = ['tag': '%' + request.params.tag[] + '%' ]
def result = mgr.queryList( 'GET_BY_TAG', args)
```

Connection Pooling

For those of you who have developed high-performance classic JDBC style applications, you are likely pondering how pureQuery performs. pureQuery is designed for ease of use and simplicity. This means that, by default, connections are opened on request, statements processed, and the connection closed. Opening and closing connections are relatively expensive and can at times cause a noticeable delay in an application, especially under heavy loads. In standard JDBC applications, connection pools are used to hold open database connections that are reused by multiple requests. This greatly reduces the time spent creating and destroying connections.

WebSphere sMash currently does not support connection pooling of database resources, but by using the appropriate pooling driver classes or custom code, this can be easily achieved. Refer to the "Cookbook" entry discussing connection pooling on the Project Zero website for more information on implementing pooling in your application.

Data Access Using Java

There is effectively no difference between using Groovy for data access and Java. With Java, you just supply the appropriate class types for each return type. All the methods and processes are the same. By default, query results are returned as a map or list of maps. You can still coerce results into beans or "native" types by passing in the class type for the response within the query call. As an example, Listing 8.30 shows a sample block that performs a query and returns the results.

Listing 8.30   Selecting Data into a List of Beans

```
Manager data = Manager.create("bookmark");
String sql = "SELECT * FROM bookmark WHERE tags like ?";
String tag = "%smash%";
List results = data.queryList(sql, tag);
for( int x = 0; x < results.size(); x++ ) {
    System.out.println("Row: " + x+1 + " = " + results[x]);
}
System.out.println("Total rows returned: " + results.size() );
```

Data Access in PHP

Access relational data using PHP is performed essentially the same as with Java and Groovy, with just a slightly different syntax (see Listing 8.31).

Listing 8.31   Database Access Using PHP

```
//-- Create a manager reference
$manager = dataManager("bookmark");
$sql = "select * from bookmark where tags like ?";
$result = dataExec($manager,$sql, array("php") );
foreach ($result as $row) {
    foreach($row as $column => $value) {
        echo "$column = $value\n");
    }
}
```

PHP data access supports positional parameters, as shown here, as well as mapped parameters (for example, `:key`). You can see an example of a mapped parameter handling in the next sample. The other PHP data manipulation SQL statements are performed in a similar manner. Samples of these can be seen in Listing 8.32.

Listing 8.32   Sample PHP Data Manipulation Calls

```php
//-- Create a manager reference
$manager = dataManager("bookmark");

//-- Perform an Insert, using mapped parameters
$sql = "INSERT INTO bookmark (url, description, tags) VALUES (:url,
:description, :tags)";

$data = array(
    'url'          => 'http://www.w3schools.com/sql/default.asp',
    'description' => 'W3Schools SQL tutorial',
    'tags'         => 'sql'
);

$insertedRows = dataExec($manager,$sql,$data);

echo "Rows inserted: ".$insertedRows."\n";

// An Update (Reset all visited counts to zero.)
$sql = "UPDATE bookmark SET visited=0";

$updatedRows = dataExec($manager,$sql);

echo "Rows updated: ".$updatedRows."\n";

//-- A Delete action, because we have to clean out bad stuff
$sql = "DELETE FROM bookmark WHERE tags like ?";

$deletedRows = dataExec($manager, $sql, array("asp") );

echo "Rows deleted: ".$deletedRows."\n";
```

Error Handling

Errors in PHP database access can be checked by obtaining a reference to the `dataLastError` method. This returns a map of the last error condition encountered during a SQL operation. As shown in Table 8.3, there are several fields that can be queried to determine the cause of the failure.

Table 8.3 Query Fields

dataLastError() Object Key	Description
functionName	The name of the failing function
type	Error type generated
message	Reason message for the failure

A sample application that can test the error object is shown in Listing 8.33.

Listing 8.33 Sample PHP Query with Error Handling

```php
//-- Create a manager reference
$manager = dataManager("bookmark");
$sql = "select * from bookmark where id = 999999";
$result = dataExec($manager,$sql) );
if ( $result === null || count($result) === 0 ) {
    echo "Failed to locate any data\n";
    $error = dataLastError();
    echo "Error Function: ".$error['functionName']."\n";
    echo "Error Type: ".$error['type']."\n";
    echo "Error Message: ".$error['message']."\n";
}
```

Standard JDBC Database Access

The great thing about pureQuery is that it's still using JDBC under the covers. So, when you need to do complex data access work, or simply have legacy code you want to bring into a WebSphere sMash application, it's all good. As long as you have the database driver in your classpath, or in the application's lib directory, and import the required classes, you can do anything with JDBC that you would in a normal Java application. This is true of both Java and Groovy.

To utilize native JDBC, and still use the WebSphere sMash conventions of defining your database connection, obtain a database manager reference, as seen in all the pureQuery samples.

After you have the manager object, you now have full access to all the JDBC interfaces. Just remember to properly clean up your Connections, ResultSet, and Statement objects when using normal JDBC to avoid stale connections and memory leaks.

Let's cover a few useful ways to introspect your application's environment. Although you probably won't need to use these topics often, they can come in handy on those rare occasions. Some may be quite obvious, whereas others require a little more digging.

Locate All Database Definitions and Details

This method returns a list of all the databases defined in the config file, as shown in Listing 8.34. We grab several details for each database. The main thing to notice is how we obtain a manager reference, open a connection from the manager, get the details, and then close the connection.

Listing 8.34   Method to Return All Defined Databases

```
def getDatabases() {
    def dbs = zlist("/config/db", true)
    def list = []
    dbs.each {
        logger.INFO{"DB Key name: : + (it - '/config/db/') }
        def mgr = Manager.create( dbKey )
        def con = mgr.retrieveConnection()
        DatabaseMetaData dbMetaData = con.getMetaData();
        list << [
            'db_url'         : dbMetaData.getURL(),
            'db_name'        : dbMetaData.getDatabaseProductName(),
            'db_version'     : dbMetaData.getDatabaseProductVersion(),
            'driver_name'    : dbMetaData.getDriverName(),
            'driver_version' : dbMetaData.getDriverVersion()
        ]
        mgr.closeConnection()
    }
    logger.INFO {"getDatabases: ${list}"}
    return list;
}
```

Obtain Database Schema Details

The code sample shown in Listing 8.35 obtains a connection from the manager and returns a list of objects containing the schema entity. We'll use this result in the next tip to build up more information.

Listing 8.35   Method to Obtain Database Schema

```
def getSchemas(String dbKey) {
    def mgr = Manager.create( dbKey )
    def con = mgr.retrieveConnection()
    def list = []
    ResultSet schemas = con.getMetaData().getSchemas()
    while (schemas.next()) {
        String schema = schemas.getString("TABLE_SCHEM");
        list << ['uid':schema, 'name':schema, 'type':'schema']
    }
    mgr.closeConnection()
    logger.INFO {"getSchemas: ${list}"}
    return list;
}
```

Obtain Tables from Schema Entry

The code module shown in Listing 8.36 returns a list of tables within a schema, which we
obtained in the preceding example.

Listing 8.36   Method to Obtain Tables for a Schema

```
def getTables( String dbKey, String schema) {
    def mgr = Manager.create( dbKey )
    def con = mgr.retrieveConnection()
    def tables = []
    ResultSet rs = con.getMetaData().getTables(null, schema, "%",
null)
    while (rs.next()) {
        def table = rs.getString("TABLE_NAME")
        logger.INFO {"Got table: ${schema}.${table}" }
        tables << ['uid': "${schema}.${table}",
            'name': table,
            'type': 'table',
            'tableType': rs.getString("TABLE_TYPE") ]
    }
    mgr.closeConnection()
    logger.INFO{ "${schema} tables: ${tables}" }
    return tables
}
```

Get Columns for a Table

The function shown in Listing 8.37 returns a list of all the columns in the given table. We simply attempt to pull in a single record from the table and iterate over the resultsetMetaData for the column labels and column type names.

Listing 8.37   Method to Obtain Fields for a Table

```
def getTableColumns( String dbKey, String table) {
    logger.INFO{ "called for: ${ds}::${table}" }
    def cols = []

    //-- Check DB vendor, and adjust SQL to get single record
    def sql
    def dbInfo = getDbInfo( ds )
    if ( dbInfo.db_name.startsWith("DB2") ) {
        sql = 'select * from '+table+' FETCH FIRST 2 ROWS ONLY'
    } else if ( dbInfo.db_name.startsWith("SQL") ) {    //SQL*Server
        sql = 'select top 1 * from '+table
    } else if ( dbInfo.db_name.startsWith("Ora") ) {    //Oracle
        sql = 'select * from '+table+' where rownum=1'
    } else {
        // Just grab it all and bail out
        sql = 'select * from '+table
    }

    Connection con = null
    def stmt = null

    try {
        def manager = Manager.create( ds )
        con = manager.retrieveConnection()
        stmt = con.createStatement()
        stmt.execute( sql )
        ResultSet rs = stmt.getResultSet()
        ResultSetMetaData rsMetaData = rs.getMetaData();

        for (int x = 1; x <= rsMetaData.getColumnCount(); x++) {
            cols << [
                name : rsMetaData.getColumnLabel(x),
                type : rsMetaData.getColumnTypeName(x)
            ]
        }
    }
```

```
    } catch ( Exception e ) {
        logger.INFO {'Error on SQL processing' + e}
        cols = ["name":"ERROR", "type":"Error during SQL processing:
${e}"]
    } finally {
        try { stmt.close() } catch (Exception e) {}
        try { con.close()  } catch (Exception e) {}
    }
    logger.INFO{ "COLS: " + cols }
    return cols;
}
```

Process Dynamic SQL

OK, we know it is insanely dangerous to allow dynamic SQL calls into your database. Never create your SQL in the client browser and submit it to the server for execution. Yes, I've seen this done before on public websites. Talk about inviting the wolves into the hen house! You can't call this SQL injection—it's more like SQL mainlining. In any case, this is displayed in Listing 8.38.

Listing 8.38   Method to Run Dynamic SQL

```
def runSql(dbKey, sql) {
    logger.INFO {"RunSql Starting for ${dbKey}: ${sql}"}
    def map = [:]
    Connection con = null
    def stmt = null

    try {
        def manager = Manager.create( dbKey )
        con = manager.retrieveConnection()
        stmt = con.createStatement()
        if ( stmt.execute( sql ) ) {
            def headers = [
                ['name':'Row #', 'field':'_id_', 'type':'number' ]
            ]
            ResultSet rs = stmt.getResultSet()
            ResultSetMetaData rsMetaData = rs.getMetaData();
            for (int x = 1; x <= rsMetaData.getColumnCount(); x++
) {
                def type
                switch (rsMetaData.getColumnType(x)) {
```

```
            case Types.BIGINT:      case Types.INTEGER:
            case Types.NUMERIC:     case Types.SMALLINT:
            case Types.TINYINT:     case Types.DECIMAL:
            case Types.DOUBLE:      case Types.FLOAT:
                type = "number"
                break;
            case Types.BINARY:      case Types.BIT:
            case Types.BOOLEAN:
                type = "boolean"
                break;
            default:
                type = "string"
                break;
            }
            headers << [
                name    : rsMetaData.getColumnLabel(x),
                field   : 'C'+x, 'type':type
            ]
        }
    map.put( 'headers', headers )

    //-- Process result set
    def content = [
        'identifier' : '_id_',
        'label'      : 'C1',
        'items'      : []
    ]
    def rowCntr = 1
    while (rs.next()) {
        def row = [ '_id_': rowCntr ]
        for( int c = 1; c <= rsMetaData.getColumnCount(); c++ ) {
            def cellData = zero.util.XMLEncoder.escapeXML(
                            rs.getString(c) );
            row.put( [ ('C'+c), cellData ] )
        }
        content.items << row
        //-- Sanity check!
        if ( rowCntr++ >= 10000 ) {
            break
        }
    }
```

```
            map.put('content', content)
            if ( rowCntr > 1 ) {
                map.put('message', "Successfully retrieved ${rowCntr}
                        records")
            } else {
                map.put('message', "No records found")
            }
        } else {
            //-- Assume an "update" (insert, update, delete)
            def cnt = stmt.getUpdateCount()
            map.put('message', "${cnt} records processed.")
        }
    } catch ( Exception e ) {
        logger.INFO {'processSql: Error on SQL processing' + e}
        map.put('message', "Error during SQL processing: ${e}")

    } finally {
        try { stmt.close() } catch (Exception e) {}
        try { con.close()  } catch (Exception e) {}
    }
    return map
}
```

The extra processing performed on the `ResultsetMetaData` is to build up a header section so that when we return the results back to the browser, we can build a nicely formatted table.

WebSphere sMash DBA—The Database Administrator Application

If you have not guessed by now, we have all the makings of a DBA-style application. We can get a list of data sources with connection details, obtain the schemas and tables for each data source, get the columns for a table, and then enable a user to execute SQL based on all the information we've provided. All that's needed is to front these methods with REST accessors.

To support the DBA application, the JDBC scripts defined previously need to be made available as REST services. Start by creating a new WebSphere sMash application called `Book.Database.DBA` and then create a single file. Because all the database access logic is encapsulated in the /app/scripts are of the application, the only logic needed by the REST services is to parse any parameters, pass them to the appropriate method, and format the results into a usable response. To make it easy on the WebSphere sMash DBA application, all responses are formatted in a Dojo-specific DataStore JSON layout, which consists of a list of rows called items. Within each item is a map of all the field-value pairs. There are a couple meta-fields that define the ID member and the fields to be used as a label for presentation. Listing 8.39 provides a sample

GET call for the list of DataSources for this application. This entry is located in /app/resources/ds.groovy. All the other database functions are also configured with appropriate resource definitions, as shown in Table 8.4. Because several services are dependent on a specific DataSource, binding files (.bnd) are also defined as needed.

Table 8.4   REST Resources for Database Access

REST Service	Call Type	Site Specific
/resources/ds	GET (list)	Get list of all available DataSources
/resources/ds/{ds}	GET (singular)	Get Schema details for a DataSource
/resources/dbInfo/{ds}	GET (singular)	Get Driver details for a given DataSource
/resources/ds/{ds}/table/{table}	GET (singular)	Get columns for Table within DataSource
/resources/ds/{ds}/sql	POST	Execute SQL within a DataSource

Listing 8.39   REST Resource to Obtain All DataSources

```
/*
 * Obtain all available DataSources
 * Returns:
 *    ItemFileReadStore Json object, with hierarchical format
 *    {"label":"uid","identifier":"uid","items":}
 */
def onList() {
    logger.INFO {'onList called'};
    def dbs = invokeMethod("dba", "getDataSources", null)
    def map = ['label':'uid', 'identifier':'uid']
    def items = []
    dbs.each { items << ['uid': it] }
    map.put('items', items)
    invokeMethod('sendResponse', 'json', map)
    logger.INFO {'onList finished'}
}
```

In Chapter 12, "Client-Side Programming with the Dojo Toolkit," we'll be creating a front end that will take advantage of all these database-related REST services. Feel free to skip ahead, or wait to savor the goodness.

Command-Line Database Management

WebSphere sMash comes with several commands that can be accessed from the console or command line. These lend themselves particularly well to testing and building scripts. Let's go over each command and see how they work.

validatedb {dbKey}

This command is used to verify a database's configuration. The CLI attempts to establish a connection to the database manager defined in the first argument. If everything is OK, the command says so; otherwise, it displays an appropriate error message. As an example, Listing 8.40 shows two calls to `validatedb`. The first is to our properly defined `bookmark` configuration, and the second is to another configuration called `bad`, which has an improper driver defined.

Listing 8.40   Two Runs of validatedb Command: One Good and One Bad

```
command> zero validatedb bookmark
CWPZT0600I: Command validatedb was successful

command> zero validatedb bad

[pdq][0][1.3.110] CWPZC9044E: Manager create failed for
/config/db/bad -> [pdq][0][1.3.110] com.mysql.InvalidDataSource;
Caused by: java.lang.ClassNotFoundException:
com.mysql.InvalidDataSource ;
  Caused by: com.ibm.pdq.runtime.exception.DataRuntimeException:
[pdq][0][1.3.110] com.mysql.InvalidDataSource
```

runsql {dbKey} {sqlFile}

The `runsql` command is rather self-explanatory. You pass in a filename relative to the application home directory, and the CLI will execute it. The SQL commands in the file can be any combination of the following:

- Table data modifier queries, such as INSERT, UPDATE, and DELETE (but not SELECT)
- Database alter methods, such as CREATE, DROP, and ALTER
- Database vendor-specific SQL commands to define databases, tables, indexes, and so on

You may opt to place all actions into a single SQL file or break them up into logical units. Typically, you want a script that will reinitialize or create from scratch an entire database. Because all actions within a SQL file are run under a single database transaction, a failure anywhere in the chain of statements will result in a rollback of the entire transaction.

By convention, you should place these SQL files into vendor-specific directories. These files should be located within your project as follows:

```
{app_home}/config/sql/{db_vendor}/{app_name}_{action}.sql
```

As an example, we may have SQL files to create, drop, and populate the MySQL-based bookmark table. We would end up with three files like those shown in Listing 8.41.

Listing 8.41   Database Manipulation Scripts

```
/config/sql/mysql/bookmark_create.sql
/config/sql/mysql/bookmark_populate.sql
/config/sql/mysql/bookmark_drop.sql
```

Now you can script your build process to run each of the SQL files in the proper order. This sample assumes that your current directory is the application's root folder (see Listing 8.42).

Listing 8.42   Running Database Scripts

```
zero runsql bookmark config/sql/mysql/bookmark_drop.sql
zero runsql bookmark config/sql/mysql/bookmark_create.sql
zero runsql bookmark config/sql/mysql/bookmark_populate.sql
```

Conclusion

This chapter has explored the various ways you can easily back your WebSphere sMash applications with relational databases. The Zero Resource Manager can deftly handle the process of designing and populating databases, as well as handling all the standard database access and modifier REST patterns, with literally a single line of code. When your needs grow beyond the design simplicity of ZRM, using pureQuery to access your data provides a powerful and streamlined API for data processing. Low-level database access and manipulation is always available through normal JDBC calls.

We hope that you can recognize the power and development efficiencies that come with using ZRM and pureQuery to empower your applications with WebSphere sMash. When compared with standard JDBC and other data access APIs, WebSphere sMash ranks right up there with popcorn and cotton candy. So, you've been able to deliver that marketing request to gain insight into the company's data by the end of the day, and its not even lunch time! Take the rest of the day off, and take your kids to the circus. Just stay clear of those creepy clowns.

CHAPTER 9

Security Model

Web application security is an obvious requirement in essentially any corporate project, but one that is often underestimated or forgotten. WebSphere sMash provides a rich set of features to assist in hardening your projects to meet today's stringent requirements. In this chapter, we discuss the different areas where WebSphere sMash security is used to prevent the bad guys from running roughshod over your site and accessing your company's private data. There are several facets of the security model that we need to cover, as shown in Figure 9.1.

Secure messaging consists of the following four characteristics:

- **Confidentiality**—Only the authorized party can access defined content. This is also referred to as authorization.

- **Integrity**—Only the authorized party can modify the data content, and those changes can be detected.

- **Authentication**—The identities of the sender and receivers of the content cannot be disguised.

- **Non-repudiation**—The sender cannot deny a message's origination. This is managed through the digital signing of the data content.

Authentication is addressed in several different ways later in the chapter. The first two of these security entities can be managed effectively through the transport layer using Secure Socket Layer (SSL) encryption. SSL is the standard solution for web application security. For web applications, we simply request the https protocol over the basic non-encrypted http protocol. SSL is built-in in all browsers, so there are no setup requirements on the client side. Another benefit of SSL is the ease of configuration for firewalls.

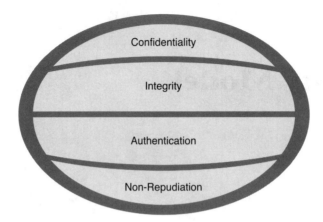

Figure 9.1   Security characteristics

SSL works by encrypting all data that passes between the client and the server. Only these two endpoints are capable of decrypting each other's data content. As we said earlier, SSL provides confidentiality, integrity, and authentication through the use of certificates. SSL has no provision to prove the authenticity of the originator of a message. Just because a message says it came from the expected server, there is no way to prove that it actually did. The other limiting factor with SSL is intermediary sites. There may be a secure link from the browser to the main server, but there are no guarantees that connections from the server to other sites (such as in a proxy situation) are secure, or that the data content was not corrupted in one of these secondary connections.

Digital signing of content between the browser and server(s) is possible, but there are no real cross-browser solutions available. Because most web application activity is defined as a point-to-point connection between the browser and the server, you have to trust that server anyway. As a client, you have to trust the server to be responsible to handle any sensitive data appropriately when communicating with other systems.

As you can see, we've been somewhat non-specific on the actual content that we want to secure. That's because it applies across the board, in that it can be static assets such as HTML and JavaScript files, or it can be dynamic data being accessed through a browser AJAX call to a REST resource, or the server making external calls to other systems.

Do you need to protect everything with SSL? Well, no, not if you are building an application that does not contain sensitive information and does not require any user authentication. In these applications, keep it simple, and let your anonymous users have a good time.

In the business space, and even within the confines of a company intranet, encryption and authentication are frequently needed for authorization and accounting needs. Let's go through the ways in which WebSphere sMash can assist in securing your application.

To properly configure a WebSphere sMash application to use user authentication, we need to make some changes to the zero configuration file. These settings include the following:

- Enabling SSL
- Defining a secret key for encryption
- Turning on security
- Defining the authentication type
- Defining the resources to protect

We need to assemble together all the pieces of our security puzzle before we can appreciate the final solution.

SSL Configuration

As stated at the beginning of this chapter, SSL encryption of the connection solved two of the four security concerns: confidentiality and integrity. Security and SSL go hand in hand in all web-based connections. Setting up SSL within WebSphere sMash is rather trivial when you have a keystore file. In a real-world environment, you would normally purchase an SSL key from a trusted authority, such as VeriSign or a similar entity. By obtaining your key in this manner, the key provider is vouching that you are a reputable party. For our purposes, we'll create a self-signed certificate for enabling SSL connections to our application. As its name suggests, a self-signed certificate should not be trusted outside your immediate sphere of influence, because you are simply stating that you created your own key, and you are only as good as your word. In a business sense, production servers should always be backed by legitimate certificates provided by a trusted authority.

Let's get into the meat of creating a certificate and configuring our application to use SSL encryption. We're just going to go through the bare minimum on key creation, as it can be a rather intricate subject. If you need more details, read up on Java Secure Socket Extensions (JSSE) for your particular Java provider. Your company's network administrators may also be able to provide you with custom certification keys for your application; otherwise, just follow these steps, and we'll get things going rather quickly.

First, it is assumed that you have already created a new WebSphere sMash application or have an existing application that you want to secure. Go to a command line and change to the application's `config` directory. When there, assuming you are using IBM's Java, run IBM's ikeyman utility to create the keystore. If you are using an alternative Java runtime, such as Oracle's Sun Java, use the appropriate keytool utility, as described in the vendor's documentation. Execute the `ikeyman` command, and click the Create icon, as shown in Figure 9.2. Verify or correct the Location field to point toward your application's `config` directory. Click OK, enter your preferred password, and click OK again to create the store. Remember this password, as we'll be using it again shortly.

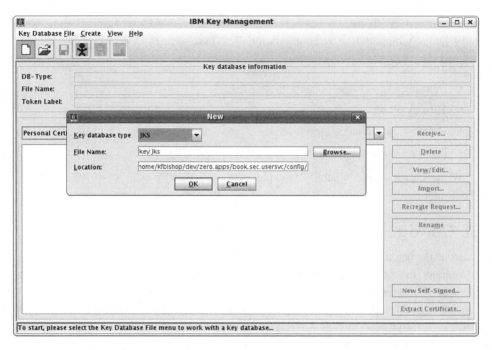

Figure 9.2   IBM ikeyman utility: Create self-signed cert.

Next, click the New Self-Signed button to create the certificate. In the dialog, enter in the Key Label field and Common Name field, as shown in Figure 9.3. All the other fields can be left blank or filled in as you see fit. Click OK to close this dialog. Exit out of the ikeyman utility. The result will be a new keystore file called `key.jks` located in the application's `config` directory.

The next task is to set up the SSL configuration for the application. Open the `zero.config` file and add the following stanza, as shown in Listing 9.1, somewhere in the file. The first non-comment lines define our HTTP and HTTPS (SSL) ports we'll be using—in this case, 8443. You may optionally disable the normal HTTP port by setting it to a value of `0`. The second block defines the SSL configuration. We set the keystore to point to our newly created keystore file (key.jks). The keystore password must be the same one you used to create the keystore itself. Although not required, it's a good practice to enter this (and all passwords) as an XOR-encoded string. This is done by running the `zero encode mypassword` command from within your application's directory tree. Copy the resulting XOR string as the value of the keystore password. The final entry is the type of store we are using, which in this case is JKS (Java Key System). The final stanza is required because we have an insecure self-signed certificate. Set the trust value to false while using this cert; when you obtain a real certificate, you can set it to false or simply remove this stanza altogether.

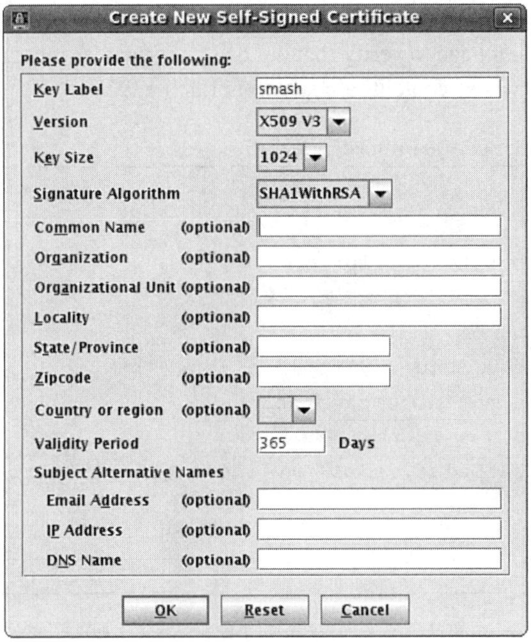

Figure 9.3 Create a self-signed certificate.

Listing 9.1 SSL Configuration Settings

```
#----------------------------------------------------------
#-- SSL Config
#----------------------------------------------------------
/config/http/port  = 0
/config/https/port = 8443
/config/https/sslconfig = {
 "keyStore":         "keystore.jks",
 "keyStorePassword": "<xor>Lz4sLCgwLTs=",
 "keyStoreType":     "JKS"
}

#-- Add this for any self-signed certs.
#-- Remove/comment out for production certs
/config/connection/https/defaultConfig +={
  "disableTrustVerification" : true
}
```

At this point, our application is ready to serve pages using the HTTPS protocol. Let's create a simple index.get landing page to verify that our SSL certificate is recognized. Create a new file called /public/index.gt, whose contents are shown in Listing 9.2.

Listing 9.2   Main Landing Page (/public/index.gt)

```
<html>
<head>
  <title>sMash Security</title>
</head>
<body>
  <h1>Welcome to the Security Application</h1>
  <h3>This page is not protected</h3>
  <h2>Try going to a
    <a href="<%= getRelativeUri('my/index.gt') %>">Protected page</a>.
  </h2>
</body>
</html>
```

Open your browser to https://localhost:8443/ (note the https protocol, and the special port number we defined earlier). You should first get a warning from your browser that the connection is untrusted, due to using a self-signed certificate. This is a good behavior, as it's validating that WebSphere sMash was able to process the certificate, and your browser just doesn't approve its validity. Click through the warning to acknowledge this issue and optionally add this as an exception to your browser. You should then be taken to our main landing page, as shown in Figure 9.4. We'll build on this shortly to add a secured page, as well as login and logout pages. That wasn't so bad, was it? Next, let's go over user authentication and how we actually protect various resources in our application.

Figure 9.4   Main landing page

Enabling Security

A single setting enables security within a WebSphere sMash application. A secure application by default protects all resources addressable by URL, and simply requires users to be authenticated, but no other restrictions are applied. We'll walk through fine tuning which resources should be protected, and for which users and groups, later in this chapter. To enable security, add the line shown in Listing 9.3. This provides a single location to quickly disable security during debugging, by just commenting out this one line, regardless of any other security-based configurations defined in the configuration.

Listing 9.3   Enable Security Configuration Setting

```
#-----------------------------------------------------------
#-- Security Config
#-----------------------------------------------------------
@include "security/enableSecurity.config"
```

Application Secret Key

Each application that will enable security needs to have a secret key defined. This key is used to provide a seed for encrypting sensitive data. By utilizing a secret key value within the application, the potential for Cross Site Request Forgery (CSRF)[1] and other external attack vectors is greatly reduced. The actual value of the secret key has no meaning, other than it is nearly impossible for an attacker to guess it to use in an exploit.

To create a secret key, run the `zero secretkey` command from within your application's directory. Alternately, if you are using the AppBuilder, select the Console tab, and run `zero secretkey` at the prompt, as shown in Figure 9.5. In either case, the results will be an encoded secret key string. Copy this value and add it as a value to the `/config/security/secretKey` entry in the application's `zero.config` file, as shown in Listing 9.4.

Listing 9.4   Adding a Secret Key to the Application's config File

```
#-----------------------------------------------------------
#-- Security settings
#-----------------------------------------------------------
@include "security/enableSecurity.config"
/config/security/secretKey="iZBIC6dB2pWBURIW/UEVSw=="
```

For advanced scenarios where you may want to have two or more WebSphere sMash applications share common tokens, generate a secret key in one of the applications, and copy this common value to each of the other applications.

---

[1] CSRF: http://en.wikipedia.org/wiki/Cross-site_request_forgery

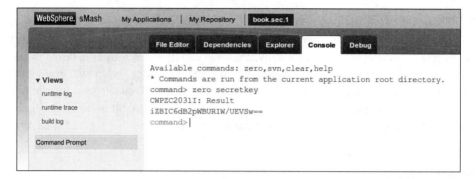

Figure 9.5   Create a secret key in AppBuilder's console.

Authentication Types

All resources in WebSphere sMash are protected by URLs. Patterns can be used to define which URLs require authentication. When you define a rule for a URL or URL pattern, you may also limit it to be accessed by certain users and/or groups. The default value for any authenticated user is membership within the group: ALL_AUTHENTICATED_USERS. The default security rules, when enabled as described previously, restrict access to all URL patterns. Most applications will probably want to allow anonymous users to at least access a welcome page or other introductory pages, which is explained further later in the chapter.

There are a few different methods for authentication within WebSphere sMash, as described in the following sections:

1. Basic authentication prompts the user with a simple browser-styled pop-up similar to Figure 9.6, which will request the username and password when a non-authenticated user requests a protected URL. See RFC 2617[2] for details on basic authentication.

Figure 9.6   Basic authentication login prompt

---

[2] RFC 2617: http://tools.ietf.org/html/rfc2617

2. Form-based authentication provides a better user experience in that when a protected resource is requested, a custom login page is presented to the user that can be tailored to match the overall business styling of the rest of the application.

In this setup, we'll be using form-based authentication, which is a common means for defining how a user is authenticated against a user registry. Other types of authentication include single-sign on services, OpenID, and custom programmatic solutions. We'll touch on these other authentication types and features later in the chapter.

The generalized authentication flow for the types of authentication mentioned previously is shown in Figure 9.7.

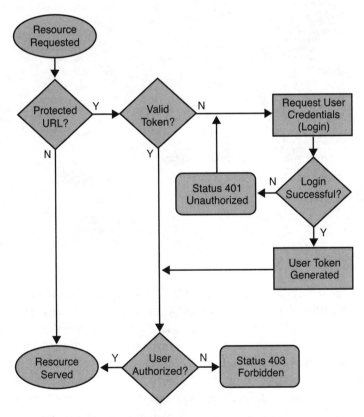

Figure 9.7 General authentication logic flow

Form-Based Authentication Configuration Settings

Table 9.1 lists the various settings available to define the form-based authentication environment within the WebSphere sMash application. Each of these is a member of the `/config/security` object in the `zero.config` file.

Table 9.1   URL Protection Values

Member	Description	Default
conditions	This defines the URL-based resource(s) to be protected. You may also define the HTTP methods (GET, POST, and so on) allowed as well.	`"/request/path =~ /(.*)?"` This pattern defines all possible URL paths.
users	Array of user IDs allowed to access this resource.	All authenticated users may access this resource.
groups	Array of groups whose members are allowed to access this resource.	`["ALL_AUTHENTICATED_USERS"]` This is a pseudo-group that all members belong to.
roles	Array of roles whose members are allowed to access this resource.	Unset
realm	Default realm used for basic authentication. This is an advanced LDAP environment setting.	Unset

Let's put these settings into the `zero.config` file for our application. In the configuration fragment shown in Listing 9.5, we define the following settings. In the first stanza, we define a new rule that protects any URLs that are located under the /my tree. When an URL matching this pattern is requested from the browser, the basic authentication mechanism checks for a valid token and if not found will request that the user log in. Upon successful authentication, the user is checked to see if he is a member of the listed groups for authorization. We are allowing any authenticated user, based on the default pseudo-group called `"ALL_AUTHENTICATED_USERS"`. The second stanza defines the form page URL, which in our case is located at `"/login.gt"`.

Listing 9.5   Form-Based Authentication Configuration

```
#------------------------------------------------------------
#-- URL Protection
#------------------------------------------------------------
#-- Conditions define what path(s) are to be protected (req login)
#-- Groups list the groups that are allowed access to this url path
@include "security/rule.config" {
   "conditions": "/request/path =~ /my(.*)?",
   "authType"   : "Form",
   "groups"     : ["ALL_AUTHENTICATED_USERS"]
}


#-- Login form
@include "security/form.config" {
   "formLoginPage" : "/login.gt"
}
```

Login Form

Next, we need to create our login page that will be used exercise the security configuration. By using basic authentication, if the user does not have a valid token defined, he will be redirected to the defined login page. The login page itself consists of three fields within a POST form. You can dress up this form as desired to meet any stylistic needs. The basics of this page consist of that shown in Listing 9.6. Here, we have a standard HTML form with a POST method. There are two required input fields: `"zeroUserName"` and `"zeroPassword"`. There is also an optional third field called `"postLoginTargetURI"`; if set, this field will be used as the target page when the login is successful and is used for the redirect target. If this field is not present, the originally requested resource will be the target page used after successful authentication.

Listing 9.6   Login Form Page (/login.gt)

```
<html>
<head>
   <title>Login Test</title>
   <style>
     @import "<%=getRelativeUri('/theme.css')%>";
   </style>
</head>
<body>
```

```
<% if( zget("/request/headers/in/Referer") =~ zget("/request/uri") ){ %>
  <div class='error'>
    <h2>Invalid user ID or password</h2>
    Please verify your ID and password and try again.
  </div>
<% } %>

  <p>Login using your normal user ID and password:</p>
  <form method="POST" action="" name="loginForm">
    <!-- optional hidden field to force the target redirect
         after login -->
    <!--
    <input type="hidden" name="postLoginTargetURI" value="/my">
    -->

    <label for="zeroUserName">User ID:</label><br/>
    <input type="text" name="zeroUserName" size='20' /><br/>

    <label for="zeroPassword">Password:</label><br/>
    <input type="password" name="zeroPassword" size='12' /><br/><br/>

    <input type="submit" value="Submit" />
  </form>

</body>
</html>
```

If you examine the code on the login page, there is an obscure check to determine if the referring page is the same as this page. This is done to determine if the user has been to the login page already. If a user attempts a login and enters a bad username or password, the login fails, and the user is returned to the login page.

Another error condition that we need to tackle based on the flow diagram is when the user successfully logs in but is not authorized to view the resource based on the URL in the configuration settings. In this case, a 403 error will be returned by the login process. To handle this situation, we have to create a `/app/errors/error403.gt` file to inform the user of what went wrong. You can see a sample of this in Listing 9.7. You should provide the user with a means of returning to a clean state, such as a link to the application's home page, when this error condition is encountered.

Listing 9.7   /app/errors/error403.gt

```
<html>
<head>
  <title>Login Error</title>
  <style type="text/css">
    @import "<%=getRelativeUri("/theme/style.css")%>";
  </style>
</head>
<body>
  <div class='error'>
    <h2>Unauthorized access (Code: 403)</h2>
    You are not allowed to access this portion of the application.
    Please contact the application owner and request access.
  </div>
</body>
</html>
```

Knowing Your Users

When you allow a user to access sensitive information, it is important to know who that person is. It is important to maintain various levels of control over who can access different types of documents. This control is done through authorization, where typically the user will log into the application with a uniquely identifying username and password. When you know who you are dealing with, you can also determine other information for this user, such as his name and what groups he belongs to. You can then use this information to provide a custom experience tailored specifically to his rights, privileges, and preferences.

There are many different systems available for managing users. Some of the more common include the Lightweight Directory Access Protocol (LDAP), such as IBM's Tivoli® Directory Server, Microsoft® Active Directory, and some relatively new solutions, such as OpenID. WebSphere sMash uses standard Java Authentication and Authorization Service (JAAS), to authenticate users and also provides a minimal file-based user management solution for basic user authentication.

We'll start out by building a simple file-based user authentication solution. After this is fully built and working, we will then modify the solution to use an LDAP server and take a peek into defining an OpenID environment as well.

Basic Zero Users Configuration

By default, WebSphere sMash provides an embedded user registry that can be used for small to medium applications or testing that does not require an external authentication resource. This file-based service maintains a list of users, their passwords, and the groups they belong to. The file is called `zero.users` and is located in the application's `/config` directory. To create or edit entries in the user service, run `zero user` from the command line or from the command prompt within AppBuilder. A series of prompts guide you through the process of creating or editing users, as shown in Figure 9.8. For advanced usage, you can supply all the parameters on the command line, which would facilitate creation of users through a script or other build process.

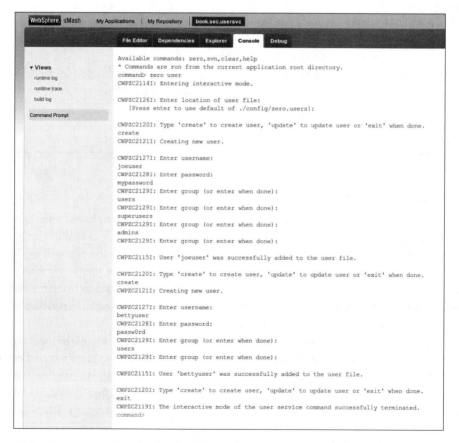

Figure 9.8   Creating users using the file-based zero user command

After you have created your users and assigned them a password and group memberships, the `zero.users` file will be created. Groups can be used to restrict users based on some arbitrary collection, such as team membership or management level. Figure 9.9 shows the resulting user file after creating a couple users.

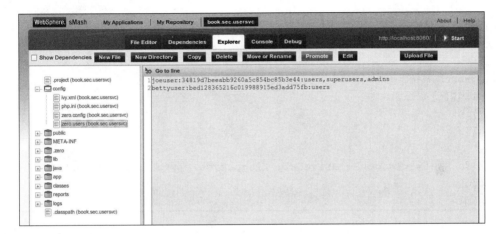

Figure 9.9 Listing of zero.users file

Additional Files for Our Application

Before we can test out this secure application, we need to create a couple more files. The first is a protected index page, and the next is a logout page for when the user actively clicks a logout link.

The first page we need to create is our protected page, located at /public/my/index.gt. The contents of this file are shown in Listing 9.8. On this page, we can be assured that the user is logged in successfully, and we then show some details about the user. As you can see, we are limited to the username and the groups of which he is a member. If you need more details than that, you need to step up to an LDAP or similar solution or create your own custom user profile within the application itself to retrieve this kind of information from an external identity resource—for example, a directory server (LDAP server) or even your self-built identity information database.

Listing 9.8 Secured Landing Page (/public/my/index.gt)

```
<html>
<head>
 <title>Protected Page</title>
</head>
<body>

<%
```

```
def user    = request.subject.remoteUser[]
def groups = []+request.subject.groups[]
%>

<h1>Hello ${user}</h1>
<h2>Your group(s):</h2>
<ul>
<% groups.each { g -> %>
  <li>${g}</li>
<% } %>
</ul>

<h2><a href="<%= getRelativeUri('/logout.gt')%>">Logout<a></h2>
</body>
</html>
```

The final page we need to add is a logout page. It is always a good practice to provide a means to enable your users to log out of an application. Listing 9.9 creates a logout page. You often should do some housekeeping on the "user" Global Context and remove any session-like variables that you do not want to persist into the user's next access to the site. This could include sensitive data that should not be persisted or just as a means of good housekeeping.

Listing 9.9   Logout Page (/public/logout.gt)

```
<html>
<head>
  <title>Logout</title>
</head>
<body>
<%
zero.core.security.LoginService.logout();
%>
  <h1>You have been logged out</h1>
  <h2>Return to
    <a href="<%= getRelativeUri('/index.gt') %>">Home page</a>.
  </h2>
</body>
</html>
```

Testing the Secure Application

At this point, we have all the pieces required to test our secure application. Start the application, and open your browser to the secure https port defined in the configuration file. In the preceding example, we had chosen port number 9443, so your URL is https://localhost:9443/. You should be presented with our insecure main landing page without being prompted for a login, as shown in back in Figure 9.4.

Click the link to go to the secure page. If everything is configured properly, you will be redirected to the login page (see Figure 9.10) for user authentication. On subsequent attempts to access the secure page after logging in, you will have a valid browser token and will not need to log in again. To test out our failed login logic, enter either a bad username or wrong password, and click Submit. You will be returned to the login page and an appropriate error message will be displayed, as seen in Figure 9.11. At this point, log in using your correct username and password and verify that you are able to log in. We now look at our secured page with information about your user, as shown in Figure 9.12. To close out our test, click the logout link, which will put you on the logout page shown in Figure 9.13. To verify that you are actually logged out, manually enter the secured landing page URL: https://localhost:9443/my/index.gt. You should be redirected to the login page once again. You've done it! A nice, clean user-secured application.

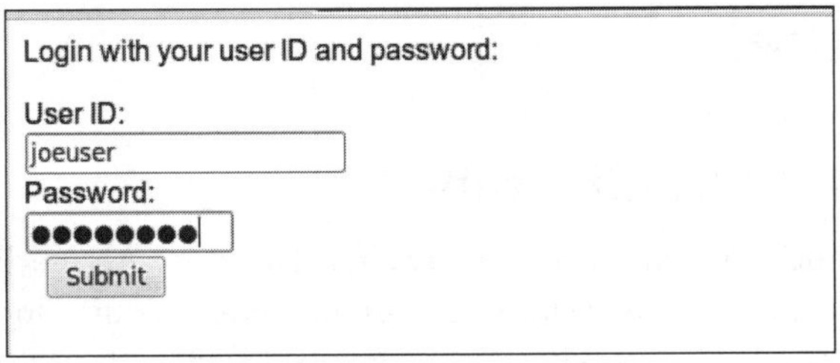

Figure 9.10   Login page

Figure 9.11   Login page after failed login

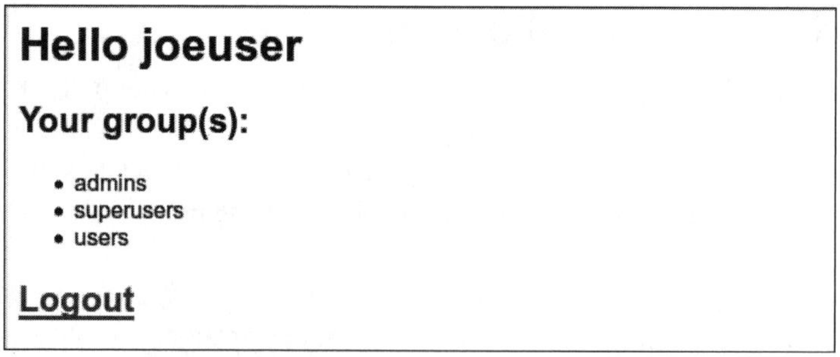

Hello joeuser

Your group(s):

- admins
- superusers
- users

Logout

Figure 9.12   Secured landing page

You have been logged out

Return to Home page.

Figure 9.13   Logout page

Directory Server Configuration

Directory servers, which implement the Lightweight Directory Access Protocol (LDAP), are probably the most common user repository in most enterprises. A directory server consists of a hierarchical database that stores user information or users' profile information by a unique distinguished name (DN), which is equal to a path and through which an application is able to search and retrieve information. Based on this information, a directory server is an ideal ID source for this application functionality. Other than the WebSphere sMash configuration settings, you'll see that this is very similar to the solution we just built. Although there are some syntax contortions that are necessary to deal with LDAP, it is very effective in what it does.

Namely, directory servers store user information with quick and secure identification access. Because many LDAP installations are unique in how they store and define the data structure, we can't cover all situations. Consult your directory server's documentation and site administrator for more details about the required search and filtering constraints.

We show a generic configuration and leave it as an exercise for you and your LDAP administrator to determine the proper arguments to access your site's LDAP particulars.

The first thing we need to do is enable the application for LDAP authentication. After a user is logged in, the only attributes we have by default are the unique user ID, which (depending on the LDAP configuration) may be different than the user ID used to log in and the group memberships, as shown in Table 9.2. In almost any situation, you'll want more information than what is provided here, so we'll also look to see how to obtain extended LDAP attributes for a given user.

Table 9.2   User Authentication Variables

LDAP Attribute	Global Context Entry
Unique user ID	`request.subject.remoteUser[]`
Group membership	`request.subject.groups[]`

Let's define the configuration settings to authenticate with the LDAP server. Edit your application's `zero.config` file and add the information, as shown in Listing 9.10. You need to get the actual LDAP values from your friendly system administrator.

Listing 9.10   LDAP-Specific Configuration Settings

```
#--------------------------------------------------------
#-- LDAP Settings
#--------------------------------------------------------
/config/security/userservice/registryType="ldap"

#-- General LDAP Auth
/config/security/userservice/ldap += {
  "jndiProviderUrl"                   : "ldap://ldap.acme.com:389/",
  "ldapUserIdSearchFilterPattern" :
"(&(mail={0})(objectclass=inetOrgPerson))",
  "ldapGroupSearchFilterPattern"  : "(&(member={0})
(objectclass=groupOfNames))",
  "ldapUserIdBaseDn"                  : "ou=people,o=acme.com",
  "ldapGroupBaseDn"               :
"ou=memberlist,ou=groups,o=acme.com"
}

#-- Token Support - Pick Simple or LTPA2.
#-- SimpleToken support
/config/security/token/simple += {
    "tokenExpiration": 120,
    "ssoDomains" : ["acme.com"]
}
```

```
#-- LTPAToken2 support
#-- Referenced key is relative to /config dir.
#@include "security/token/ltpa2.config"{
#    "keyImportFile": "myLTPA.key",
#    "keyPassword" : "myPassword",
#    "ssoDomains" : ["acme.com"]
#}
```

These are the only configuration items we need to add to the existing values in the security sample application. Everything else remains as it is. Let's take a quick walk-through of these settings. First, we need to set the security registry type to LDAP. The second stanza defines the LDAP server host, its port, and its query settings. Again, the actual values here are dependent on the server installation you want to use.

Directory Server User Details

Next, we need to create a method to assist us in obtaining more details about the authenticated user. To do this, we'll need to obtain the Groovy-Ldap package from the Apache project.[3] To use Groovy-Ldap, download and extract the package to a temporary directory. Copy the included JAR file to your project's /lib directory. Next, create a new groovy file in your application named /app/scripts/helpers/ldap.groovy, and populate it with the code shown in Listing 9.11. You will need to alter the LDAP-specific variables to match your environment. A second and even better approach would be to put these values into the application's zero.config file and reference the settings appropriately. In this LDAP helper method, we establish a connection to the LDAP server, set up a search query, and cache the results into the user context object for future use. Be watchful of the objects that are returned from these LDAP calls, as the query might return an array of objects, and the values for the entries will be either a string or an array of strings. It's best to first test the type of the values before using them. For details on how to use Groovy-Ldap, and to see how you can perform advanced searches, add, updates, and deletes, refer to the documentation on the Apache.org website.

Listing 9.11   LDAP User Details Function

```
package helpers

def getUser() {
  if ( ! user.me[] ) {
```

[3] GroovyLdap: http://cwiki.apache.org/DIRxSBOX/groovy-ldap.html

```
  //-- Replace these with your site specific values
  def ldapServer       = 'ldap://acme.com:389/ou=people,o=acme.com'
  def ldapSearchFilter = '(&(objectClass=person)(uid={0}))'

  def uid = request.subject.remoteUser[]
  def ldap =
    org.apache.directory.groovyldap.LDAP.newInstance( ldapServer )
  def search = new org.apache.directory.groovyldap.Search()
  search.filter = ldapSearchFilter
  search.filterArgs = [ uid.toLowerCase() ]
  def results = ldap.search(search)
  if ( results != null && results.size() > 0 ) {
    user.me = results[0]
    logger.INFO{ "Me: ${user.me[]}" }
  }
 }
 return user.me[]
}
```

Now we have everything we need to deal with our user, and all his personal attributes. Because we protected the /my URL in the initial configuration, let's create an index.gt file there and see what our LDAP server can tell us about our user. Place the code shown in Listing 9.12 into /public/my/index.gt.

Listing 9.12   Enhanced User and Group Details Page

```
<%
def uid    = request.subject.remoteUser[]
def groups = ( []+request.subject.groups[] ).sort()
def user   = invokeMethod('helpers/ldap.groovy','getUser', null)
%>
<table border='1' width="100%" cellspacing='0px' cellpadding='0px'>
  <tr>
    <th colspan='2'><h2>Hello ${uid}</h2></th>
  </tr>
  <tr>
    <th><h2>Your LDAP details</h2></th>
    <th><h2>Your Groups</h2></th>
  </tr>
  <tr>
    <td>
```

```
      <table border='1' width='100%'>
<% user.keySet().sort().each { key -> %>
        <tr><td>${key}</td><td>${user[key]}</td></tr>
<% } %>
      </table>
    </td>
    <td>
     <ul>
<% groups.each { g -> %>
        <li>${g}</li>
<% } %>
     </ul>
    </td>
  </tr>
</table>
```

The code should be self-explanatory, but we simply pull out our user's unique ID, his groups, and the user object from our helper method. Then we sort the keys of the user object to improve readability and dump its contents. Finally, we dump the groups as well. The results are rather voluminous and potentially confidential in nature, depending on your LDAP's configuration. You have to try this yourself to see the results—when I ran this on myself at my company, there was little that I'd be comfortable showing the world. Run this sample application using your own companies' LDAP server, and examine the details maintained about you as an employee.

OpenID Configuration

One of the newer and more exciting authentication concepts is called OpenID. It is a decentralized process, where essentially any service provider can act as an trustee for user authentication.

Although the concept is that you would have a single login identity that would work across the Internet, its common to have several different identities spread across different service providers. You actually might already have an OpenID—many social sites such as Facebook, Google, and Yahoo!, to name a few, also act as OpenID providers.

To find out if you have an ID, or want to create one, point your browser to www.openid.net. Here, you can see which sites support OpenID, as well as create your own personal OpenID. You then can build an OpenID-based WebSphere sMash application and impress all your friends.

As with other authentication schemes, we have a little configuration setup that we need to make, and then it is simply a matter of creating a custom Login form. First, we need to add a dependency to the zero.security.openid module into the project. To do this in AppBuilder, select the Dependencies tab, click the Add button, search for "opened," and click Add. In Eclipse, open the project's /config/ivy.xml file, click Add, search on zero:zero.security.openid, and click OK. Additionally, we need to enable security to our zero.config and define a few OpenID-specific settings, as shown in Listing 9.13. This is a fairly generic setup, and specific details can be found in the Project Zero documentation under the security section of the developer guide.

Listing 9.13 OpenID Security Configuration

```
#---------------------------------------------------------
#-- OpenID Settings
#---------------------------------------------------------
/config/security/userservice/registryType="openid"

# specify the OpenID loginPage and associated login related
# configuration
@include "security/openidLoginURL.config" {
  "openidLoginPage": "/openidlogin.gt",

  #-- [optional] require these openid profile entries
  "sregRequired": ["email","nickname","gender"],

  # optionally send date of birth, full name, country,
  # timezone and language if available
  "sregOptional": ["dob","fullname","country","timezone","language"],

  # URL describing how application will leverage simple registration
  # required and optional attributes
  "sregPolicyURL" : "http://www.projectzero.org",
  "allowedOpenidDomains" : ["myopenid.com"]
}

#specify the security constraints
@include "security/openidAuthentication.config"{
  "conditions": "/request/path =~/my(/.*)?"
}
```

OpenID also supports standard profile information that may be optionally requested by consuming applications. This is meant to provide a better web experience and not to expose any confidential user information. Most OpenID providers allow the entry of one or more profile sets that you can specify to be used by consuming websites. The currently defined profile fields are listed in Table 9.3. More information can be found at the OpenID Simple Registration Extension.[4]

Table 9.3   OpenID Profile Fields

OpenID Profile Fields	Description
nickname	User's preferred nickname.
email	User's email address.
fullname	User's full name.
dob	User's data of birth (YYYY-MM-DD). Zeros may be used for non-revealed values, such as birth year, which might result in something similar to: 0000-07-04.
gender	User gender: either "M" for male, or "F" for female.
postcode	UTF-8 string-free text that *should* conform to the end user's.
country	The end user's country of residence in standard two-digit country code format.
language	End user's preferred language
timezone	ASCII string from TimeZone database. For example: "Europe/Paris" or "America/Los_Angeles."

Securing Outbound Connections

Up until this point, we have been discussing how to secure connection requests from external browsers or applications coming into your applications services.

Let's shift gears a bit and deal with securing outbound connections to other services. Typically, you will be using the Connection class to make outgoing connections. These can be normal, insecure HTTP-based calls, and authenticated requests to secured HTTPS-based services. The solution here is to pre-define the secure connections in the `zero.config` file, including the required username and password; then we can make the calls as needed from our application code.

Start by defining your secure outbound connection(s) in the `zero.config` file, as shown in Listing 9.14. Here, we define a connection URL pattern, and the user and password values. You can enter the password in clear text, but it's better to obfuscate it using XOR encoding. Even with encoding, storing passwords in a configuration is a concern, and you should make an effort to

---

[4] OpenID Simple Registration Extension: http://openid.net/specs/openid-simple-registration-extension-1_0.html

ensure that this file is protected from unauthorized viewing. To encode the password, just run the `zero encode {password}` command from either the command line or from the console tab in AppBuilder, as shown in Figure 9.14.

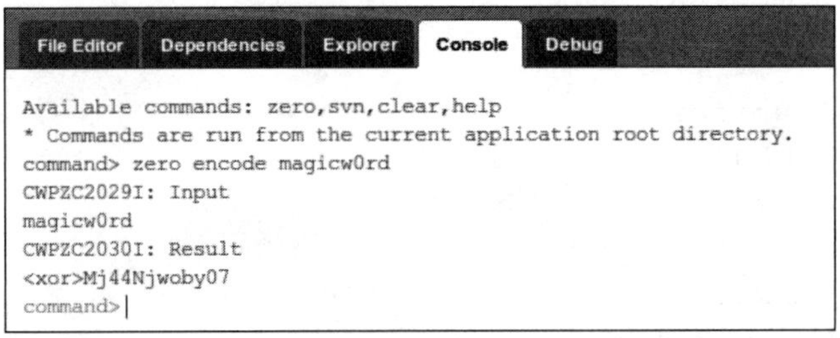

```
 File Editor    Dependencies    Explorer    Console    Debug

Available commands: zero,svn,clear,help
* Commands are run from the current application root directory.
command> zero encode magicw0rd
CWPZC2029I: Input
magicw0rd
CWPZC2030I: Result
<xor>Mj44Njwoby07
command>|
```

Figure 9.14   Password encoding using AppBuilder console

Listing 9.14   Defining Outbound Connections in Configuration File

```
/config/connection/destinations += {
  "https://crownjewels.acme.com/*" : {
    "connection" : {
      "protocol" : "https",
      "config" : {
        "userid": "wecoyote@acme.com",
        "password":"<xor>Mj44Njwoby07"
      }
    }
  }
}
```

After we have our outbound connection pattern defined, all we have to do is to set up a new connection call to our desired service.

WebSphere sMash compares the outbound connection URL with the pre-defined destination patterns, and if a match is made, will automatically apply the appropriate user and password credentials to the connection. This keeps our credentials external to our application logic, which is always a good thing. Listing 9.15 shows a code fragment that makes a connection to the remote server.

Listing 9.15   Application Code to Call a Secured Service

```
def callDataService( args ) {
  logger.INFO {"Starting with: ${args}"}
  def URL = "https://crownjewels.acme.com/resources/${args.service}"
  if ( args.id ) {
    URL += "/${args.id}
  }
  args.remove('service')
  args.remove('id')
  args.eachWithIndex() { it, idx ->
    URL += (idx == 0 ? '?' : '&' ) +
           URLEncoder.encode(it.key, "UTF-8") + "=" +
           URLEncoder.encode(it.value, "UTF-8")
  }
  logger.INFO {"URL: ${URL}"}
  def response = Connection.doGET(URL)
  def doc = new XmlParser().parse( response.responseBody )
  logger.INFO {"Results : ${doc}"}
  return doc
}
```

In this example, we make a dynamic call to some service as defined by the method parameters, and receive an XML document as a response. It is a big assumption that we will be receiving an XML response, but this serves for this example. If you are expecting a response other than XML, adjust the response handler to process the correct data type.

Let's examine this bit of reusable code a little more. In the first several lines, we build up the base URL. The static part of that URL should really be defined as an entry in the application config file, and not a static string as shown in this example.

We supply the actual service to be called in the args.service entry, and if supplied, we add on the resource ID.

Next, we remove the service and ID entries from the argument map, and then walk the remaining args and append them to the URL as parameters. Encoding the parameters is necessary because the parameters might include characters that are not transmittable in their original encoding.

Finally, we open a GET connection to the URL and pull in the results as an XML document. There is a lot more we could do to improve this method, such as dynamically handling different response data formats, but at least you should be able to see how easy it is to make secure connection calls to remote services.

Conclusion

In this chapter, we have taken a whirlwind tour of various security subsystems within the WebSphere sMash environment. There is a lot we didn't cover about various configuration options within each security scenario. The documentation provided on the Project Zero website goes deeper into the security details. The goal of this chapter was to give you the basics needed to create a secure WebSphere sMash application. The information learned in this chapter is directly usable in real-world applications.

## CHAPTER 10

Event Processing

In this chapter, we discuss a variety of WebSphere sMash capabilities and provide an insight as to when you can use these features to add greater flexibility to your application. For instance, there are often times when an application cannot simply rely on the standard request/response cycle dictated by the user's browser. You may want to perform some preparation work upon application initialization and not force the first user in to bear the brunt of the extra processing delay. There may be times where you want your application to periodically check in with another server, pull in news feeds, or send usage statistics to a monitoring site. The scenarios are limitless and may not fall within the normal traffic patterns of your users.

WebSphere sMash provides several features to assist you in processing data based on various events. These events can be regular and cyclical in nature, where a timer can initiate an event, or you may need to watch a file system for changes and process those files. There are also facilities for watching POP mail accounts for new mail, and queues can receive asynchronous messages as part of the Reliable Transport Extension (RTE).

A large network of connected applications can also use WebSphere sMash to communicate without any users or browsers being involved in the mix. This opens the door to a wide array of internetworked applications that can stay in contact with each other.

Timers

A *timer* is used to fire re-occurring events. The timer ticks at predetermined intervals, and a handler event method called `onTimer()` can then take any required actions.

To use timers, you need to add the zero.timer dependency to the application's ivy.xml file. Then, for each process you want to execute, add a timer task entry and event handler into the zero.config file. By convention, you should place your timer handler scripts into a directory called /app/scripts/timers. This is just a recommendation; you can organize your code as you see fit.

In the configuration snippet shown in Listing 10.1, we define a timer named "heartbeat," which fires every 30 seconds, and call the onTimer method of the /app/scripts/timers/ heartbeat.groovy file. In the first line, we define the timer task. A *timer task* is an object that has a single property called a "delay," or the tick time in seconds. When the task ticks, it fires a "timer" event, and sets the event task name to the ending name of the timer task, which in our sample is "heartbeat." For every timer task, there is a corresponding handler block. The handler block consists of an events type of timer, with conditions matching the event's task name to the timer's task name. The handler determines the script to call for the doTimer method. The instanceData member contains a map of arguments that are passed into the onTimer method.

Listing 10.1   Timer Configuration

```
/config/timer/tasks/heartbeat = { "delay" : 30 }/config/handlers += [{
    "events"        : "timer",
    "conditions"    : "/event/_taskName =~ heartbeat",
    "handler"       : "timers/heartbeat.groovy",
    "instanceData" : {
        "myArg1"       : "someConfigurableValue"
    }
}]
```

So, what do we put into our doTimer method? Well, that can basically be whatever you want. The instanceData variables are accessible from the "event" global context. So, in our sample configuration, the doTimer method can grab the instance data using zget("/event/myArg1"). Listing 10.2 shows our handler code located in the file: /app/scripts/timers/heartbeat.groovy.

Listing 10.2   /app/config/timers/heartbeat.groovy

```
package timers
def onTimer() {
  logger.INFO{"Heartbeat timer fired"}
  logger.INFO{"Event name: " + zget("/event/_taskName")}
  logger.INFO{"Event Instance Data MyArg1 : " + zget("/event/myArg1") }
}
```

Start the application, and let's see what we get produced to the console. Nothing. Hmm, even waiting 30 seconds, and we get...nothing. The reason for this is that the timer is not fired until a request comes into the ZSO, which then actually starts up the application. So, use your browser to access the application (http://localhost:8080). The browser displays the normal sMash "up and running" page, whereas the console log shows our logging output. We can take away a few things from this test. First, timers by default start only when the ZSO has activated the application, and by consequence, they also stop firing when the ZSO idles the application. We'll address this seemingly erratic behavior momentarily. The other thing to notice on this little sample is that a timer event fires immediately when the application is initialized, and then upon each tick's delay value. This can be used to our advantage for using a timer to perform a one-time application initialization.

By default, the timer will not start until the first request comes in and the ZSO initiates the application. If you need the timer to start as soon as the application initializes, set the following in the zero.config; the timer fires immediately and then at the defined intervals:

```
/config/zso/immediateStart=true
```

By default, the ZSO starts an application when a request comes in on one of the listening ports. At this point, ZSO starts the application and subsequently the timer service. After a period of inactivity, ZSO closes down the application and therefore the timers that are running within that application. If you set the ZSO `immediateStart` flag, ZSO immediately starts the application and allows the timer to fire. Depending on the delay time of the timer, the ZSO may still shut down the application, but the timer(s) continues to fire at the appropriate intervals, forcing the ZSO to bring the application back up into listening mode.

Application Initialization Using Timers

One common use of a timer is to perform a one-time application initialization. As stated earlier, a timer is fired immediately upon application startup and then at each delay interval. So, to force an application to perform a single startup, set the delay time to a very large value. It will fire one time, and remain dormant thereafter. The only issue to resolve is to ensure that initialization has completed before any user requests are processed. When the application is run under the ZSO, this race condition is even more likely. The solution is to use an initialization flag.

When a request comes into the ZSO for an application, the ZSO starts up the application, which immediately fires the timer event. The timer event and the servicing of the request happen in parallel, which means that each entry point or starting page of the application needs to check for initialization before continuing and actually servicing the request. Let's go through a quick example of using an initialization flag.

First, create a new `init` timer, with a delay time of 9999999 (or any ridiculously large value) and an event handler stanza, as shown in Listing 10.3. A value this large (~3 years) will ensure that our timer never fires again. This is essentially the same as our first example, but this time, we are not defining any `instanceData` values.

Listing 10.3   Initialization Timer Configuration

```
/config/timer/tasks/init = { "delay" : 99999999 }

/config/handlers += [{
    "events"        : "timer",
    "conditions"    : "/event/_taskName =~ init",
    "handler"       : "timers/init.groovy"
}
```

The `/app/scripts/timers/init.groovy::onTimer` method shown in Listing 10.4
performs whatever initialization processes our application requires. In this sample, we just put the
thread to sleep for several seconds to simulate some rather long database activity. After the initialization has completed, we set an application-level context flag to indicate that we are fully initialized and ready to accept incoming requests. This is all well and good, but what if a request comes in
before our flag is set? We need to create a blocking method that holds the request(s) until the application is initialized. This is represented in the `"waitForInitialized"` method. This method
simply enters a time-delayed loop waiting for the proper initialization flag to be set. Although it is
probably not a great practice to sleep your request threads, it can come in handy in this situation.

Listing 10.4   /app/scripts/timers/init.groovy

```
package timers

def onTimer() {
  try {
    if ( ! zget("/app/initialized") ) {
      logger.INFO{ "Initializing application - " +
        "from timer task (${event._taskName[]})" }
      Thread.currentThread().sleep(30000) // 30 sec.
      zput( "/app/initialized", true )
      logger.INFO{ "Initialization completed." }
    }
  } catch ( e ) {
    logger.SEVERE{ "Initializing error - ${e}" }
  }
}

def waitForInitialized() {
  def x = 0
  while ( ! app.initialized[] ) {
    logger.INFO{ "Waiting for initialization to complete...${++x}" }
```

```
      Thread.currentThread().sleep(1000) // 1 sec.
   }
   return true
}
```

The only thing we have left to do is to add the call to our `waitFor` method in each possible web page of the application. We show a sample of this in Listing 10.5, showing us a simple index.gt file. Although this sort of waiting for initialization process becomes cumbersome to manage if there are many potential entry pages into your application, it does solve a rather thorny issue.

Listing 10.5   /public/index.gt

```
<% invokeMethod("timers/init.groovy", "waitForInitialized", null ) %>
<html>
   <head>
      <title>Init Test</title>
   </head>
   <body>
      <h1>Hello!</h1>
   </body>
</html>
```

Test out our initialization process by starting the application and quickly attempting to access the main page. The browser should be forced to wait several seconds before the ready flag is set and the rendering is permitted to continue. Check the log file to verify that the proper sequence of events has taken place.

There are other ways that you can explore to gain both a functional application initialization and still maintain the benefits of using ZSO to manage overall application resources. One entails having a dedicated "timer" application that is always running and firing events. This assumes that the initialization is for more generic resources, such as databases, file systems, or other remote resources. The timer application can also "kick" other applications and delivery information at regular intervals. We discuss kickers in the next section. If you have a cluster of related applications on a single host, organizing timed events around a single long-running "timer" application can solve a lot of issues with the individual applications running cyclical events, while still allowing the ZSO to manage the other application instances.

Kickers

There are several different styles of kickers that we cover in this chapter. The purpose of a *kicker* is to "kick" or notify a remote application that an event has occurred. This kick is done via a POST connection. The connection is automatically retried as necessary until a successful POST has been made, or the number of configured retries has been exceeded. Kickers use the timer subsystem discussed previously to perform a kick, or test for conditions that will invoke a kick action. The kick call returns either success or failure based on the status code returned from the POST call to the remote application.

To enable kicker support in your application, you need to add the appropriate zero.kicker module into the ivy.config. There are a few new `instanceData` variables that go into the event stanza for each type of kicker, which we need to define in the configuration file. Other kicker types also have their own `instanceData` variables, which we'll point out shortly. The variables that are shared among all kickers are shown in Table 10.1. We'll look at sample configurations for each kicker.

Table 10.1   Common Kicker InstanceData Members

InstanceData Configuration Members	Description
`receiverURL`	The target URL to receive the "kick" notification. This is a required variable for all kickers. Despite its name, you may also use a connection name instead of an actual URL for this field.
`maxRetries`	The number of times to attempt to kick the remote application. The default is five retries.
`maxDelay`	This is the delay time between failed kick attempts. The default is 5 seconds between retries.
`config`	You can supply custom Connections variables using the config map. This is typically used to supply the username and password under basic authentication connections. This is an options setting based on your requirements.

As a matter of consistency and convention, it is recommended that you place all kicker handlers under the `"/app/scripts/kickers"`. Of course, you are free to place them wherever makes sense to you and your application structure.

Simple Kicker

The most basic kicker simply calls a handler on each timer tick, passing in the variables defined in the `instanceData` block from the configuration file. It's simply a matter of calling the kick function from your custom handler. This will perform a POST to the designated `receiverUrl`, passing in a map of the parameters passed into the kick method.

Let's build a simple kicker to illustrate this concept and look at what the receiving application delivered. First, add the `"zero.kicker"` module to the ivy.config file. Next, create a timer and event stanza in your application's configuration file, as shown in Listing 10.6. Remember that timers will not fire when the application is idled by the ZSO, so make sure you set the `immediateStart` flag to true.

Listing 10.6 Simple Kicker Configuration

```
/config/zso/immediateStart=true /config/timer/tasks/myKicker = { "delay"
: 120 }

/config/handlers += [{
    "events"          : "timer",
    "conditions"      : "/event/_taskName =~ myKicker",
    "handler"         : "kickers/mySimpleKicker.groovy",
    "instanceData"    : {
        "receiverUrl": "http://localhost:8080/resources/kickReceiver"
    }
}]
```

We create a standard timer with a two-minute tick delay, and a corresponding handler that calls `"mySimpleKicker.groovy"`, which is shown in Listing 10.7. Notice how we define the `receiverUrl`. Under normal circumstances, this would point to a different application, likely residing on a different host. For this sample, we'll just call a resource in the same application.

Listing 10.7 /app/scripts/kickers/mySimpleKicker.groovy

```
import zero.kicker.Kicker
def onTimer() {
  def args = [
    "arg1": "Test message",
    "number1" : "234"
  ]
  logger.INFO{ System.currentTimeMillis() +
    ": mySimpleKicker: sending: " + args }
  def kickOk = Kicker.kick( args );
  logger.INFO{ System.currentTimeMillis() +
    ": mySimpleKicker: kickOk: " + kickOk }
}
```

There is actually a lot to inspect in this little bit of code. First, we import our Kicker class, which contains several variations of the `kick()` method. This simplest and most common class accepts a map of arguments to be sent to the remote host. The URL is automatically retrieved from the `receiverUrl` value in the event handler. The next thing to note is that the map may only consist of string values. The kicker does not perform any object morphing and will balk if not presented with all proper strings. Finally, we have the kick method itself. We've surrounded it by logger statements including timestamps. The kick method holds until the POST has either completed successfully or fails after the defined number of retries and delay times. Therefore, in theory at least, the kick method could take a fair amount of time to complete. The issue you could run into is that if your timer ticks occur faster than the kick method under failure/retries, you could easily end up with an ever-growing stack of kicks attempting to fire concurrently. As a general rule of thumb, ensure that your timer tick delay is greater than the number of retries times the max retry delay time. This will keep you out of this sticky mess.

Let's take a mental trip over to the receiving application for a moment, forgetting that it's actually residing within the same application on this sample. As you can see in the kicker event configuration, we are calling `"/resources/kickReceiver"`, which in this sample is another groovy script, shown in Listing 10.8. All we are doing here is dumping out the various parameters we received.

Listing 10.8   /resource/kickReceiver.groovy

```
def onCreate() {
  logger.INFO{"Got kicked by: " + zget("/request/params/appName") }
  logger.INFO{"Parameters found: " + zlist("/request/params") }
  zlist("/request/params", false).each{ key ->
    logger.INFO{">> " + key + ": " + zget("/request/params/${key}") }
  }
}
```

The log output is shown in Listing 10.9. We can see the two expected parameters that we supplied to the kick method, but we also see two extra parameters that were provided that tell us the kicker and the application name that originated the kick.

Listing 10.9   Log Output of /app/resources/kickReceiver.groovy

```
2009-09-01 21:22:18 app.resources.kickReceiver.groovy::onCreate
Thread-2
        INFO [ Got kicked by: Book.Async.SimpleKicker ]
2009-09-01 21:22:18 app.resources.kickReceiver.groovy::onCreate
Thread-2
        INFO [ Parameters found: [/request/params/appName,
/request/params/arg1, /request/params/kickerName,
/request/params/number1] ]
2009-09-01 21:22:18 app.resources.kickReceiver.groovy::onCreate
Thread-2
```

```
        INFO [       appName: Book.Async.SimpleKicker ]
2009-09-01 21:22:18 app.resources.kickReceiver.groovy::onCreate
Thread-2
        INFO [       arg1: Test message ]
2009-09-01 21:22:18 app.resources.kickReceiver.groovy::onCreate
Thread-2
        INFO [       kickerName: myKicker ]
2009-09-01 21:22:18 app.resources.kickReceiver.groovy::onCreate
Thread-2
        INFO [       number1: 234 ]
```

That's about all there is to the simple kicker. Next, we'll go over some slightly more advanced kickers that can help us check files and mailboxes and work with message queuing systems.

File Kicker and Receiver

A file kicker/receiver is built into WebSphere sMash. This built-in kicker/receiver gives your application the opportunity to respond to changes in the file system. The file kicker periodically examines the file system and sends an HTTP POST request when the specified element in the file system has changed. The HTTP POST is received by the built-in receiver, which in turn fires a fileUpdate event and places data about the file system change into the global context. Application logic to respond to the event should be placed in the fileUpdate event handler. To set up the file kicker, we need to modify the zero.config file to add the file kicker timer handler. In Listing 10.10, we configure the file kicker to watch "c:/zero/fileKicker/file1" whenever this file is modified; the service defined in the receiverURL will be called.

Listing 10.10   File Kicker Configuration

```
/config/handlers += [{
"events" : "timer",
"handler" : "zero.file.kicker.FileKicker.class",
  "conditions" : "/event/_taskName =~ myFileKicker",
  "instanceData" : {
    "fileName" : "C:/zero/fileKicker/file1",
    "receiverURL" : http://localhost:8080/file/FileReceiver
  }
}]
```

Next, we need to configure the file receiver that will handle the HTTP POST sent by the file kicker. We demonstrate this in Listing 10.11.

Listing 10.11   File Receiver Configuration

```
/config/handlers += [{
  "events" : "POST",
  "handler" : "zero.file.receiver.FileReceiver.class",
  "conditions" : "/request/path =~ /file/FileReceiver(/.*)?"
}]
```

The receiver is configured to handle any HTTP POST event that is sent to the `FileReceiver` in the file virtual directory. When an HTTP POST is made to this path, the receiver is activated and then fires a `fileUpdate` event for which we need to configure a handler. To configure a handler for this event, we can do as shown in Listing 10.12.

Listing 10.12   File Update Event Handler Configuration

```
/config/handlers += [{
  "events" : "fileUpdate",
  "handler" : "FileUpdateHandler.groovy"
}]
```

As you can see, the `FileUpdateHandler.groovy` is configured to respond to the `fileUpdate` event. The `FileUpdateHandler.groovy` file should be placed in our `app/scripts` directory. In this file, the `onFileUpdate` method will be called when the event is triggered by the file receiver. In this method, we need to put whatever application logic is needed to appropriately respond to the file being updated. In our case, we'll just print out the data that is returned from the receiver to the info logger, as seen in Listing 10.13.

Listing 10.13   File Update Event Handler

```
def onFileUpdate(){
  def kickData = zget("/event/kickData")
  logger.INFO {"kickData="+kickData}
}
```

As you can see, the data from the kicker is received by the receiver and placed in the `"/event/kickData"` global context entry. This entry contains a variety of information, such as when the file was updated, the filename that was updated, the name of the kicker, and so on. See the output of our event handler in Listing 10.14.

Listing 10.14   File Update Event Handler Output

```
2009-10-01 04:43:24 app.scripts.FileUpdateHandler.groovy::onFileUpdate
Thread-11
INFO [ kickData=[
        fileData:[fileName:C:/zero/fileKicker/file1,
        msg:file found, lastModified:1254244143625],
        fileName:C:/zero/fileKicker/file1,
        appName:fileKicker,
        kickerName:myFileKicker] ]
```

So, to go over the course of events once again, the file is updated, which activates the file kicker. The file kicker is a timer that watches a particular file or directory. The file kicker calls the file receiver, which converts the POST data from the kicker into a global context entry and then generates a `fileUpdate` event. This event is handled by our `FileUpdateHandler.groovy`, which outputs the data into the info log file. As you can see, this enables us to create a great many file-oriented handlers with just a few lines of configuration and whatever code you need to handle the file changes.

Events

WebSphere sMash has several built-in events for requests. We've created handlers for GET and POST requests in this and previous chapters. There are also events that surround every GET, PUT, POST, and DELETE request. Those built-in events let you execute code before a request and after a request, and log when a request has been serviced. To hook into these events, we simply need to configure handlers for the specific events. For demonstration purposes, we'll create a handler that handles all three of these events and logs a message. The events are named `requestBegin`, `log`, and `requestEnd`. Listing 10.15 shows how to configure a handler for all of these events.

Listing 10.15   Configure Event Handlers for the requestBegin, log, and requestEnd Events

```
/config/handlers += [{
  "events" : "requestBegin",
  "handler" : "LogEvent.groovy",
  "conditions" : "/request/path =~ /foo(/.*)?"
}]

/config/handlers += [{
  "events" : "log",
```

```
  "handler" : "LogEvent.groovy",
  "conditions" : "/request/path =~ /foo(/.*)?"
}]

/config/handlers += [{
  "events" : "requestEnd",
  "handler" : "LogEvent.groovy",
  "conditions" : "/request/path =~ /foo(/.*)?"
}]
```

Notice that we've defined the same handler for all three events. We can do this because each event will call its own on<EventName> method. Note also that we're restricting our handlers to firing only when we execute something in the /foo path. You can modify this condition to be any particular path or any path if desired. We create the LogEvent.groovy handler in the app/scripts directory with the code shown in Listing 10.16.

Listing 10.16   LogEvent.groovy Handler to Handle Several Events

```
def onRequestBegin(){
  logger.INFO {"onRequestBegin"}
  def tmp = zget("/event/_name")
  logger.INFO {"/event/_name="+tmp}
}

def onLog(){
  logger.INFO {"onLog"}
  def tmp = zget("/event/_name")
  logger.INFO {"/event/_name="+tmp}
}

def onRequestEnd(){
  logger.INFO {"onRequestEnd"}
  def tmp = zget("/event/_name")
  logger.INFO {"/event/_name="+tmp}
}
```

The code in Listing 10.16 handles all three events with the onRequestBegin, onLog, and onRequestEnd methods. All we're doing in this demonstration is logging to the info logger, but we do access the event zone of the global context to retrieve the event name. We could also access any of the other event zone properties for the fired event. Just to be complete, the logged output of this code is shown in Listing 10.17.

Listing 10.17   LogEvent.groovy Handler Output

```
2009-10-01 16:14:41 app.scripts.LogEvent.groovy::onRequestBegin
    Thread-11
    INFO [ onRequestBegin ]
2009-10-01 16:14:41 app.scripts.LogEvent.groovy::onRequestBegin
    Thread-11
    INFO [ /event/_name=requestBegin ]
2009-10-01 16:14:42 app.scripts.LogEvent.groovy::onLog Thread-11
    INFO [ onLog ]
2009-10-01 16:14:42 app.scripts.LogEvent.groovy::onLog Thread-11
    INFO [ /event/_name=log ]
2009-10-01 16:14:42 app.scripts.LogEvent.groovy::onRequestEnd Thread-11
    INFO [ onRequestEnd ]
2009-10-01 16:14:42 app.scripts.LogEvent.groovy::onRequestEnd Thread-11
    INFO [ /event/_name=requestEnd ]
```

As we can see, the `requestBegin` event is fired, followed by the log event and finally the `requestEnd` event. This all assumes there is some sort of handler behind /foo—for example, an HTTP GET handler. One thing to note is that these events can be configured and handled by multiple handlers. For example, you may have a couple of different log event handlers: One could log accesses to a local log, and another could call a remote logging application to record live statistics about your application. However, the HTTP GET, PUT, POST, and DELETE events may only have one handler. In the next section, we take a look at custom events, which enable you to extend the cast of events to couple together your handlers with events of your choosing.

Custom Events

WebSphere sMash provides a complete event infrastructure for loosely coupling handlers. As we saw in the "File Kicker and Receiver" section, a `fileUpdate` event was fired by the file receiver and handled by another handler. This gives advanced developers tremendous flexibility and extensibility of WebSphere sMash by allowing developers to add their own event types and configuring multiple handlers to listen for those events. Let's write a resource that kicks off an event of its own and a couple of handlers to handle the event. To start with, we'll write an HTTP GET handler named `Foo.groovy` in Listing 10.18.

Listing 10.18   Foo.groovy HTTP GET Event Handler

```
import zero.core.events.EventEngine

def onGET() {
  logger.INFO {"scripts/Foo onGET called"}
```

```
    def eventData = ["fooData": "value, could be a map of data"]
    EventEngine.fire("foo", eventData);
}
```

Foo.groovy goes into the scripts directory. We start by importing the EventEngine class, which gives us the ability to fire events. For our new event, we create some event data called fooData that will be the payload we'll retrieve in our event handlers. The event we're firing is called "foo" and is fired by calling the EventEngine.fire method. This is all kicked off by the built-in HTTP GET event. We configure our Foo.groovy handler to be triggered when the /foo path is called, as can be seen in the configuration in Listing 10.19.

Listing 10.19   Foo Event Configuration

```
/config/handlers += [{
  "events" : "GET",
  "handler" : "Foo.groovy",
  "conditions" : "/request/path =~ /foo(/.*)?"
}]

/config/handlers += [{
  "events" : "foo",
  "handler" : "FooHandler.groovy"
}]

/config/handlers += [{
  "events" : "foo",
  "handler" : "FooHandlerTwo.groovy"
}]
```

When the request path has /foo in it, the Foo.groovy handler is triggered, which in turn fires the foo event. The foo event is then handled by two other handlers that we have configured: FooHandler.groovy and FooHandlerTwo.groovy. When these two handlers are triggered, the onFoo method in each is executed. For the purpose of our example, they both simply log to the info logger, as shown in Listing 10.20.

Listing 10.20   Foo Event Handler Code

```
FooHandler.groovy:
def onFoo(){
  logger.INFO {"onFoo invoked for FooHandler"}
  def fooData = zget("/event/fooData")
```

```
  logger.INFO {"fooData="+fooData}
}


FooHandlerTwo.groovy:
def onFoo(){
  logger.INFO {"onFoo invoked for FooHandlerTwo"}
  def fooData = zget("/event/fooData")
  logger.INFO {"fooData="+fooData}
}
```

Both `foo` event handlers have access to the payload data and can act on it accordingly. Finally, if we hit the `/foo` URL of our application, we'll see what's listed in Listing 10.21.

Listing 10.21   Foo Event Output

```
2009-10-01 15:39:37 app.scripts.Foo.groovy::onGET Thread-11
     INFO [ scripts/Foo onGET called ]
2009-10-01 15:39:37 app.scripts.FooHandler.groovy::onFoo Thread-11
     INFO [ onFoo invoked for FooHandler ]
2009-10-01 15:39:38 app.scripts.FooHandler.groovy::onFoo Thread-11
     INFO [ fooData=value, could be a map of data ]
```

We see that we handle the HTTP GET event and generate our `foo` event, which is handled by a couple of different handlers. Don't forget that you can have at most one handler for GET, PUT, POST, and DELETE events, but custom events and the other built-in events allow multiple handlers to be defined. So, using an HTTP GET handler to generate a custom event would allow you to use multiple handlers for every GET event.

Conclusion

We covered a variety of ways to communicate and process data asynchronously. The manner in which these events occur is based largely on the situation and reliability requirements of your application. We hope that this chapter has provided you with the tools needed to expand the capabilities of your application through the use of a variety of built-in and custom timers, kickers, and events.

References

For more information on setting up SSL, refer to the following resources:

For IBM Java key management using the Ikeyman tool, refer to
http://download.boulder.ibm.com/ibmdl/pub/software/dw/jdk/security/50/GSK7c_SSL_IKM_Guide.pdf.

For Sun's keytool utility, refer to http://java.sun.com/j2se/1.5.0/docs/guide/security/jsse/JSSERefGuide.html#CreateKeystore.

For another good resource for defining a secure environment using key stores, see the "Using the Java Secure Socket Extension in WebSphere Application Server" article from the IBM WebSphere Developer Technical Journal by Messaoud Benantar at http://www.ibm.com/developerworks/websphere/techjournal/0502_benantar/0502_benantar.html.

While we are providing references to more information on SSL, see the following articles for IBM at http://www.ibm.com/developerworks/java/jdk/security/50/secguides/jsse2Docs/JSSE2RefGuide.html, and from Sun at http://java.sun.com/j2se/1.5.0/docs/guide/security/jsse/JSSERefGuide.html.

## CHAPTER 11

Framework Components

In this chapter, we introduce some WebSphere sMash components that are useful, if not necessary, for developing robust WebSphere sMash applications. We touch on these components only to make you aware that they are there for you to use. We encourage you to seek more information in the product documentation for the components that you find most useful in your application. In particular, we touch on URIUtils (which are used to create URIs that reference your WebSphere sMash application), validators (which assist in validating cached content), and Active Content Filtering (which helps to secure your site against cross-site scripting). Finally, we introduce Assemble Flow, which allows nonprogrammers to create conversation applications in WebSphere sMash.

URIUtils

URIUtils are a set of cross-language utility methods for creating relative and absolute URIs for your application. These URIs can be used to create references to images, cascading style sheets, hyperlinks, and other page resources within your application. Generally, you should use relative URIs so that they are robust enough to survive the rigors of security and client-side manipulation such as reverse proxy servers and mashups.

We look at the particulars of each language in turn to reveal any nuisances between them and learn what the API can do to help you with your application development.

Java APIs

To get access to the URIUtils class, you'll need to import it:

```
import zero.core.utils.URIUtils;
```

All the methods we use in this class are static methods. The methods you will probably be using most are the relative URI methods, and they are shown in Listing 11.1.

Listing 11.1 Java Relative URI API

```
static java.lang.String getRelativeUri(java.lang.String path)

static java.lang.String getRelativeUri(java.lang.String path,
  boolean encode)

static java.lang.String getRelativeUri(java.lang.String path,
  java.util.Map<java.lang.String,java.lang.String> queryParams)

static java.lang.String getRelativeUri(java.lang.String path,
  java.util.Map<java.lang.String,java.lang.String> queryParams,
  java.lang.String fragment)
```

The relative URI methods each take in a path. The path can come in two flavors: relative to the context root or relative to the current script. The context root relative path is denoted with a starting /. So, if our calling script was located at http://localhost:8080/path/uriutils.gt, we would get the URIs shown in Listing 11.2.

Listing 11.2 Using the Java Relative URI API

```
URIUtils.getRelativeUri("/images/happy.jpg");  evaluates to
../images/happy.jpg
URIUtils.getRelativeUri("images/happy.jpg");  evaluates to
images/happy.jpg
```

The leading / signals all the relative URI methods if your intention is to generate a URI that is relative to the context root. The API used in the preceding examples automatically encodes the URI. It is a convenience method for a call to the method that takes in a true boolean value for the encode parameter, as shown in Listing 11.3.

Listing 11.3 Using the Java Relative URI API

```
URIUtils.getRelativeUri("/space images/happy.jpg", true);
  evaluates to ../space%20images/happy.jpg
```

If, for some reason, you want to suppress the encoding, simply set the encode boolean parameter to false. The other variants of the API enable you to add parameters or a particular fragment to the URI. They are exemplified in Listing 11.4.

Listing 11.4 Using the Java Relative URI API

```
HashMap params = new HashMap<String,String>();
params.put("key0","value 0");
params.put("key1","value 1");
URIUtils.getRelativeUri("images/happy.jpg", params);
  evaluates to  images/happy.jpg?key1=value+1&key0=value+0
URIUtils.getRelativeUri("images/happy.jpg", params, "fragment");
  evaluates to  images/happy.jpg?key1=value+1&key0=value+0#fragment
```

As you can see, the methods allow for the creation of many different URIs for use in your application. There are analogous APIs to create absolute URIs, shown in Listing 11.5.

Listing 11.5 Java Absolute URI API

```
static java.lang.String getAbsoluteUri(java.lang.String path)

static java.lang.String getAbsoluteUri(java.lang.String path,
  boolean encode)

static java.lang.String getAbsoluteUri(java.lang.String path,
  java.util.Map<java.lang.String,java.lang.String> params)

static java.lang.String getAbsoluteUri(java.lang.String path,
  java.util.Map<java.lang.String,java.lang.String> params,
  java.lang.String fragment)
```

URIs generated with this set of APIs return a string in the form of the following:

```
schema://server-name:port/context-root/[path][?query-
string][#fragment]
```

The same rules apply for absolute URIs as for relative URIs. If a path starts with a /, it indicates that the URI should start from the context root. If not, it will be relative to the current script path. If we call a script at http://localhost:8080/path/uriutils.gt, the following code will return, as shown in Listing 11.6.

Listing 11.6 Using the Java Absolute URI API

```
HashMap params = new HashMap<String,String>();
params.put("key0","value 0");
params.put("key1","value 1");
```

```
URIUtils.getAbsoluteUri("images/happy.jpg");
  evaluates to http://localhost:8080/path/images/happy.jpg

URIUtils.getAbsoluteUri("/space images/happy.jpg");
  evaluates to http://localhost:8080/space%20images/happy.jpg

URIUtils.getAbsoluteUri("space images/happy.jpg", true);
  evaluates to http://localhost:8080/path/space%20images/happy.jpg

URIUtils.getAbsoluteUri("space images/happy.jpg", false);
  evaluates to http://localhost:8080/path/space%20images/happy.jpg

URIUtils.getAbsoluteUri("images/happy.jpg", params);
  evaluates to
http://localhost:8080/path/images/happy.jpg?key1=value+1&key0=value+0

URIUtils.getAbsoluteUri("images/happy.jpg", params, "fragment");
  evaluates to
http://localhost:8080/path/images/happy.jpg?key1=value+1&key0=value+0#f
ragment
```

As you can see, the absolute path URIs return similar results as their relative path analogues. Finally, the URIUtils enable us to get the current URI with the following API:

```
static java.lang.String getRequestedUri(boolean
includeQueryString)
```

With this URI, you can retrieve the current URI with or without including the query string, as shown in Listing 11.7.

Listing 11.7   Using the Java Requested URI API

```
URIUtils.getRequestedUri(false);
URIUtils.getRequestedUri(true);
```

If this code was called in for an application located here,

```
http://localhost:8080/path/uriutils.gt?key=value
```

the following URIs would be returned, as shown in Listing 11.8.

Listing 11.8   Results of Using the Java Requested URI API

```
http://localhost:8080/path/uriutils.gt
http://localhost:8080/path/uriutils.gt?key=value
```

There is also a convenience method for retrieving the URI without the query string, shown here:

```
static java.lang.String getRequestedUri()
```

This API is the same as calling the previous API with false as the parameter. In other words

```
URIUtils.getRequestedUri();
```

and

```
URIUtils.getRequestedUri(false);
```

are the equivalent.

Groovy APIs

Groovy provides a similar set of APIs that work in the same way. They are automatically imported, so they don't require extra work on your part to use them in your script. You need to call them only directly, without the static class name. For example, Listing 11.9 shows the relative URI version of the URIs shown previously in Listing 11.6.

Listing 11.9   Using the Groovy Relative URI API

```
def params = ["key0":"value 0","key1":"value 1" ]
getRelativeUri("images/happy.jpg");
  evaluates to  images/happy.jpg

getRelativeUri("/space images/happy.jpg");
  evaluates to  space%20images/happy.jpg

getRelativeUri("space images/happy.jpg", true);
  evaluates to  space%20images/happy.jpg

getRelativeUri("space images/happy.jpg", false);
  evaluates to  space%20images/happy.jpg

getRelativeUri("images/happy.jpg", params);
  evaluates to  images/happy.jpg?key1=value+1&key0=value+0

getRelativeUri("images/happy.jpg", params, "fragment");
  evaluates to  images/happy.jpg?key1=value+1&key0=value+0#fragment
```

The resultant relative URIs are the same as the Java versions. Likewise, similar APIs are available for absolute URIs and the requested URI.

PHP APIs

Some of this functionality is also provided by PHP using a similar set of APIs. However, to enable this functionality, you must add the URIUtils extension to the php.ini file by adding the following line:

```
extension = zero.php.URIUtilsExtension
```

This enables three functions that can be directly called from PHP, as shown in Listing 11.10.

Listing 11.10   PHP URIUtils API

```
get_absolute_uri(path);
get_relative_uri(path);
get_requested_uri([boolean includeQueryString]);
```

The PHP API doesn't have as many convenience methods, but it can still get the job done. Specifically, you'll have to append your own parameter and fragments. In Listing 11.11, you'll see how it works and what it returns.

Listing 11.11   Using the PHP URIUtils API

```
get_relative_uri("images/happy.jpg");
  evaluates to   images/happy.jpg

get_relative_uri("/space images/happy.jpg");
  evaluates to   ../space%20images/happy.jpg

get_absolute_uri("images/happy.jpg");
  evaluates to   http://localhost:8080/path/images/happy.jpg

get_absolute_uri("/space images/happy.jpg");
  evaluates to   http://localhost:8080/space%20images/happy.jpg

get_requested_uri();
  evaluates to   http://localhost:8080/path/uriutils.php

get_requested_uri(true);
  evaluates to   http://localhost:8080/path/uriutils.php?key=value

get_requested_uri(false);
  evaluates to   http://localhost:8080/path/uriutils.php
```

As you can see, these methods work exactly as the analogous methods in Groovy and Java.

Validators

Caching content in HTTP improves application performance and can offload content delivery to intermediate devices. HTTP uses entity tags (ETags) and last-modified dates to identify content and determine content expiration. An ETag is meant to be used as a unique identifier for content from a particular site, and the last-modified date indicates the currency of the content. Intermediate devices, such as caching proxy servers, can use ETags to return cached content instead of initiating content generation on the back-end HTTP server. ETags in association with the last-modified date can also be used to conditionally render new content. WebSphere sMash provides support called validators for generating ETags and last-modified dates.

The creation of ETags is supported by the ETag Java class that is part of the WebSphere sMash core. An ETag is created from the concatenation of all time-sensitive content that is to be set to the client. For example, if we were building a service that returned an RSS feed that was updated only occasionally, perhaps the ETag would be computed based on the titles of the feed. If we were building a stock feed resource, perhaps the ETag computation would consist of a concatenation of the stock symbol and the date-time stamp of the last price update. We could also use the complete content to be returned and compute the ETag if that is apropos. In Listing 11.12, we see an example of how to create an ETag and set it in the HTTP header.

Listing 11.12   Creating an ETag Validator

```
import zero.core.etags.Etag
def onList()
{
    def stockSymbol = "ACME"
    def currentPrice = "127.50"
    def currentDateTimeStamp = "09/05/2009"
    def content = stockSymbol + currentDateTimeStamp
    def etag = Etag.computeHashedValue(content);
    Etag.setEtagHeader(etag);
}
```

If the preceding code is placed into a resource, we can try it on our web browser or any other tooling. In Figure 11.1, we've used the Poster add-in for Firefox to show the ETag that's been set by this code.

The other validator provided by WebSphere sMash is the ability to set the last-modified date in the HTTP header. To set the last-modified date, you need to use the classes provided by Java and then use the WebSphere sMash classes to format the date properly for use in the last-modified header. For example, in Listing 11.13, we generate a last-modified date and set it in the header.

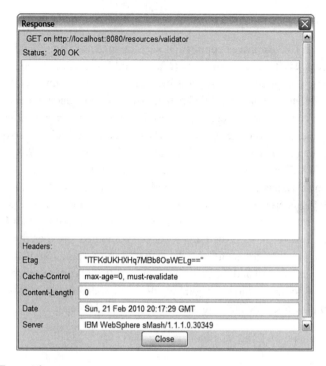

Figure 11.1   ETag set for resource

Listing 11.13   Creating the Last-Modified Header

```
import java.text.DateFormat
import zero.core.etags.Etag

def onList()
{
    def currentDateTimeStamp = "09/05/2009"
    DateFormat df = DateFormat.getDateInstance(DateFormat.SHORT);
    Date date = df.parse(currentDateTimeStamp );
    request.headers.out.'Last-Modified' = date.toString();
}
```

In Figure 11.2, we use Poster again to take a look at the last-modified header we've set with our resource.

As you can see, we now have a last-modified header set for our resource. Using these techniques will help your application's performance and take a load off your back-end server. IBM

WebSphere sMash also provides APIs for checking validators when presented. Take a look at the product documentation for further information.

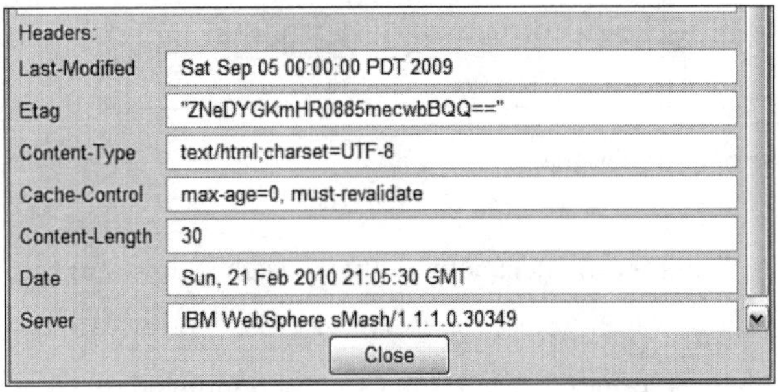

Figure 11.2 Last-modified set in Poster

Active Content Filtering

Active Content Filtering (ACF) filters potentially harmful content from being displayed on the user's screen. This can be used to prevent cross-site scripting. Cross-site scripting (XSS) is a type of website security vulnerability that enables the injection of potentially malicious content into a web page or application. The simplest incarnation of a cross site is naïve parameter handling. This is when developers neglect to verify that parameters passed to an application are valid input and not some form of script. In computer security, the people who attack sites and attempt to exploit security holes left by developers are sometimes called "black hats" (in reference to old western movies in which the bad guys tended to wear black cowboy hats). Let's take a look at an example of XSS, shown in Listing 11.14.

Listing 11.14 Naïve Parameter Handling

```
<html>
<head>
 <title>Test ACF</title>
</head>
<body>
 Hello <%= request.params.name[] %>
</body>
</html>
```

Usually a parameter such as this would come from a form submit. A typical user would have submitted his or her name and the URL; for example:

```
http://localhost:8080?name=Bob
```

This would result, as expected, in what is shown in Figure 11.3.

Figure 11.3   Results of a regular user

A black hat user might try to inject active content, such as JavaScript:

```
http://localhost:8080?name=<script>alert("Bob was here!")</script>
```

The result of this JavaScript injection is not simply printing all the text that was part of the name parameter. The JavaScript alert function is executed in the client, the results of which are shown in Figure 11.4.

Figure 11.4   JavaScript injection

This is a pretty innocuous "malicious" attack that affects only the user experience of the person making the attack. However, if the parameter had been placed in a database and later recalled in product comments, reviews, and other such user-submitted content, you could imagine how this would affect your site.

Malicious users can inject more than just JavaScript. Any HTML tag can be used. Other good examples are the image and iframe HTML tags. Combined with JavaScript, you could literally rewrite an entire page by injecting the right JavaScript and HTML tags into a page:

```
http://localhost:8080/?name=<iframe
src="http://www.acme.com"></iframe>
```

This could be used to discredit your site or misinform your users. Perhaps the most insidious of all is to use JavaScript to simply redirect users away from your site:

```
http://localhost:8080/?name=<script>location.href=
"http://www.acme.com"</script>
```

In this example, the site that your users were redirected to could look exactly like the one they are used to. Maybe it's their online bank. They attempt to login, and the black hats are collecting user IDs, passwords, bank account numbers, and so on, all for their own nefarious uses.

In WebSphere sMash, this is a fairly easy attack to prevent. You simply need to add the zero.acf dependency to the project. In the Application Builder, go to the Dependencies tab, as shown in Figure 11.5.

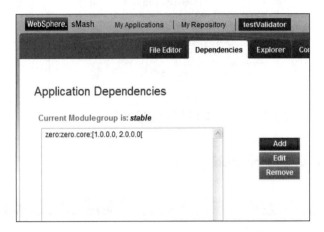

Figure 11.5 Dependencies tab

When you're on the Dependencies tab, click the Add button and the Add Dependency dialog will appear, as shown in Figure 11.6.

In Figure 11.6, the ACF module, `zero:zero.acf`, is already in our repository. We select the module and then click Add. It then shows up in our dependency list for the project. If it's not there, you'll need to click the Manage Repository button to add the ACF module to your repository, as shown in Figure 11.7.

In the Manage Repository dialog, type **zero** into the organization text box and **zero.acf** into the module text box. Next, click Search. The list returns with a number of different versions of the module. Select the version that matches your version of WebSphere sMash; then click the << button to add the module to your local repository. After the module downloads, close this dialog, and you can now add the module to your project from the Add Dependency dialog, as shown previously in Figure 11.6. When the ACF module is added to your dependencies, all parameters coming into your application will be scanned for active content before your application has access to them. This completely eliminates any chance of cross-site scripting or other active content disrupting your application. If we go back and try what we showed in Figure 11.4, we now get a different result. Figure 11.8 displays that result.

Figure 11.6   Add Dependency dialog

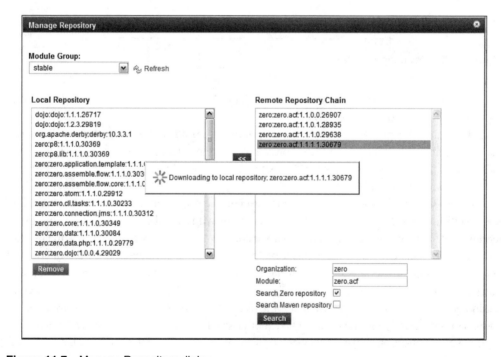

Figure 11.7   Manage Repository dialog

Figure 11.8   ACF dependency added

As you can see, we no longer get the alert dialog. It is as if the parameter were never passed and, as far as our application is concerned, it wasn't. Adding this one little dependency to our application secured it from a multitude of black hat mischief. By default, ACF also filters inbound and outbound JSON data streams. So, including this will not only prevent malicious content in URL parameters but also data sent to your resources. There is also support to protect against Cross-Site Request Forgery (CSRF) and an ACF API for those who'd like to have finer grain control and insight into the active content that is passed to or from your application. Please see the WebSphere sMash documentation for more details (http://www.projectzero.org/sMash/1.1.x/docs/zero.devguide.doc/zero.acf/Overview.html).

Assemble Flow

Assemble Flow provides the capability for constructing feeds or conversational applications with a minimum amount of programming. A *flow* is a program created by nontechnical people that acts on data. A flow can aggregate and manipulate data in various ways. Flows can be created with either a graphical tool or manually in XML. Flows are created by linking together activities. WebSphere sMash comes with several powerful built-in activities. Custom activities can also be created to extend the Assemble Flow system. Let's start with building a simple flow.

To start, you'll need to add the Assemble Flow dependency to your project. The module name is zero.assemble.flow. Remember that if it's not in your local repository, you'll need to add it via the Manage Repositories button. After the Assemble Flow module is added to your project, you'll be able to create and run flows. To create a flow in the Application Builder, select New File > "Flow in /public". Flows are always placed in the public directory or one of its subdirectories. When created, your new file will be opened in the Flow Editor.

Notice that there's a palette of activities on the right side of the Application Builder (see Figure 11.9).

The activities palette, by default, shows a list of all the built-in activities. Custom activities can be added to this palette as they are created. You'll also notice that there's a toolbar at the top of the page, as shown in Figure 11.9.

Start by clicking the Properties item in the toolbar and setting a name for this flow. In this example, I've set the name to Hello, as shown in Figure 11.10. We're going to start by building a simple flow that mimics what we did in the previous section. That is an application that takes in a parameter and responds with a simple Hello parameter.

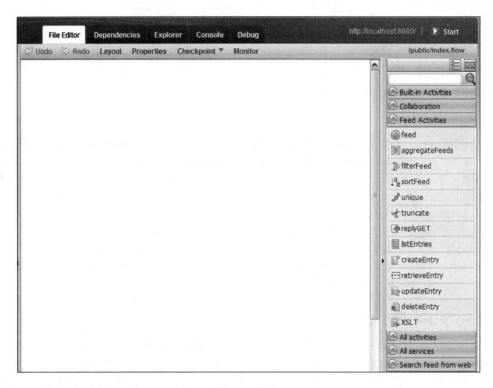

Figure 11.9   Activities palette and Flow Editor toolbar

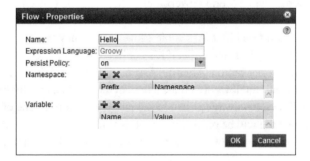

Figure 11.10   Set the flow name property

Now we can start adding activities to our flow. The first activity we should add is the receiveGet activity, which is found under the Built-in Activities section in the activities palette. We simply click and drag the activity from the palette to the editor canvas, as shown in Figure 11.11.

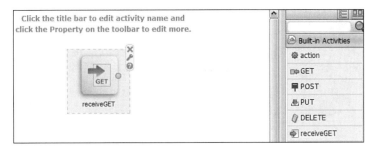

Figure 11.11   Drag the receiveGET activity from the palette to the editor canvas

The receiveGET activity is how we listen for an HTTP GET request from a client so that we may begin processing that request. Click on the small wrench icon to bring up the properties of the receiveGET activity and set the name of this activity. For our purposes, we'll name it receiveName, as shown in Figure 11.12.

Figure 11.12   Setting the activity name property

Now that we're listening for an HTTP GET request, we need to respond to the request. To do this, we need to drag the replyGET from the palette to the canvas. This enables us to respond to the HTTP GET request in any way we'd like. Again, we should click the wrench icon and set the name of the replyGET to something meaningful, like replyName. Now, click your receive-Name activity, and you'll notice a little blue ball on the right side of the activity, as shown in Figure 11.11. If you hover over the little blue ball, it turns orange, and when it does, you can click and drag from your receiveName activity to the replyName activity. This links the two activities into a flow—that is, data from the receiveName activity flows to the replyName activity, as shown in Figure 11.13.

Now that the data is flowing, we can finish the replyName activity by filling in the input property. Again, click the replyName activity and then the wrench icon. You may have noticed that there was more than just a name property when you set the name. The input property tells the activity what to do with the incoming data. In this case, the incoming data is from receiveName, and we simply want to take a parameter from that request and pass it back to the client. We'll be passing it back as plain text, as shown in Figure 11.14, although we could choose to use HTML or any of the other content types depending on our situation.

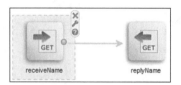

Figure 11.13   Linking receiveName to replyName

Figure 11.14   Setting input properties in replyName

Now we can start up our application and give it a try by passing it the name parameter:

`http://localhost:8080/index.flow?name=Bob`

You may have noticed that flow files end with the dot flow extension. So, we must make sure to put that in our URL. The results are exactly what you'd expect and are shown in Figure 11.15.

Figure 11.15   Results of the name flow

This has been a very simple example of how to use Assemble Flow. Assemble Flow contains many built-in activities. There are activities for every type of HTTP request (GET, PUT, POST, and DELETE). The HTTP request activities allow flows to consume requests and respond to the client. There are built-in activities for looping, flow control, sending email, and calling out to Java classes and scripts. Beyond the built-in activities, there are activities for retrieving feeds, such as RSS and ATOM feeds, and aggregating, truncating, sorting, and filtering those feeds. There's also an activity to apply XSLT to XML from a feed and activities for creating, retrieving, updating, and deleting feed entries. When put together, these activities make it possible to build robust and interesting services with a minimum of programming skill. The IBM WebSphere sMash team has provided many interesting examples on their website, as well as on YouTube.

If you can't find an activity that fits your needs, you are also able to create new activities. This is one of the more attractive use cases for Assemble Flow. A team of software engineers creates a set of activities specific to the business. Perhaps there are activities around retrieving orders, creating orders, setting orders fulfilled, client management, and so on. After these activities are created and tested, a less-technical person or even the development team could then use flow to string together new applications around these new activities. Perhaps one application is a web-based reporting application that is used by sales and marketing to see what items are most popular in their region. Another application could be built as a point of sale application to be used in retail stores. Yet another application could be used by the store management to see what they might need to order. After the building block activities are created, there are a number of applications that could arise from them.

Using this approach, it's quite easy to quickly put together these applications from the created activities. This also gives rise for ad-hoc applications to easily be built. Consider when the VP of a particular country wanted to see the aggregate of items sold in his country. If you've already built a feed to show the quantity of item orders regionally, it would be fairly easy to aggregate those feeds into a national feed. Instead of days, it would take only hours to do that aggregation. Assemble Flow is an interesting and powerful part of WebSphere sMash that could vastly improve productivity in today's fast-paced, agile world.

Conclusion

We've taken a brief look at several components of WebSphere sMash:

- URIUtils are a set of cross-language utility methods for creating relative and absolute URIs for your application. You should be using these utilities for the creation of all the URIs within your application. This enables you to create robust applications that withstand the rigors of the web.

- Validators, which assist in validating cached content and can help improve application performance.

- Active Content Filtering, which helps to secure your site against cross-site scripting in a manner that is easy for developers to use.

- Assemble Flow, which allows nonprogrammers to create conversation applications in WebSphere sMash.

It is our hope that if any of these components are interesting or helpful, you will dig into WebSphere sMash and use them to your advantage.

CHAPTER 12

Client-Side Programming with the Dojo Toolkit

WebSphere sMash enables you to rapidly create RESTful applications. This is all well and good, but in today's environment, you need to create a really sexy Web 2.0 style client that is capable of consuming your application's content. You can think of your client-side development as the face of your enterprise SOA. By enabling good client-based application logic, you can free up valuable server resources. The more work you can offload to the browser, the more requests the server can handle. In the RIA/Web 2.0 world, the server is permitted to focus on handling data requests via RESTful resources and not having to continually serve intermittent pages as part of the old school request/response cycle. Now the server can send the initial payload, including the page markup and client-side application logic, and then it's left to service data requests. After the user has entered all the required data for an application, a single submission is sent to the server for processing. There is no server-side state management (that is, session state), as all of this is handled on the client. In the Web 2.0 space, data is the new HTML.

In its purest sense, a Rich Internet Application (RIA) consists of a single HTML page that dynamically changes its content based on user input. Examples of this are the advanced mail applications from Google, Yahoo!, and others. Traditional web applications maintain a single HTML page per request/response cycle. In most real-world enterprise Web 2.0 applications, you typically will have a hybrid solution that combines that interactivity of the Web 2.0 application with an occasional page reload during major context switches. You have to find the proper balance point based on your environment and the skills of your developers.

WebSphere sMash has a tight integration with the Dojo Toolkit (http://www.dojotoolkit. org). Dojo is a JavaScript environment that provides a wealth of programming logic that assists in the browser's DOM manipulation, as well as powerful AJAX communications and many custom widgets. Although we can't cover the full scale of the Dojo Toolkit—there are plenty of good books that do that—we explore how to effectively use Dojo in your WebSphere sMash applications.

Enter the Dojo

Dojo is a leading enterprise-class, open-source JavaScript toolkit. It provides a broad set of features and functionality beyond general-purpose JavaScript, which enables you to create highly engaging and interactive Web 2.0 applications. IBM and several other companies endorse the Dojo foundation with financial and personnel support to advance its quality and feature set. Dojo is the best-in-class product for enterprise-ready features, which include Accessibility (A11Y), Internationalization (I18N), encapsulation of browser idiosyncrasies, and forward-looking API structure.

Dojo is delivered as three main packages. These are called dojo, dijit, and dojox. As an application developer, you can then add your own custom module groups, using whatever package namespacing fits your purpose. Typically, you want to follow a minimalist package-naming convention similar to Java packages. You can locate your custom Dojo classes anywhere under the /public directory and then register the custom package with Dojo, so it knows where to find them. Let's review the standard module groups provided by Dojo to gain a better understanding of what's available within each and to grasp the scale of what Dojo can provide the application developer.

The main dojo package consists of base libraries that provide smart modules loading, DOM query and manipulation functions, event handling, Asynchronous JavaScript and XML (AJAX) and RPC I/O, browser detection, CSS style manipulations, simple animation, and many other useful tools. That's a lot of functionality immediately available with a single call to load the core /dojo/dojo.js file. Dojo enables you to start small and grow your applications as your skill set grows.

All of the Dojo widgets (dijits) are available, somewhat obviously, under the dijits package. There are a huge number of widgets that provide data input, display, and management capabilities. All the dijits ensure a consistent visual user experience no matter what browser you are using. There are a complete set of form-based input widgets, including text, numbers, dates, filtering selects (such as Google Suggest), menus, buttons, and enhanced widgets that provide for client-side validation of user entry prior to submitting the data to the server. This greatly enhances the user experience, by catching input errors early and allowing the user to correct the mistakes before being sent to the server. This does not alleviate server-side validation but does prevent all the basic missing, or improperly entered, required fields style of error handling that has historically been relegated to the server, post submission. Another feature of dijits is the ability to instantiate the widgets either through programmatic logic (for example, `new dijit.Dialog()`), or through declarative tagging in the HTML itself (for example, `<div dojoType="dijit.form.Tooltip">`). This allows strong JavaScript developers to do their thing, as well as classic HTML developers to easily build up custom Dojo-enabled pages. In practice, you will likely use a combination of declarative and programmatic dijit creation.

The third main Dojo package is called dojox, which stands for Dojo eXperimental. This is somewhat of a misnomer but serves its purpose. The classes available under dojox are deemed not ready for prime time but include some powerful functionality. Some classes are robust and can safely be used in production code, whereas others are still a work-in-progress and may go through changes before they can eventually graduate to the stable dojo or dijit package groups. Read the documentation included with the classes, because they usually state the expected stability and known issues. By all means, do not dismiss the dojox package group, because this is where you can find some exciting and sexy classes to enhance your applications.

The final package group within the Dojo structure, which was not mentioned previously, is called util. As the name suggests, in this package, you will find the tools needed to perform custom Dojo builds and create API documentation and other useful, um, utilities. We discuss the value of performing custom Dojo builds later in the chapter, because they can provide a dramatic improvement in page load times. This is, without a doubt, the number-one best practice in any Dojo application.

Enabling Dojo in Your Application

To use the facilities provided by the Dojo Toolkit, you need to add the proper Dojo dependency. WebSphere sMash includes an up-to-date Dojo distribution within the normal repository locations. This dependency includes the basic Dojo Toolkit, minus a few modules that have questionable licenses, as well as some extra widgets and integration features specific to WebSphere sMash. We explore shortly how to install your own version of Dojo from dojotoolkit.org, as part of the custom build procedure, but for now, we use the bundled version of Dojo available with WebSphere sMash.

Let's start out by creating a new project in the AppBuilder. Call this application `Book.Client.Vacation`, and accept the remaining defaults. Because Dojo is specifically a client-side solution, we do most of our work within normal HTML files. Click into the application and create a new HTML file under the /public folder. Name this file `index.html`. Be sure to leave the template as `default.html` so that we get a nice boilerplate page. AppBuilder offers to automatically add the Dojo dependency, as shown in Figure 12.1. Accept this recommendation to have the latest Dojo module added to the application's ivy.xml file.

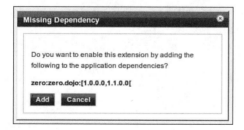

Figure 12.1   Adding Dojo dependency

If you have an existing application that you want to Dojo-enable, simply go into the Dependencies tab of the project, search for and add the latest `zero:zero.dojo.*` module, and you're ready to go!

Take a look at the newly created `index.html` page (see Listing 12.1). Open this page and select the Source tab. There are several things that WebSphere sMash has provided that are needed to properly use Dojo on the page. The first thing of interest is on lines 7 and 8. In these lines, we are importing two style sheets. The CSS on line 8 provides a clean visual environment, with small fonts and normalized default page settings. The CSS on line 7 holds massive power. Dojo comes with several themes that provide a unified look to all of your Dojo application. By default, WebSphere sMash enables the light blue-hued soria theme, as shown in Listing 12.1. Dojo also provides gray-hued tundra and nihilo themes, as well as a darker noir and a high visibility a11y theme. To change themes, simply change the CSS import statement and the main class name defined with the body tag, as shown on line 16. Changing the theme is applied automatically to all the dijits in the application as well. It is also possible to import multiple theme style sheets and enable your user to select and change themes on-the-fly without ever reloading the page. Eventually, you will want to create your own theme that matches your company's web color scheme. Just pick a base theme tree and alter the CSS files for the dijits you use, and you are all set. Changing the color scheme of a website can have a dramatic effect on the user experience.

Listing 12.1   Dojo-Enabled index.html Page

```
<!DOCTYPE html PUBLIC "-//W3C//DTD XHTML 1.0 Transitional//EN
     "http://www.w3.org/TR/xhtml1/DTD/xhtml1-transitional.dtd">
<html xmlns="http://www.w3.org/1999/xhtml">
<head>
    <title>New page</title>
    <style type="text/css">
        @import "/dijit/themes/soria/soria.css";        // Line 7
        @import "/dojo/resources/dojo.css";
    </style>
    <script type="text/javascript" src="/dojo/dojo.js"   // Line 10
        djConfig="parseOnLoad: true"></script>
    <script type="text/javascript">
        dojo.require("dojo.parser");                     // Line 13
    </script>
</head>
<body class="soria">                                         // Line 16
</body>
</html>
```

Let's continue on to the parts that actually instantiate Dojo, which are located on lines 10 and 11 and are contained within a single script tag. At first glance, it's just a script tag that loads in the /dojo/dojo.js file, but continuing onto line 11, you see an unusual attribute called `djConfig`. This is a pre-initialization configuration setting for Dojo. This attribute enables you to set several options for Dojo. By default, WebSphere sMash just sets the `"parseOnLoad"` value to true. This instructs the `dojo.parser` to go through the DOM tree, look for any tags that contain the `"dojoType"` attribute, and if found, instantiate the type defined into a true Dojo widget. This is how the declarative markup version of Dojo works. Because `dojo.parser` is not part of the core `dojo.js`, we need to tell Dojo that we will be using it. This is done on line 13 with the `dojo.require` statement. Any time you use a noncore element of Dojo, you need to tell Dojo to load it using this syntax. You can think of this statement like a Java import. Dojo is smart enough to not load duplicates of any required modules, so there is no risk in overusing this statement.

Let's get back to the `djConfig` attribute on the Dojo loader line 11. One important option that you should always include in your development environment—but never in your production environment—is the `"isDebug:true"` value. This is so important; add it to the `index.html` source now, as shown in Listing 12.2. Setting this flag to true opens up a simple console on any browser that does not have an embedded JavaScript console. The Firebug debugger for Firefox, which is a must-have plugin during development, provides a console for you. For other browsers, that lack a console, such as Microsoft's Internet Explorer, a mini-console opens up that outputs any logging messages. For obvious reasons, you do not want your end users seeing a debugging console appear when they load your application, so prior to going into production, or as part of your production build process, you need to remove or disable the `isDebug` flag.

One other change that you should make to the default page generated by WebSphere sMash concerns the URLs. In the CSS and Dojo script statements, sMash adds the URLs as root-based absolute paths. This is a bad practice, and you should make the URL references relative to the current page. For this index page located at the top level of the public directory, this just means adding a period before the initial slash, as shown in Listing 12.2. Although making this change will not have an impact on this application, it saves you debugging time should you decide to add a context root to the application. For groovy and groovy template (.gt) files, you should always use the `<%= getRelativeUri("url") %>` syntax to reference local resources. Get in the habit of always using relative paths in your URLs, and you'll be better off in the long run.

Listing 12.2 Enabling the Debug Console on the index.html

```
<script type="text/javascript" src="./dojo.dojo.js"
    djConfig="parseOnLoad:true, isDebug:true"></script>
```

We now have a proper Dojo-enabled page, and when you run the application and load this page in your browser, you get exactly...nothing. This won't do at all. Let's add a bit of code that shows we are actually doing something. For now, we code our page manually. Later, we take a look at the drag and drop approach provided by AppBuilder's visual page developer to add some cool widgets. The first thing we want to do is add an initializer to the page. Immediately under the `dojo.require()` statement on line 12, add the following block of code, shown in Listing 12.3. Let's also add some markup within the body tag, as shown in Listing 12.4.

Listing 12.3   Adding Some Logic to the Page

```
<script type="text/javascript">
  dojo.require("dojo.parser");

  dojo.require("dijit.form.DateTextBox");
  dojo.require("dijit.form.Button");
  dojo.require("dijit.Dialog");
  dojo.addOnLoad( function() {
    console.debug("Application starting!");
    dojo.connect( dojo.byId("bookitBtn"), "onclick", function() {
      var startDate = dojo.byId("startDate").value;
      console.debug("Vacation booked for: ", startDate);
      var dia = new dijit.Dialog({ title : "Vacation start date" });
      dia.setContent("Woohoo! You're leaving on:"+
        "<h1>"+startDate+"</h1>");
      dia.show();
    });
  });
});
</script>
```

Listing 12.4   Including a Custom Dojo Widget to the Page

```
<body class="soria">

<h1>Let's go on vacation</h1>
Enter start date:
<input dojoType="dijit.form.DateTextBox" id="startDate"
  value="2010-03-15" required="true" />

<button dojoType="dijit.form.Button" id="bookitBtn">
  Book it Dano!
</button>

</body>
```

The first few lines added in Listing 12.3 should be obvious—we are telling Dojo that we intend to use a DateTextBox, Dialog, and Button dijits on our page. The Button and DateTextBox dijits are used declaratively using the dojoType attribute, as seen in Listing 12.4. The Dialog is created programmatically after the button is pushed. Back in Listing 12.3 comes the mucky "what in the world kind of syntax is this" statement block. Let's break it down slowly, because this is a common paradigm in Dojo development and important for you to embrace if you want to become a true Dojo "black-belt developer." My apologies to butchering this metaphor—I shall try not to digress again. First, we are telling Dojo that after the page is loaded and the initial parsing of dijits is complete, we want to run a function. Because we will never run this function again, there is no sense in polluting the DOM's global namespace with a named function, so we use an inline, anonymous function call. The first thing we do is output a console message stating the application is starting up. The console class has several levels that signify severity. These include debug, info, warn, and error and are styled appropriately within Firebug.

The next task is making an event connection between the `bookitBtn` button's `onclick` event and another anonymous function that creates and displays our dialog box. The `dojo.byId()` function is shorthand for the more verbose `document.getElementById()` call. Within the connect target function, we simply grab the date input's value and then instantiate and show a dialog box with the information.

Novice JavaScript developers may be asking themselves: Why not use the `onclick` attribute on the button tag itself? You could, but this is a bad practice. What if you want multiple actions to occur when you click a button? What if these actions are in a nonobvious areas of the application? You could create a single target function that is called on the button click, that then calls these different functions, but now you have a tight binding of nonrelated events. Using Dojo's connect feature, you provide a stackable, loose coupling of events and actions. It's not the button's concern what happens when it is clicked—it's the concern of the logic that is executed. Using this connect function provides a clean MVC-based separation of concerns between the Button (View), Handler function (Model), and the connection (Controller.) Different areas can each create their own connections to the button without knowledge of the other events.

If the syntax in Listing 12.3 is really bothering you, look at Listing 12.5. This has the same equivalence, with the major disadvantage of polluting the global namespace with two zombie functions that will never be used again. But admittedly, it is slightly easier to read and comprehend. Learn to accept the nested syntax of anonymous functions and do it the "Dojo way." No enlightened Zen puns will be applied here.

Listing 12.5 The BAD Way to Use One-Off Functions

```
<script type="text/javascript">

var init = function() {
  console.debug("Application starting!");
  dojo.connect( dijit.byId("bookitBtn"), "onclick", btnAction );
};
var btnAction = function() {
  var startDate = dojo.byId("startDate").value;
  console.debug("Vacation booked for: ", startDate);
  var dia = new dijit.Dialog({ title : "Vacation start date" });
  dia.attr("content", "Woohoo! You're leaving on:"+
```

```
    "<h1>"+startDate+"</h1>");
  dia.show();
};


dojo.addOnLoad( init );


</script>
```

Now that we have added these few lines of Dojo code to the page, start the application and run it in your browser. You should see a simple text input box and a pretty blue button. If the button is the standard gray browser button, something is wrong, and Firebug should give you a good idea of where the problem is located. Assuming that you are using Firefox and have installed the Firebug plugin, you can click the little insect icon in the bottom right of your browser. This opens up the Firebug console. Now when you reload the page, you should see a lot of Dojo modules being loaded and then our console statement that the application is starting. Dojo's module loading system is intelligent. It starts with the modules you required, it inspects those modules and loads any modules that they require, and so on.

Now, click the date text box, and the magic begins. You should see a nicely styled calendar, where you can navigate and select any given date, as shown in Figure 12.2. For grins, try typing an invalid date into the text area. A warning tooltip displays, stating that you have entered an invalid value. All this with a single `<input>` tag!

Figure 12.2   Date selection input

After you have selected a date, click the Book it Dano button and a dialog box displays the value you entered, as shown in Figure 12.3. The dialog is truly modal with the rest of the page grayed out. You can close the dialog by clicking the x icon in the upper-right part of the title bar. Experiment with trying the tundra theme (changing the css import and body tag class) or another theme. Also, you can experiment with setting your browser to a different language to verify that the date selector is properly internationalized. In Firefox, you can change the desired language by selecting Edit > Preferences > Languages > Choose. Finally, test out your code on different browsers. Notice how the pages are rendered almost exactly the same. We made a lot happen with little effort. As we progress through the rest of this chapter, you hopefully will grasp the full potential of Dojo-based RIA applications.

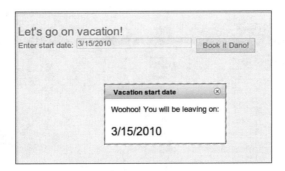

Let's go on vacation!
Enter start date: 3/15/2010   Book it Dano!

Vacation start date   ⊗
Woohoo! You will be leaving on:

3/15/2010

Figure 12.3   Dialog displaying selected date

AppBuilder Page Designer

The WebSphere sMash AppBuilder development environment provides a visual way to drag and drop Dojo widgets onto your page. This should come as a natural way to create visual application to those familiar with other IDE-based GUI builders, such as VisualStudio or Eclipse. This is a nice tool to use for creating simple forms and basic pages. A listing of available dijits and HTML artifacts are shown on the right side of the page pallet, as shown in Figure 12.4. The tool does show some weakness when it comes to advanced pages, because it does not handle nested layout widgets, which are crucial in any complex application.

Input form

Input number 1
| Item 1 | ▼ |

Input number 2
| Item 1 | ▼ |

Input number 3
| Item 1 | ▼ |

Input number 4
| Item 1 | ▼ |

Dialog
Context Menu
Title Pane
Toolbar
Tooltip
Editor
Inline Edit Box
Tree
Progress Bar
Color Palette
Dojox (1.1)
Grid
Multi Combo Box
Checked Multi Select

Figure 12.4   Visual builder sample

One helpful feature is the ability to right-click a widget and update its properties. This ability to view the manageable attributes for the widgets is a nice relief from the more manual way of reading the API documents, on what properties can be applied to various dijits. JavaScript, due to its loosely typed nature, makes exposing class properties through tooling difficult. You can see a sample of the properties on a dijit in Figure 12.5.

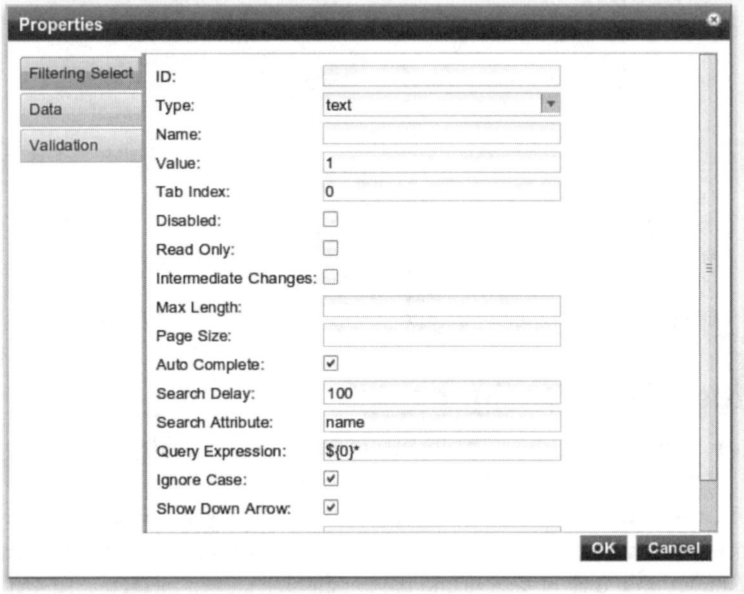

Figure 12.5   Dijit Properties editor

The visual page builder is handy for quickly prototyping pages with widgets, and those coming up to speed on the available dijits and attributes. However, it has several inherent flaws that limit its use in real development scenarios. In our opinion, one of the main disadvantages of the visual builder is its insistence to set absolute location placement for all dropped widgets. This is bad in web applications for several reasons, as the application has no knowledge of the browser's size or if it's part of a larger mashup of other views. By stating absolute positioning, it is essentially killing the browser's capability to flow the layout of items on the page. Additionally, most of the time, you want layout widgets such as BorderController, ContentPanes, TitlePanes, and such to consume all the available space within their parent container. The AppBuilder sets fixed sizes on all widgets, so the developer is forced to always go in and edit these properties. Another issue with this absolute positioning is that a well-written web application would have all these visual definitions within the cascading style sheets (CSS), referencing back to the ID or class of the widgets, rather than inlining it within a style attribute of the dijit itself. The final issue with the visual builder is that it's unnervingly easy to delete the containing layout dijit and all its contained dijits, when all you want to do is remove a simple text field. Not having an undo action for this sort of misstep is a critical limitation.

For these reasons, we typically end up forgoing the visual builder in favor of the source editor tab. Although we don't want to discourage your using the visual page builder for initial layout and page generation, we think that experienced Dojo developers are likely to be more productive without it. You should expect that, over time, these issues will be resolved or minimized, so revisit the visual builder from time to time to reevaluate its capabilities and features. Give the visual page builder a fair shake, and depending on your development style, you may find that it quite adequately meets your needs.

Put a Dojo Face on ZRM and Application Data

In Chapter 8, "Database Access," we discussed how to utilize the Zero Resource Model (ZRM) to easily represent relational data within WebSphere sMash. As part of the ZRM process, you can create a resources delegate that provides all the standard REST verbs to access and update the ZRM using REST calls. This is a natural fit to access these resources from within Dojo and its AJAX communications. WebSphere sMash provides some custom dijits for integrating Dojo with the Zero Resource Manager (ZRM). These include two different DataStore implementations, and a grid to display the data in tabular form. Although it wasn't discussed much, these dijits were in use during the original ZRM discussions.

Dojo provides an API for dealing with abstract data types, called DataStore. Using this API, client developers can use a consistent set of calls to query, read, and write data locally without concerning themselves with the underlying data structure, Dojo provides several DataStore implementation out-of-the-box with stores for JSON, XML, ATOM feeds and many more. sMash includes its own instances of DataStore implementations called `zero.resource.DataStore` and `zero.resource.RestStore`. Using the `zero.resource.DataStore`, you can easily talk directly to a ZRM-defined database on the server. This store automatically handles the standard CRUD activities associated with a ZRM resource. The `zero.resource.RestStore` provides for more generic access to RESTful data. Another Dojo widget provided by WebSphere sMash is the `zero.data.DataGrid`, which utilizes the normal `dojox.grid` classes and includes the `zero.resource.DataStore`. It also provides some nice CRUD functionality. So, with a single dijit, you can provide full read/write access to ZRM-managed data in your application.

In the real world, you probably want to stick with one of the default DataStores and DataGrid implementations provided directly by Dojo. The two DataStores provided by WebSphere sMash are chatty with the host, limiting their benefits, and the implementations overall are not terribly flexible in either functionality or presentation layout.

Instead of creating a new application from scratch, you are encouraged to create the `zero.employee.demo` application and review the `index.gt` file to see how the `zero.resource.RestStore` is used to access and manipulate data from the host. In the App-Builder's My Applications page, click on Create from repository, and then locate and create zero.employee.demo. After the new application is created, go to the Console tab and run `zero runsql setup_db.sql`. This creates a normalized database using the built-in Derby database. Start the application and go to the index.gt page; you should see a data grid showing the data records for several employees. Feel free to add, edit, and delete records using the buttons provided. When you've tired of this, open the index.gt file and inspect the logic used to manage the data and user actions. The application is big enough to provide you with a good feel of using the Dojo DataStore API, without being overly obtuse.

Let's extend the employee sample application to show how a DataStore can be used by multiple widgets. We add our new functionality directly into the existing index.gt page. This enhancement adds a new user input that searches employees by username, and when selected, shows the details for that employee. First, add several new `dojo.require()` statements, as shown in Listing 12.6. Place these statements near the other `require` statements at the beginning of the file. Next, add the code shown in Listing 12.7 near the end of the file just before the `<div id="error">` block.

Listing 12.6   Require Statements for Added Functionality

```
dojo.require("dijit.form.FilteringSelect");
dojo.require("dijit.form.Button");
dojo.require("dijit.Dialog");
```

This block of code creates a filtering selection input driven by the available usernames in the employee DataStore (see Figure 12.6). You can verify this by adding a new employee to the grid, and it automatically becomes available to the selector. When the user clicks the button, an inline declarative script obtains the full employee record from the store and then creates a dialog to display the raw data (see Figure 12.7). Notice the metadata included with the record. We could have extracted the discreet fields, but it's nice to see what's available to us within the data source (see Listing 12.7).

Listing 12.7   New Search Widgets

```
<br/><br/>
Search for Employee by username:  
<div dojoType="dijit.form.FilteringSelect" store="employeeStore"
  searchAttr="username" name="searchInput" id="searchInput"></div>
<button dojoType="dijit.form.Button">
  Show details
  <script type="dojo/connect" event="onClick">
  var emp = dijit.byId("searchInput").getValue();
  console.debug("Username selected = ", emp );
  employeeStore.fetchItemByIdentity(
    {identity: emp, onItem: function(item) {
      console.debug("Employee = ", item );
```

```
      var dialog = new dijit.Dialog({ title: "Employee details" });
      dialog.setContent("<pre>"+dojo.toJson( item, true )+"</pre>");
      dialog.show();
  } } );
  </script>
</button>
```

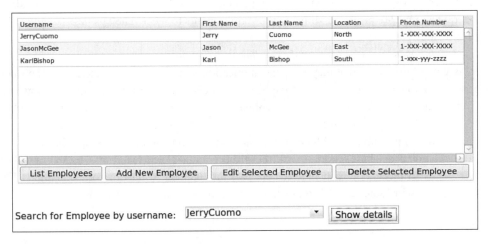

Username	First Name	Last Name	Location	Phone Number
JerryCuomo	Jerry	Cuomo	North	1-XXX-XXX-XXXX
JasonMcGee	Jason	McGee	East	1-XXX-XXX-XXXX
KarlBishop	Karl	Bishop	South	1-xxx-yyy-zzzz

List Employees	Add New Employee	Edit Selected Employee	Delete Selected Employee

Search for Employee by username: JerryCuomo   ▾ | Show details |

Figure 12.6   Employee sample with added input

Employee details   ⊗

```
{
        "firstname": "Jerry",
        "lastname": "Cuomo",
        "location": "North",
        "username": "JerryCuomo",
        "phonenumber": "1-XXX-XXX-XXXX",
        "_S": {
                "resourceUri": "resources/employees",
                "memberLabel": "username",
                "memberIdentifier": "username",
                "_arrayOfItems": [
                ],
                "preamble": null,
                "declaredClass": "zero.resource.RestStore",
                "_storeRef": "_S",
                "_changedItems": null
        }
}
```

Figure 12.7   DataStore details for selected record

Using DataSources in your Dojo applications provides a standardized way to read, write, and search back-end resources without direct knowledge of how the data is structured. For any data that contains many rows, DataStores will greatly enhance your data access concerns.

DBA—A Complete RIA Using WebSphere sMash and Dojo

At this point, we're ready to take all the knowledge gained and build a complete and usable Rich Internet Application (RIA). Let's approach this application like a typical business project, where we are provided with a list of requirements to meet. The business has requested the following:

A web-based, cross-vendor database administration utility

We have also heard that they want the application up and running by the end of the week! We know that the only way we can accomplish this task is to use our freshly acquired knowledge of WebSphere sMash combined with the Dojo Toolkit. Lucky for us, a few days ago, you happened to be wearing your DBA hat, while reading through Chapter 8 of this book, and you have already provided us with a set of RESTful resources that can be utilized to access the company's various relational databases. Along with the project request, we received a list of functional requirements to meet. For each requirement, we just happen to have a corresponding REST resource, shown in Table 12.1. It's funny how these things fall together so cleanly!

Table 12.1   Functional Requirements and Related REST Calls

Business Requirement	Corresponding REST Service
View available data sources	/resources/ds
View all schemas / tables (by type) for a data source	/resources/ds/{ds}
View database driver details	/resources/dbInfo/{ds}
View columns and types for a table	/resources/ds/{ds}/table/{table}
Perform free-form SQL queries and view results	/resources/ds/{ds}/sql

We have enough information to sketch out a flow diagram of the application. Figure 12.8 provides a basic flow, including the REST calls and user interaction. Building up an application flow diagram is always a good idea as it illustrates key criteria to address. If you can't easily draw a flow diagram, you need to rethink how you plan to build your application.

Because we're using Dojo to build up the application's front-end, let's take a quick inventory of some of the widgets that will come in handy. These include the following:

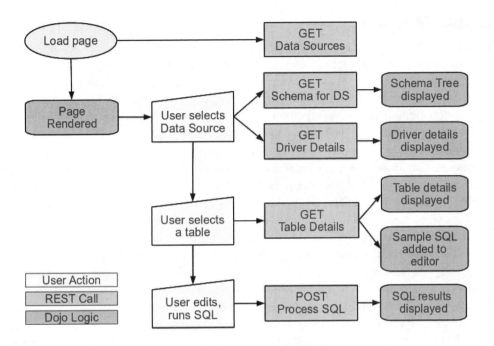

Figure 12.8   DBA flow diagram

- **Layout:** `BorderContainers, ContentPanes, AccordionContainer, Themes`
- **Data Management:** `ItemFileReadStore`
- **Data Presentation:** `Tree, DataGrid, ProgressBar, Toaster`
- **User Input:** `Buttons, Checkbox, FilterSelect, Editor`

Project Creation

Create a new WebSphere sMash project, and name it `Book.Client.DBA`. Next, open the `/config/ivy.xml` file, add a dependency on Dojo, and also add a dependency on the `book:Book.Database.DBA` project. This gives us direct access to the REST services we'll be using to actually access our databases. This works out quite well because we have a clean separation of concerns between the two projects; as long as the REST contract—URLs, request parameters, and response payloads—remain the same, the back-end can be maintained separately from our front-end presentation layer. Ensure that the project resolves properly and we're ready to begin construction of the sMash DBA application. Remember, the clock is ticking on delivery, and we want to impress the business.

Layout Mockup

The first thing that needs to be accomplished is defining and constructing the application's physical layout. For complex layouts, this is generally managed by using Dojo's `dijit.layout.BorderContainer` widget, which for those familiar with general GUI design is similar to a grid bag layout component. A `BorderContainer` defines up to five general regions: Top, Bottom, Leading (Left), Trailing (Right), and Center. The Top and Bottom regions require a fixed height value, the Leading and Trailing regions require a fixed width, and the Center region fills in whatever is left over. Not all regions need to be defined, but the Center region is mandatory. Additionally, the `BorderContainer` is configured to use either a Headline design, where the top and bottom regions consume the full width of the available area, or it can use a Sidebar design, where the leading and trailing regions take up the full height of the available area. Finally, you can define regions to contain a splitter, which allows the user to dynamically alter the height or width of a region by dragging a splitter bar.

The other key layout widgets to know about for this application are the `dijit.layout.AccordionPane` and `dijit.layout.ContentPane`. The `AccordionPane` provides a visually engaging stack container where only a single content area is visible at a time. The `ContentPane` is a general-purpose container where content can be placed directly within it, or reference external HTML files to be retrieved and rendered within it. Each `BorderContainer` region is defined by a layout widget, which is typically a `ContentPane`. Other layout widgets can also be used as region containers, such as `BorderContainers` and `Accordions`. So, it's possible to have a `BorderContainer` within a `BorderContainer`. By combining and nesting `BorderContainers`, you can create a sophisticated application layout with very little effort.

The DBA application's layout follows a typical multipaned application layout similar to that used in classic email and file manager clients. A logical layout diagram for the DBA application is shown in Figure 12.9. With Dojo's declarative layout containers, it's easy to mark this up in HTML, as shown in Listing 12.8. You can view the basic layout design in the `Book.Client.DBA` application source code in the `/public/example_layout.html`.

Listing 12.8   Layout Markup

```
<div id="main" dojoType="dijit.layout.BorderContainer"
   design="headline" livesizing="true">

   <!-- ########## Header ########## -->
   <div dojoType="dijit.layout.ContentPane" region="top" id="header">
      Header</div>

   <!-- ########## Footer ########## -->
   <div dojoType="dijit.layout.ContentPane" region="bottom"
      id="footer">Footer</div>
```

```
<!-- ########## Left Column ########## -->
<div dojoType="dijit.layout.AccordionContainer" region="leading"
    id="left" splitter="true">
    <div dojoType="dijit.layout.ContentPane"
        title="Data Source Selection" selected="true"></div>
    <div dojoType="dijit.layout.ContentPane"
        title="Database Layout"></div>
    <div dojoType="dijit.layout.ContentPane"
        title="Table Details"></div>
    <div dojoType="dijit.layout.ContentPane"
        title="Driver Details"></div>
</div><!--AC -->

<!-- ########## Right Content Area ########## -->
<div dojoType="dijit.layout.BorderContainer" region="center">
    <div dojoType="dijit.layout.ContentPane" region="top"
        id="RightTop" splitter="true"></div>
    <div dojoType="dijit.layout.ContentPane" region="center"
        id="RightBottom"></div>
</div>
</div>
```

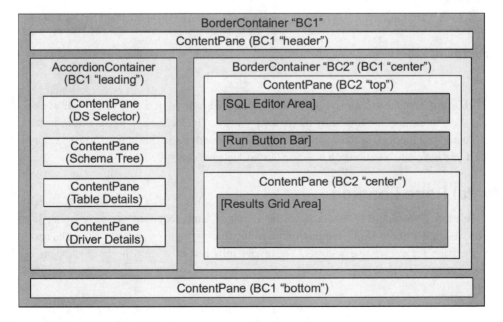

Figure 12.9 DBA logical layout

If you start the application and load this file in a browser, you can see that we have the beginnings of a professional-looking application, as seen in Figure 12.10. There isn't any content yet, but the layout is well defined, with an active `Accordion` area on the left and three resizeable content areas. Dojo makes its incredibly easy to do complex layouts with little effort. We won't actually use this file in the application because we'll be transposing this layout into the main `index.html` page and adding in more content.

Figure 12.10   DBA example layout mockup

For this application, all styling details are located in the `/public/style/dba.css` file. Style-sheet references are linked by ID to make it easy to locate the appropriate rules in the CSS file. There are a lot of style rules applied to the various widgets in this application, so refer to the CSS if you have any questions on how various widgets are controlled.

Initial Page Loading

As with any Dojo application, we have the standard setup requirements of bringing in style sheets, loading the core Dojo, defining our used modules with `dojo.require()` calls and parsing the page for declarative widgets. These can all be seen within the head element of the `index.html` page, as shown in Listing 12.9.

Listing 12.9 DBA Page Initialization

```
<style type="text/css">
  @import "/style/dba.css";
</style>

<script type="text/javascript" src="/dojo/dojo.js"
    djConfig="parseOnLoad:true, isDebug:true" ></script>

<script type="text/javascript">
    console.info(">>>>>  sMash DBA starting up  <<<<<");
    console.debug("Loading required Dojo modules");

    dojo.require("dojo.parser");
    dojo.require("dijit.layout.BorderContainer");
    //... Other dojo.require()s not shown ...

    console.debug("Loading custom dba module");
    dojo.registerModulePath("dba","../js/dba");
    dojo.require("dba");

    dojo.addOnLoad( dba.init );
</script>
```

Near the end of the script tag is a new feature we have not yet addressed. We are telling Dojo about a new module path that contains our custom code. This essentially provides a namespaced directory tree we can use just as you would any other defined Dojo object. This is a best practice to place all your custom code within an externally defined directory location. It is important to note that the module path's location is relative to the dojo.js file and not the index.html file where it is being called. Because WebSphere sMash Dojo support puts the dojo tree directly under /public, the /js/dba path is one directory above the /dojo/dojo.js file. We can now dojo.require() our custom code, and the Dojo loader will locate it and bring it into memory. Within the dba tree, there is a file called dba.js. We inform Dojo of our intent to use this file, and finally when the page is loaded and parsed, we tell Dojo to run the dba.init() function.

Examine the rest of the index.html. The majority of it should resemble the layout sample provided earlier, but we have added a fair amount of extra content. Although space does not permit us to describe everything going on in this file, it should all be relatively decipherable. If you can't figure out what a particular widget definition is providing, try looking up the widget name in the Dojo documentation. Several items are merely placeholders for later functionality injected by the dba controller (dba.js).

Application Initialization

Let's move on to the /js/dba.js script. This is where most of the action occurs for the this application. Listing 12.10 shows the beginning of the script. The first line registers this module with the Dojo loading system so that any future requires for this module will show as available and not cause a reloading of this file. After that are several more require statements. Although we could have put all the require statements either in the index.html or in this file, it's a good practice to put the requires in the file that directly instantiates or uses a class. The next line of code immediately executes an anonymous function that encloses a rather large object definition for the dba object. The dba object contains many variables and functions. In this application, we made the dba object effectively a static global object. We could just as easily have made this an instantiable class but opted for the more direct approach instead; the reasoning for this is that a single static object is easier to manage. We don't have to be concerned about object scoping, and because we have a single instance for the entire application, there's not a need for a unique instance object.

Before we move on to heavy stuff, let's explain a few items. At the beginning of the dba object, we define a few variables. The first is a map of the URLs that are used to retrieve data. Keeping all the URLs in a single location makes it easy to know what services will be called and makes maintenance of these much easier. Notice how a few have embedded tokens. These are replaced at runtime with the actual values using the dojo.string.substitute function. Next are a few more variables that simply hold the DataStore instances that will be used, a reference to the currently selected data source, and finally a list object that holds the current activities that we show in a progress bar at the bottom of the application. See the dba.busy() function and the footer section of the index.html to see how the progress bar is utilized for showing activity.

Let's walk through the initialization process of the DBA application. As shown previously, when the page is loaded and the declarative widgets are rendered, the OnLoad event calls the dba.init() function. In this function, all we're effectively doing is calling another function to load the available data sources. Notice, though, that each function defines an F variable. This is simply a convention we've used so that when writing console output, we can start with the F variable, and we always know what function the message came from. This can also be used in error reporting, as seen in several areas of the application where there are try/catch blocks that call dba.error(F,e) to report on the caught "e" Error object. As an interesting side note, when the page and dba objects are loaded, you can use Firebug to call any function directly; to test out the dba.error function, and the resulting toaster widget display of the error, type the following into the Firebug console's input area:

```
dba.error("Blah(): ", new Error("Ker-Blamo") );
```

Listing 12.10   DBA Script Initialization

```
dojo.provide("dba");

dojo.require("dijit.Tree");
dojo.require("dojox.string.Builder");
```

```javascript
//-- Remote REST URL's used by the application.
//-- Parameters are replaced at runtime.
(function(){

dba = {

  urls : {
    DS:      "/resources/ds",
    SCHEMA:  "/resources/ds/${ds}?showSysTables=${showSysTables}",
    DBINFO:  "/resources/dbInfo/${ds}",
    SQL:     "/resources/ds/${ds}/sql",
    TABLE:   "/resources/ds/${ds}/tables/${table}"
  },

  //-- Data stores used within the application
  stores : {
    dataSources: null,
    schema: null,
    tableDetails: null
  },

  dataSource : null,
  busyMessage : [],

  //-------------------------------------------------------------
  init : function() {
    // summary:
    //   Start DBA application
    var F = "dba.init(): ";
    console.debug(F, "Starting...");
    dba.loadDataSources();
    console.debug(F, "finished");
  },

  //-------------------------------------------------------------
  loadDataSources : function() {
    // summary:
    //    Load initial Data Source list
    var F = "dba.loadDataSources(): ";
    console.debug(F, "Starting...");
```

```
    dba.busy("Data Sources", true);
    dba.stores.dataSource = new dojo.data.ItemFileReadStore({
       url: dba.urls.DS} );
    dba.stores.dataSource.fetch({
       sort: ,
       onComplete: function(items, request) {
          console.debug(F, "Data Sources loaded. #:", items.length);
          var key = dba.stores.dataSource.getValue(items[0], "uid");
          console.debug( F, "Setting DS default to: ", key );

          var dsInput = dijit.byId("dataSource");
          dsInput.attr({
             store : dba.stores.dataSource,
             value : key,
             disabled : false
          });

          var dsButton = dijit.byId("loadDataSourceButton");
          dojo.connect(dsButton, "onClick", dba, "loadDatabaseInfo");
          dojo.connect(dsButton, "onClick", dba, "loadDatabaseSchema");
          dsButton.attr( "disabled", false );
          dba.busy("Data Sources", false);
          console.debug( F, "Finished" );
       }
    });
  },
  //...
 Other functions removed ...
};


}() );
```

It's time to tackle the loadDataSources() function. This function defines a new Data-Store (ItemFileReadStore) passing in a target URL to the data source service on the host. The next task is to perform a query on the data. This is the action that actually causes the DataStore to go out and fetch the data from the server. Because DataStore use asynchronous AJAX calls to obtain the data by URL, we need to provide a callback function to run when the data has been fully retrieved. Within the onComplete callback, we obtain a reference to the data source dijit. This is the FilteringSelect drop-down widget. Notice how we used the dijit.byId(), which returns an instance of the widget, rather than the `dojo.byId()`, which simply returns the DOM node of the ID. It is important to understand the difference, because we need the widget instance to call the appropriate methods to populate the widget. After we have the input's widget reference, a call is made to update several attributes at once. The first is to assign the DataStore to the input. We also set the default value and enable to the widget for user interaction. The final task within this function obtains a reference to the load button, enables it, and sets up two event handlers to call other functions when it is clicked. The data source `FilteringSelect` and the load button are shown in Figure 12.11.

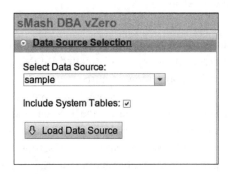

Figure 12.11 Data source selector and loading button

Driver Details and Schema Loading

As shown in the logic flow diagram, two simultaneous asynchronous events are initiated when a data source is selected. These event handlers make calls to the appropriately named `dba.loadDatabaseInfo` and `dba.loadDatabaseSchema` functions. Because we don't want to completely fill this book with source code samples, we talk generally about the activity in the remaining functions, and you can review the actual logic in the provided source code.

First, a call is made to retrieve the driver details used for this data source. A normal `xhrGet` call is used to fetch this data. This is an AJAX call and, as such, needs a callback function named `load` for when the results are received. This data is returned as a normal JSON data object, and the individual values are placed into a table within the Driver Details accordion pane, as seen in Figure 12.12. There is also an associated error callback that can be used to process any failures in an AJAX call. For more information on `xhrGet`—and its sister functions, such as `xhrPost`—as well as the more general topic of asynchronous processing and callbacks, read up on the topic of `dojo.Deferred`.

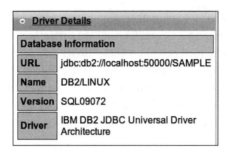

Figure 12.12   Database driver details

The second process started when a data source is selected fetches the database schema. The schema service returns a `ItemFileReadStore`-formatted JSON data, which contains a hierarchical structure that is perfect for representing in a tree widget. The process flow should be predictable at this point. We define a new DataStore, fetch the data, and when received, the `createSchemaTree` function is called to generate the Tree widget. This function checks to see if there is already a tree defined from a previous data source and, if so, destroys it. Then it creates a new Tree instance, passing in the backing DataStore, and setting up a handler for when a leaf node on the tree is clicked. Back in the load schema function, the accordion container is advanced to show the schema tree to the user, as seen in Figure 12.13, as well as updating the contents of the SQL editor area with an informative message.

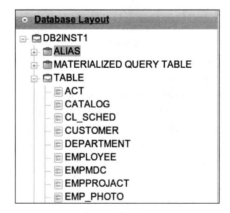

Figure 12.13   Database schema tree listing

Notice the use of the `onError` function to report any errors that occur during this process. One common mistake would be to place a try/catch around the entire `fetch` function. This typically does not do what you would think, as the `fetch` is asynchronous and effectively returns immediately. Any errors that occur happened within the context of the `Deferred` and therefore must be handled in the error path. Always use the appropriate error path (also known as the errback path) when dealing with `Deferreds`. Otherwise, errors can occur that will otherwise go unreported, even if there are try/catch blocks surrounding the asynchronous function calls.

Table Selection and Running SQL

The rest of the application flows are essentially variations of what we have described already. When the user clicks on an entry in the schema tree, the `dba.tableSelected` function is called. This function creates another DataStore containing the table columns and types, which are then shown in a `DataGrid` widget, as seen in Figure 12.14. These table details are also used to define a sample SQL query statement that is then placed into the editor.

Table Details

DB2INST1.EMPLOYEE

Column Name	Column Type
EMPNO	CHAR
FIRSTNME	VARCHAR
MIDINIT	CHAR
LASTNAME	VARCHAR
WORKDEPT	CHAR
PHONENO	CHAR
HIREDATE	DATE
JOB	CHAR
EDLEVEL	SMALLINT
SEX	CHAR
BIRTHDATE	DATE
SALARY	DECIMAL
BONUS	DECIMAL
COMM	DECIMAL

Figure 12.14 Table columns and values

The SQL editor allows freeform queries or update statements. When the user clicks the Execute SQL button, the `dba.executeSql` function is called. This function uses a regular expression to strip embedded HTML tags from the editor's value, and then makes an `xhrPost` call to send the query to the host for processing. The results of the query are then passed on to the `dba.processSqlResults` function. This function destroys any existing results grid, defines a DataStore based on the results, builds up a new layout, and creates a new results grid. Some update SQL statements return only a message indicating the number of rows updated, or even an error message may be returned. This functions handles and displays them appropriately as well.

Final Product

We have covered the entire DBA application flow. It took us only a few days to write and debug, and with WebSphere sMash, the deployment was quick and painless. You presented the application as seen in Figure 12.15, and the business couldn't be happier with the results. Your boss, basking in the glory that is your success, has offered to take you out to lunch and let you have Friday off! WebSphere sMash and the Dojo Toolkit have turned you into a good-looking, geek super-hero. Enjoy your long weekend.

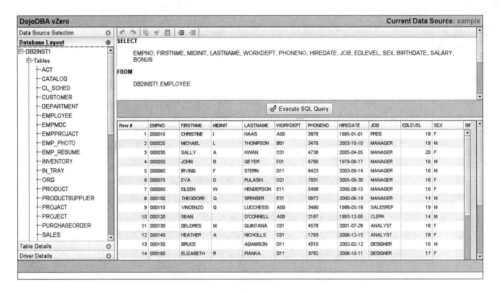

Figure 12.15   Final application

This DBA application was originally written as a WebSphere sMash proof of concept a while ago and has real-world value to examine and easily access your databases. Although the number of lines of code is a poor metric for any project, this application comes in at under 750 lines of client-side code (HTML, CSS, and JavaScript) and under 500 lines of code on the server. Even so, it provides an incredibly rich and useful user experience. Please, keep this application user protected and behind a firewall. Otherwise, all sorts of bad things could happen to your data. Remember that disgruntled DBAs eventually become evil clowns, which means that they know how to use computers and have a deep-rooted hatred of relational data. Consider yourself warned.

Creating Custom Dojo Builds for Performance

This section is somewhat advanced, but if you are deploying a WebSphere sMash application into a production environment, or simply want your application to load quickly, it is strongly recommended that you create a custom build of Dojo specific to your application. You can bundle this custom build as part of your WebSphere sMash application.

You may be asking if a custom Dojo build is necessary. In a single word—yes. A custom Dojo build can actually reduce noncached page loading time by 70% or more. A typical complex web application can go from a 30–40 second load time, down to under 5 seconds just by employing a custom Dojo build. It's hard to argue with that. The reason for this radical load difference is tied directly to Dojo's module loading scheme. In the Dojo world, you load only what you are going to use. But this comes at the cost of having to discreetly load dozens, if not hundreds, of classes. CSS and HTML template files are also modularized in the same fashion. When you create a custom build, you tell Dojo which modules your application uses, and the build process bundles them all into a single custom `dojo.js` file. HTML templates are inlined into their class files, and CSS imports are merged together. Comments and console statements are removed, and the resulting JavaScript file is safely shrunken down to minimize code size. We do not attempt to go into the minutia of the Dojo build process itself. That is all well documented on the Dojo site, and in the Dojo books.

The version of Dojo that comes bundled with WebSphere sMash does not include the build tools required to create a custom Dojo build. This is due to licensing issues with the Rhino JavaScript interpreter. To get around this, you need to download and create a local Dojo project to replace, or overlay, the standard WebSphere sMash Dojo dependency. The steps to perform this are shown in the next section.

Using Non-Supplied Versions of Dojo

There are times when the versions of Dojo supplied in the WebSphere sMash repositories are insufficient for your needs. It may be that you want to perform a custom build as described previously, or the latest and greatest version of Dojo has a killer new dijit that you must have in your next application. It's easy to add in a new version of Dojo into your project. Just as the Dojo dependencies that come with WebSphere sMash are external to your actual project, your custom Dojo additions should also be established within their own project. Then you just add the new Dojo project as a dependency to your main application. Source versions of Dojo enable you to explore the code and read the internal comments, which is a great way to learn the internal workings of various Dojo components.

Follow these steps to set up a Dojo source project:

1. Download a Source version of Dojo.
   a. Go to www.dojotoolkit.org.
   b. Locate the main Download link, select "All Download", and click on the latest version (or any version you want); then locate and download the source distribution. As an example, at the time of this writing, the latest released version of Dojo is 1.4.3, so download the file http://download.dojotoolkit.org/release-1.4.3/dojo-release-1.4.3-src.zip.

2. Create a new WebSphere sMash Project to hold the Dojo source.

    a. Call this new project something like Dojo.Source.143 (match the suffix to the version you downloaded).

    b. Edit the ivy.xml file and set the organization to dojo, and set the version to match the Dojo version you downloaded.

3. Go to a command prompt and extract the dojo zip into the /public directory.

    a. The zip extracts with an extra directory level, so you need to move some things around. Move the directories under dojo-release-1.4.3-src up one level, and then remove the base extraction directory. You should end up with four directories under /public containing: dojo, dojox, dijit, and utils, as shown in Figure 12.16.

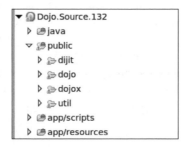

Figure 12.16   Resulting Dojo source tree under /public

You now have a new Dojo project that you can add to any project as a direct dependency. It is common to have several different versions of Dojo in your workspace using this naming convention. It makes it easy to swap versions just by changing your project's dependency.

An important note to discuss here for development environments: WebSphere sMash permits any peer projects to the main application to be dependencies. Unfortunately, the current version of AppBuilder does not recognize local projects as available modules in the dependencies tab. Therefore, to add a local project dependency, you need to edit the ivy.xml file and manually enter the dependency information. But, after you make this change, your project is flagged as not runnable. You then need to select the dependent project(s), and package them. At this point, your application is then ready to run. The WebSphere sMash plugin for Eclipse does not suffer this limitation; you can just add the local project dependencies using the module selector, and everything resolves properly.

Debugging and Best Practices in Dojo Development

If there is one thing that all JavaScript developers can agree on, it's that debugging can be a source of major frustration. Things break, and it can be hair-pulling difficult to determine where the problem lies. By using a quality debugger, and heavy console logging, you can greatly enhance your ability to resolve problems in JavaScript code. The situation has gotten a lot better in the past few years, with the adoption of better browsers, great debuggers, and tools to validate your code. We will go ahead and state that Internet Explorer, especially version 6, which is still in heavy use around the world, is pure evil. If you don't agree, fine, but most JavaScript developers are nodding their heads reading this. Do all of your primary development and debugging in Firefox and Firebug, and once things are working, test it out in IE and other browsers. Although most of the content in this section has nothing to do with WebSphere sMash, or even Dojo, it's being including because it's critical to know these nuggets of knowledge to be able to create solid JavaScript-based applications.

Debugging and Logging with Firebug

In the early days, the browser would simply state There is an Error on This Page. Developers would then typically insert dozens of I Am Here alert statements and narrow things down until eventually they located the source bug in their JavaScript. These were dark days indeed. Eventually, the Mozilla Venkman debugger became available. And when you spent the time to learn how to make it work, and then relearned it every few months, as you forgot, and needed to use it again, you could step through and properly debug your JavaScript. It was quicker and more definitive than alerts, but not by any great shakes. But, it was the only thing available, so you went for it. This could be compared to the cusp of the industrial revolution for JavaScript developers.

Then, in early 2007, Joe Hewitt released the Firebug debugger (http://getfirebug.com), and the JavaScript world was changed forever. Finally, there was a fast, intuitive, cool-as-all-get-out tool to debug your applications. Not only can it debug your code with the expected step in, step over, breakpoints, and the like, it also provides an easy way to profile performance, monitor network activity, examine the DOM, identify CSS elements, and provide console output. Read the documentation provided on the website, and soon you will be a master at JavaScript debugging. It should also be noted that Chromium and other WebKit-based browsers also have good debuggers available. Now, if we could only get a good debugger for Internet Explorer.

Code Validation with JSLint

JSLint (http://jslint.com), written by Douglas Crawford, should be at the top of your JavaScript development bookmarks. You should make it a habit to run your code through JSLint anytime you make significant changes. As the site says, it will hurt your feelings, but it will also make you a much better JavaScript programmer. Spend the time to read through the documentation and understand why it flags things as errors. When you have corrected all the reported errors, look through the rest of the report and verify that things look right. For instance, we know that we want to minimize global variables, so make sure that the reported globals are valid and not due to missing `var` qualifiers in your function variables, which is a common omission. JSLint also does a fairly good job at validating HTML and JSON data. JSLint may be that friend that says, "Yes, you do look fat in that dress," but, soon enough, it will be one of your closest and most trusted friends as well.

Data Validation with JSONLint

Along the same lines as JSLint, JSONLint (www.jsonlint.com) checks JSON data for validity. JSON is a data format widely used in Web 2.0 applications. But, just as bad JavaScript code can cause problems, so can malformed JSON data. A quick check of JSON data can verify your data, and notify you of improper quoting, trailing commas on nested lists, or any other common data issues. This site not only validates your JSON data, but also goes a step further and formats it nicely. This is especially handy if you have received a system-generated block of JSON that is compressed into a single line. This is great for minimizing bandwidth and computer parsing, but terrible for viewing by humans. This site instantly provides you with the results intended to show the data structures.

Dojo References

As we said before, Dojo is a highly capable toolkit for developing amazing applications. However, all the functionality comes at the price of a fairly steep learning curve. There are several good books available that can help you learn to become a Dojo master. Although we can't vouch for all of them, we can say that Mastering Dojo by Gill, Riecke, and Russel (Pragmatic Programmers, ISBN: 978-1-934356-11-1) and Dojo, The Definitive Guide by Matthew Russell (O'Reilly, ISBN: 978-0-596-51648-2) both should sit right next to this book and within easy reach on your bookshelf.

There are also several websites that you should bookmark, as they are invaluable when working with JavaScript and Dojo.

Here are some of our top Dojo development links:

- Dojo Toolkit Home (http://dojotoolkit.org)
- Dojo API (http://api.dojotoolkit.org/)
- Dojo API Cheatsheet (http://download.dojotoolkit.org/release-1.3.2/cheat.html)
- Dojo Campus (http://dojocampus.org)
- Dojo Campus Docs (http://docs.dojocampus.org)
- Dojo API from Uxebu (http://dojodocs.uxebu.com/)

Here are some of our top JavaScript development links:

- JSLint (http://jslint.com/)
- Firebug (http://getfirebug.com)
- W3 Schools—JavaScript (http://www.w3schools.com/js/default.asp)
- Mozilla Development Center—Core JavaScript Reference (https://developer.mozilla.org/en/Core_JavaScript_1.5_Reference)

- Mozilla Development Center—Core JavaScript Guide (https://developer.mozilla.org/en/Core_JavaScript_1.5_Guide)
- JSONLint (http://jsonlint.com/)

Conclusion

We have covered a great deal in this chapter, and hopefully have exposed a whole new world of possibilities for client-side application development within WebSphere sMash using the Dojo Toolkit. By leveraging the power of the Dojo Toolkit on the client browser, you can easily consume your enterprises data in a RESTful manner. Dojo and WebSphere sMash can put a nice face on your SOA infrastructure.

There are many quality JavaScript toolkits out there. IBM and WebSphere sMash have chosen to endorse the Dojo Foundation based on the quality, extensive capabilities, forward-looking APIs, and enterprise features. The time spent learning Dojo will pay off for you, as a developer, as well as for your company. Remember, for most users, the website *is* the company. Make sure you provide your customers with an engaging, feature-rich, state-of-the-art, and responsive experience. You will be a hero, and your customers will remain loyal.

PHP in WebSphere sMash

Why Develop in PHP Using sMash?

WebSphere sMash's PHP implementation was developed using Java SE. This means that you get the best of several environments for application development. You have the ease of use tradition-ally associated with the PHP core libraries and a wealth of available PHP extensions, but you also get the power of Java and its libraries, plus the WebSphere sMash APIs for HTTP access, REST, event, and database access. That's a lot of power at your fingertips.

WebSphere sMash provides a key benefit over normal PHP development in other environ-ments. PHP has a large following because of its ease of use and short time-to-market; however, it has not been good at providing integration with enterprise resource access programs written in other languages. By utilizing the PHP to Java Bridge provided by WebSphere sMash, you can easily extend the reach of PHP to access Message Queuing (MQ) systems, Java Messaging Sys-tems (JMS), and Web Services. This chapter exposes the various ways to use PHP and still seam-lessly work with Java and Groovy resources. These resources can be native code embedded within the application, or more commonly, JAR files or other dependent projects that your PHP application consumes.

Adding PHP to Your Application

To use PHP in your application, you must add the `zero.php` module as a dependency. After you create an application, select the Dependencies tab and then click Add. Type in `zero:zero.php` into the input box, and the filter should show you the desired dependency, as shown in Figure 13.1. After you have enabled this module, you are ready to begin writing WebSphere sMash applica-tion with PHP.

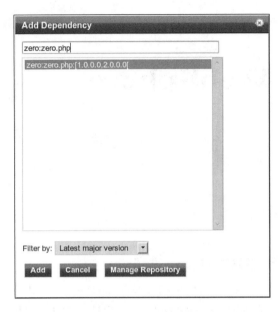

Figure 13.1   Adding PHP dependency to your application

PHP Applications

There are many PHP applications that currently run on the latest development drivers of Web-Sphere sMash. Many other applications will likely work, but there are known gaps in feature support. The WebSphere sMash development team is working hard to address these issues to provide near full support for all PHP APIs and applications. Check the Project Zero website for the latest list of applications that are known to work with WebSphere sMash. There is also information for many PHP-based applications, along with any custom setup requirements needed to make it run properly. Just search the site and community forums for the applications you are trying to install, and if it's been done, you should find the information you need. If the application package you want to use is not listed, give it a try. Post your results on the site, and if you are having problems, chances are someone will be willing to offer assistance.

The following popular PHP applications are known to work with WebSphere sMash:

- PhpBB
- WordPress
- Mediawiki
- SugarCRM
- FirePHP
- Drupal, plus many extensions
- Gallery2

- elgg
- EyeOS
- Moodle

Running PHP Applications in WebSphere sMash

To run a PHP application within WebSphere sMash, download the PHP archive and extract it into the /public directory of a new project. Ensure that you enable the zero.php dependency. If the application requires database support, you need to add the required dependencies or jar files for that as well. MySQL is very popular and is widely supported by many PHP applications. To enable MySQL support, add the mysql:mysql-connector-java module. For more information on MySQL support within WebSphere sMash, refer to Chapter 8, "Database Access." After the required modules are added to the application, run a resolve and start the application. If everything goes well, the PHP application will be available and functional. Make sure to follow any application-specific installation setup, including creating and populating databases.

There have been several sample PHP applications in this book. The rest of this chapter assumes you have a basic understanding of how to write conventional PHP applications. If needed, stop and review some of the previous samples, or check out a couple PHP tutorial sites to refresh your PHP knowledge. The Project Zero site contains many PHP example applications as well.

PHP to Java Bridge

The PHP implementation used in WebSphere sMash is written in Java (see Table 13.1). As such, there is a clean bonding capability that enables you to access native Java code from within your PHP programs. This has huge potential, especially when you are dealing with an enterprise environment, where you want the ease of rapid development of PHP for the presentation layer but still need to access remote resources using standard Java APIs or any in-house developed libraries. The WebSphere sMash PHP implementation makes it easy to call Java APIs. It's a matter of calling a custom import statement to load the Java class and then following simple conventions to access variables and make calls to Java methods.

Table 13.1 Syntax for Access Java Constructs from PHP

Syntax	Description
java_import("pkg.ClassName");	Imports a static Java class.
$var = new JavaClass("pkg.Class-Name");	Creates a variable for a static class. Using java_import() is preferred over this format.
ClassName::staticMethod()	Calls a static method of a Java class.

Table 13.1   Syntax for Access Java Constructs from PHP

Syntax	Description
`ClassName::$staticVariable`	Provides read/write access to a static variable within the Java class.
`$var = new Java("pkg.ClassName", arg1, ...)`	Creates an instance of a Java class.
`$var->instanceMethod( arg1, ...)`	Calls a method of the class instance.

The PHP-Java bridge will always try to access a bean-getter function for a request, and then failing that, will attempt to access a field member directly. So, making a call to `$obj->member` will first result in an attempt to access the `obj.getMember()` method. If that function does not exist, it will attempt to access the `obj.member` value directly. This provides for a clean accessor pattern for both instance and static member variables.

Accessing Java Classes

To directly access Java instance classes from PHP, use the following syntax:

```
$myVar = new Java("package.MyClassname", args, ...);
```

This provides the ability to instantiate Java classes and then work with the functions and members of the class instance directly through PHP. The following code sample illustrates how to instantiate a new Java classes and then work with the functions. Notice that even though you are dealing directly with PHP variables, the bridge will coerce the values into a proper Java type when applying them to the functions.

Listing 13.1   Instantiating and Using a Java Class in PHP

```
$sb = new Java("java.util.StringBuilder", 1024);
$sb.append("This is the first of many, many line of text.<br/>");
for ( $i = 0; $i <= 1000; $i++) {
  $sb.append("Line ".i.": More text added to buffer<br/>");
}
echo $sb.toString();
```

Access Static Java Class Members

To enable access to a Java class, add an import statement to the PHP file. This will provide access to all the members and functions of the imported class:

```
java_import("com.company.package.MyJavaAPI.java");
```

Care should be observed when accessing Java methods, because PHP is not case-sensitive in this regard. The PHP-Java Bridge will attempt to locate the appropriate function/member based on the normalization of the function name, as well as the number of arguments passed into the call. The bridge attempts to best match the function with the same or fewer number of arguments made in the PHP call. You must pass in the expected number of arguments to a Java function form PHP, because Java does not support default argument values.

Example: Using Apache Commons Logging in PHP

Many companies have a standard and often-complex logging mechanism to be used in all applications. Sometimes these are written using Log4J, Java Logging, or one of the many other standard logging facilities out there. The Apache Commons Logging API provides a simple API façade for these logging frameworks so that Java application developers can write to a single API without regard to the actual logging implementation. Using the WebSphere sMash PHP to Java Bridge, we can write to the Java-based Commons Logging API from a PHP page, and then our new PHP-based application will be conforming to the corporate standards for logging. That should make the Enterprise Architecture Review Board happy.

The first thing we need to do is download the Apache Commons Logging JAR and place it into the lib directory of our application. If you've gotten this far in the book, I'm sure you are well accustomed to doing this, but in case you're the type to jump around, here are the steps involved:

1. Access the Apache Commons Logging page at: http://commons.apache.org/logging/download_logging.cgi.

2. Download the latest binary release, which is 1.1.1 as of this writing. Select the archive format you are most comfortable with.

3. When downloaded, open the archive and extract the common-logging-1.1.1.jar file into a temporary directory. We don't need anything else from the download archive.

4. Start AppBuilder and open your browser to the appropriate URL (typically http://localhost:8070).

5. Click the Create New Application link and enter a name of **Book.PHP.Java**, or whatever suits your taste.

6. Click on the new application's name to access it.

7. Add the JAR file to the lib directory, by clicking the Explorer tab, clicking the lib directory on the left side, and then clicking the Upload button. In the dialog shown in Figure 13.2, browse for the location of the JAR file and make sure that the lib directory is selected as the target location.

8. Return to the File Editor tab and create a new PHP file in /public called **logging.php**. The only reason to put this into a public response file is so that it's easy to run and view the output this way.

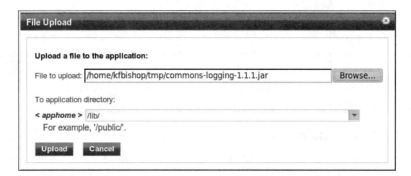

Figure 13.2   Adding JAR file to the application lib directory

9.   Enter the following block of code into this file. This code will define our logger, log sev-
     eral different log messages, and then output the logging levels supported. Note how a
     $src variable is used to define where these logs came from. This is required due to the
     reflective nature of how the PHP to Java Bridge works.

Listing 13.2   Logging PHP to Java Sample Program

```php
<?php
//-- Produce standard Log4J logging calls.
java_import("org.apache.commons.logging.Log");
java_import("org.apache.commons.logging.LogFactory");

$log = LogFactory::getLog("MyPhpLogger");
$src = "logging.php: ";

$log->fatal($src."Fatal message from PHP");
$log->error($src."Error message from PHP");
$log->warn($src."Warn message from PHP");
$log->info($src."Info message from PHP");
$log->debug($src."Debug message from PHP");
$log->trace($src."Trace message from PHP");

echo "ACL logging levels check<br/>";
echo "Fatal enabled = ".$log->isFatalEnabled()."<br/>";
echo "Error enabled = ".$log->isErrorEnabled()."<br/>";
echo "Warn enabled = ".$log->isWarnEnabled()."<br/>";
echo "Info enabled = ".$log->isInfoEnabled()."<br/>";
echo "debug enabled = ".$log->isDebugEnabled()."<br/>";
echo "Trace enabled = ".$log->isTraceEnabled()."<br/>";
?>
```

10. Start the application by clicking the green run arrow in the upper left of the AppBuilder window.

11. Open the file in a new browser window with a URL of http://localhost:8080/logger.php. There won't be much to see in the response shown in Figure 13.3, but that's not what we are concerned with.

```
ACL logging levels check
Fatal enabled = 1
Error enabled = 1
Warn enabled = 1
Info enabled = 1
debug enabled =
Trace enabled =
```

Figure 13.3 Response output of Logger sample

12. Return to the AppBuilder Window and click the Console tab. Here we should see the logging output from our PHP program, as shown in Figure 13.4.

```
2010-04-05 21:43:34 zero.core.cfadapter.ZeroServer::run Thread-10
        INFO [ CWPZC0149I: /home/kfbishop/dev/smash/apps/Book.PHP.Java running on port 8080 ]
2010-04-05 21:43:37 sun.reflect.NativeMethodAccessorImpl::invoke0 Thread-11
        SEVERE [ logging.php: Fatal message from PHP ]
2010-04-05 21:43:37 sun.reflect.NativeMethodAccessorImpl::invoke0 Thread-11
        SEVERE [ logging.php: Error message from PHP ]
2010-04-05 21:43:37 sun.reflect.NativeMethodAccessorImpl::invoke0 Thread-11
        WARNING [ logging.php: Warn message from PHP ]
2010-04-05 21:43:37 sun.reflect.NativeMethodAccessorImpl::invoke0 Thread-11
        INFO [ logging.php: Info message from PHP ]
```

Figure 13.4 Logger sample console output

13. The logger output by default goes to standard out, which in this case is the runtime logs. By manipulating the `logging.properties` file located in the classpath, or in the applications lib directory, the logging output can be directed to any proper handler, such as common log files, databases, email, or whatever your logging implementation is configured for. Testing different logging implementations is beyond the scope of this sample, but you should get the basic concept of using external Java from this example.

PHP to Groovy Bridge

The Groovy bridge enables you to connect and use Groovy classes and closures from within your PHP applications. You can also run Groovy script code directly in your PHP blocks. This mechanism provides a clean way to merge different projects as dependencies and allow developers to use their language of choice and still have the integration desired between modules.

It's quite common within WebSphere sMash applications to write simple static Groovy classes; as such, it's mostly a matter of importing the Groovy class and directly accessing its methods and variables. To enable access to a Groovy class, add an import statement to the php file pointing to the Groovy class you want to interact with, as shown here:

```
groovy_import("MyGroovyStuff.groovy");
```

At this point, you have access to all the public variables and methods contained within this class. The general syntax is the class name, two colons, and the member you want to access. This is better shown in Table 13.2.

Table 13.2   Access Patterns for PHP to Groovy Bridge

Syntax	Description
`ClassName::staticMethod()`	Calls a static method of a Groovy class
`ClassName::$staticVariable`	Provides read/write access to a static variable within the Groovy class
`$var = new ClassName()`	Creates an instance of a Groovy class
`$var->instanceMethod()`	Calls a method of the class instance
`$var->instanceField`	Provides Read/Write access to a variable within the class instance

PHP to Groovy Bridge Example

Let's go for a simple example to illustrate how a PHP application can utilize existing Groovy classes and functionality. In this scenario, let's assume that we have two developers working on a project. Developer A is a PHP developer by trade and will be working on the front-end user interface. Developer B handles the access to all the databases and other remote resources. She prefers to use Groovy for all her processing. Assuming that both developers are using WebSphere sMash, it's easy for developer A to use the PHP-Groovy bridge to access the back-end classes into the PHP-based UI portion of the project. For this example, we keep everything in a single project for simplicity, but layering different projects as dependencies for complex applications is an often-untapped strength of WebSphere sMash.

Take a look at the following PHP code shown in Listing 13.3. This example creates two instances of a Groovy Person class and processes the results. The first statement defines the Groovy class to be used in this script. From this point, we have access to all the members and methods of this class. If you don't want the fuss of actually creating a standalone Groovy file, you can also run groovy code directly within the `groovy_eval()` function.

Listing 13.3   PHP Accessing Groovy Class

```php
<h1>People</h1>
<?php
groovy_import("Person.groovy");
//-- Create and then Populate a person
$joe = new Person();
$joe->setFirstName("Joe");
$joe->setLastName("Strummer");
$joe->setBirth("1952-07-21");
$joe->setDeath("2002-12-22");
echo "$joe<br/><hr/>";

//-- Create person passing in values into constructor
$data = array(
firstName => "Jerry",
lastName => "Garcia",
birth => "1942-08-01",
death => "1995-09-05"
);

$jerry = new Person( $data );
echo $jerry."<br/>";
echo "He lived for ".$jerry->daysAlive()." days!<br/><hr/>";

// Create and execute Groovy scripts dynamically
$groovyScript = "'Johnny Cash'.reverse()";

echo "Evaluating: $groovyScript = ".groovy_eval($groovyScript);
echo "<br/><hr/>";

//-- Access static members too
echo "Class description: ".Person::$description."<br/><hr/>";
?>
```

The Groovy code for the Person class is shown in Listing 13.4. Note that there are two constructors defined in this class. GroovyBeans have two assumed constructor formats: the first taking no arguments and the second taking a map of key/value pairs that match the member variables. By default, the WebSphere sMash introspection routine assumes the zero argument constructor, which is normally fine. The definition of a constructor with explicit arguments overrides this default behavior, and therefore you must also provide a no-argument constructor signature. Otherwise, the introspection will complain that there is not a valid constructor for a no-argument constructor.

Mapping of dates between PHP and Groovy can be somewhat problematic, so a clean approach is to use an ISO string representation of a date and parse it back into a real Date object, as shown in the `setBirth` and `setDeath` methods. One of the nice convenience features of Groovy is the ability to easily perform math on dates, as represented in the `daysAlive()` method. Because this is arguably more difficult to do in PHP, it makes for a good candidate to pass off to Groovy to handle for us.

Listing 13.4   Person Groovy Class

```
class Person {
  def public static description = "Person class for working with
people data"
  String firstName
  String lastName
  Date birth
  Date death

  Person() {}
  Person(args) {
    this.firstName = args.firstName
    this.lastName = args.lastName
    setBirth( args.birth )
    setDeath( args.death )
  }
  void setBirth( dob ) {
    this.birth = new Date().parse('yyyy-MM-dd', dob)
  }
  void setDeath( dob ) {
    this.death = new Date().parse('yyyy-MM-dd', dob)
  }
  String toString() {
    return "${firstName} ${lastName} was born on: ${birth}"
  }
```

```
int daysAlive() {
  if (this.birth && this.death ) {
    return this.death - this.birth
  } else if ( this.birth ) {
    return new Date() - this.birth
  } else {
    return 0
  }
}
}
```

When we access the PHP script from a browser, we get the results shown in Figure 13.5.

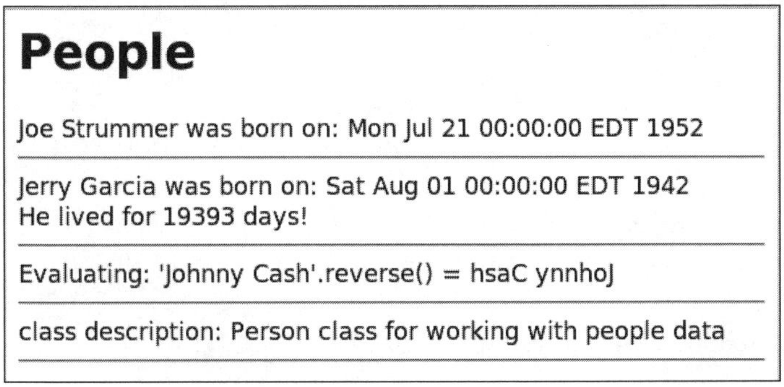

People

Joe Strummer was born on: Mon Jul 21 00:00:00 EDT 1952

Jerry Garcia was born on: Sat Aug 01 00:00:00 EDT 1942
He lived for 19393 days!

Evaluating: 'Johnny Cash'.reverse() = hsaC ynnhoJ

class description: Person class for working with people data

Figure 13.5 Output of PHP to Groovy example

Extending PHP

There are times when you may want to develop a façade over a Java or Groovy class in PHP. This allows PHP developers to access custom Java/Groovy functionality but maintain a pure PHP environment. WebSphere sMash enables you to easily create your own PHP extensions. PHP extension classes must extend the `com.ibm.phpj.xapi.ExtensionBaseImpl` class and have custom XAPI annotations defined for the class and all functions. The final restriction is `RuntimeContext` that is used to pass in function arguments and set the return value. Because all arguments and return values are actually managed by the `RuntimeContext`, all extension classes and function signatures follow a common template, as shown in Listing 13.5.

Listing 13.5   Common Template for PHP Extension Classes

```
import com.ibm.phpj.xapi.ExtensionBaseImpl;
import com.ibm.phpj.xapi.RuntimeContext;
import com.ibm.phpj.xapi.annotations.XAPIExtension;
import com.ibm.phpj.xapi.annotations.XAPIFunction;


@XAPIExtension("MyExtensionClass")

public class MyExtensionClass extends ExtensionBaseImpl {

  @XAPIArguments(MandatoryArguments = 1,
  PassSemantics = { XAPIPassSemantics.ByReference })
  @XAPIFunction("myFunction")

  public void myFunction(RuntimeContext ctx) {

    //-- Extract arguments from context
    String arg1 = ctx.getStringArgument(0).getString();

    //-- Do something here
    String something = someFunction( arg1 );
    //-- Optionally Set return value
    ctx.setReturnValue( something );

  }
  //... remaining code removed ...
}
```

A couple items are worthy of mention in this template sample. First, notice how the class and function have their own XAPI annotations. Although in this template, the annotation and the class/function names match, they do not need to. You can choose to have a public "PHP" function name, and a private "Java" name. For example, the PHP annotation of the function could be called my_function, whereas the actual Java function name could remain myfunction. The second thing of note is how we obtain the function arguments from the RuntimeContext. The context has several getXxxArgument() functions based on the type of object you are attempting to access. RuntimeContext arguments are zero-based.

The last item of interest in this template is the optional XAPIArguments annotation. This is useful when you want to explicitly require a set number of arguments by a function. The default behavior of the PHP extension's argument handling is to pass all arguments by value, meaning that the source PHP variable cannot be altered by the extension functions. If you want to enable the extension function to modify the argument source values, the XAPIArguments->Pass Semantics value needs to be set to XAPIPassSemantics.ByReference, as shown in the preceding template. Typically, you will want normal behavior and will not include this entry or even the XAPIArguments annotation for most functions.

Logger Extension Sample

The easiest way to illustrate the process is to create a sample extension. Typically, when creating extensions, a new WebSphere sMash project would be created to hold the extensions, but to keep things simple, we'll just reuse the existing project we've been using in this chapter. If we had created this Logger extension as a standalone project, the project that would be using the Logger would need to add the extension project as a dependency.

Start by creating a new Java file in a new directory called phpext, under the Java directory. Call this file Logger.java. Listing 13.6 shows the initial contents of this file. The rest is essentially a duplication of the two "fatal" functions.

Listing 13.6   Logger PHP Extension Fragment

```
package phpext;

import com.ibm.phpj.xapi.ExtensionBaseImpl;
import com.ibm.phpj.xapi.RuntimeContext;
import com.ibm.phpj.xapi.annotations.XAPIExtension;
import com.ibm.phpj.xapi.annotations.XAPIFunction;

//-- Produce standard Log4J logging calls.
import org.apache.commons.logging.Log;
import org.apache.commons.logging.LogFactory;

@XAPIExtension("Logger")
public class Logger extends ExtensionBaseImpl {

  private Log log;
  private String prefix;

  @XAPIFunction("initLogger")
  public void init(RuntimeContext ctx) {
    String arg1 = ctx.getStringArgument(0).getString();
    log = LogFactory.getLogger( arg1 );
    prefix = arg1 + ": ";
  }
```

```
/* FATAL */
@XAPIFunction("fatal")
public void fatal(RuntimeContext ctx) {
  log.fatal( prefix + ctx.getStringArgument(0).getString() );
}
@XAPIFunction("isFatalEnabled")
public void isFatalEnabled(RuntimeContext ctx) {
  ctx.setReturnValue( log.isFatalEnabled() );
}

// repeat previous two functions for:
// error, warn, info, debug, trace
}
```

When the extension is completed, we need to tell the application PHP runtime about it. This is done in the php.ini file, by adding the following line:

```
; Book Sample Commons Logging extension
extension = phpext.Logger
```

The next thing to do is write a new PHP script to perform some logging calls using the new Logger extension, as shown in Listing 13.7.

Listing 13.7   Logging_extension.php—PHP Script Using Logger Extension

```
<?php

initLogger("logging_extension.php");

fatal("Fatal message from PHP");
error("Error message from PHP");
warn("Warn message from PHP");
info("Info message from PHP");
debug("Debug message from PHP");
trace("Trace message from PHP");

echo "ACL logging levels check<br/>";
echo "Fatal enabled = ".isFatalEnabled()."<br/>";
echo "Error enabled = ".isErrorEnabled()."<br/>";
echo "Warn enabled = ".isWarnEnabled()."<br/>";
echo "Info enabled = ".isInfoEnabled()."<br/>";
```

```
echo "debug enabled = ".isDebugEnabled()."<br/>";
echo "Trace enabled = ".isTraceEnabled()."<br/>";

?>
```

All this extension does is provide a façade for the Apache Commons Logging Java code. The main advantage is that we have abstracted the actual Java code so that the PHP developer can make direct "PHP" function calls to perform his logging. As you can see, this is much cleaner from a pure PHP point of view rather than using either the Java or Groovy bridge. Figure 13.6 shows the WebSphere sMash output log from loading the `logging_extension.php` script in a browser.

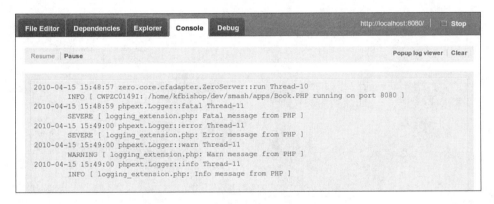

Figure 13.6 logging_extension.php—console log output

Data Conversion Between PHP and Java in Extensions

PHP and Java are different languages and have different concepts of data types. To properly pass values back and forth, data conversion on function arguments and return types must occur. The WebSphere sMash PHP Extension APIs provide a full range of conversion functions to assist in this regard as shown next.

PHP Arguments to Java Variables

Conversion from PHP variables to Java variables performs as you would expect for numeric and boolean values. Strings in PHP are handled specially due to PHP allowing nontext values in string types. The XAPIString internally holds a byte array and, using the toString() method, attempts to coerce the bytes to Unicode text. Arrays in PHP serve a dual purpose of standard indexed lists and associative array maps. The XAPIArray object has custom methods that enable you to deal with these arrays in a properly classified manner. Table 13.3 describes the full data conversion reference.

Table 13.3   PHP to Java Data Conversion Map

PHP Type	RuntimeContext Access Conversion	Java Type	Comments
Int	getIntegerArgument()	Integer	
Bool	getBooleanArgument()	Boolean	
double	getDoubleArgument()	Double	
	getFloatArgument()	Float	
string	getStringArgument()	com.ibm.phpj. xapi.XAPIString	Use toString() to convert to a Java String.
Array	getArrayArgument()	com.ibm.phpj. xapi.XAPIArray	Custom Array type with functions for other conversions, iterators, and key/value accessors.
	getArrayArgument(). getMap()	com.ibm.phpj. xapi.XAPIArrayMap	The getMap() function converts from XAPIArray to XAPIArrayMap, which implements Java Map interface, without a full copy being created.
	getArrayArgument(). copyOut()	LinkedHashMap	The copyOut() function converts XAPIArray to a LinkedHashMap. Sub-arrays are also converted to LinkedHashMap.
	getArrayArgument(). copyOutArray()	Object[]	The copyOutArray() function converts XAPIArray to an Object List. Objects are converted according to this table. Any PHP array keys or indexes are dropped, so order is not preserved.
object		com.ibm.phpj. xapi.XAPIObject	This object is not currently implemented.
resource		com.ibm.phpj. resources.Resource	This object is not currently implemented.

Java to PHP Variable Conversion

The conversion from Java variables back to PHP variables is straightforward. Any Java values not listed in Table 13.4 will throw an `XAPIException` during the conversion.

Table 13.4   Data Type Conversions Between PHP and Java

Java Type	PHP Type	Comments
`null`		
`Integer`	`int`	
`Byte`		
`Character`		
`Short`		
`Long`		
`Double`	`double`	
`Float`		
`Boolean`	`bool`	
`String`	`string`	
`Byte[]`		
`com.ibm.phpj.xapi.XAPIString`		
`Map`	`array`	All children are converted per this table, as well as child maps.
`com.ibm.phpj.xapi.XAPIArray`		
`Object[]`		
`com.ibm.phpj.resources.Resource`	`Resource`	

SuperGlobals

PHP supports the concept of SuperGlobals, which as the name implies, provides variables that are available anywhere within a PHP script. WebSphere sMash extends this concept with several custom SuperGlobals. Think of these variable sets in relation to the global context used elsewhere within WebSphere sMash applications. Examine and load the interactive `snoop.php` script located in the public directory in the provided `Book.PHP` sample. This should properly illustrate the information available from each SuperGlobal.

Here are the main SuperGlobals provided by WebSphere sMash.

$_SERVER

The $_SERVER SuperGlobal provides information derived primarily from the request object. This variable consists of a map of key/value pairs that offer insight into the request and server environment. Figure 13.7 shows a small sample of the values available within the $_SERVER SuperGlobal.

snoop.php -- Super Globals

$_SERVER

Variable	Value
$_SERVER['REQUEST_URI']	/snoop.php?a=1&b=2
$_SERVER['REQUEST_METHOD']	GET
$_SERVER['PHP_SELF']	/snoop.php
$_SERVER['SERVER_PROTOCOL']	HTTP/1.1
$_SERVER['argv']	a=1&b=2
$_SERVER['SCRIPT_FILENAME']	/home/kfbishop/dev/smash/apps/Book.PHP/public/snoop.php
$_SERVER['QUERY_STRING']	a=1&b=2
$_SERVER['SERVER_SOFTWARE']	ProjectZero
$_SERVER['SERVER_NAME']	localhost
$_SERVER['HTTP_CONNECTION']	keep-alive

Figure 13.7   snoop.php—$_SERVER SuperGlobal sample

$_GET and $_POST

The $_GET and $_POST SuperGlobals provide maps containing the key/value of the query arguments provided on the request URL. The $_GET values are those presented on the URL as query parameters, whereas the $_POST contains values as part of a POST submission of form data. Figure 13.8 shows the results of snoop passing in query arguments on the URL and submitting a form POST.

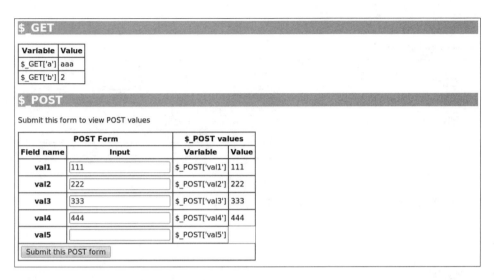

Figure 13.8   snoop.php—$_GET and $_POST sample

Be aware that when testing the snoop script, it was discovered that the $_GET and $_POST SuperGlobals do not currently support duplicate query keys. So, a GET URL of "http://local-host:8080?a=1&b=0&b=2&a=3" will produce $_GET values of "a=3" and "b=2". Likewise, duplicate input names on a form POST will truncate down to a single value. Logically, the duplicate values should be an array containing each of the duplicate values. Although this is not a terribly common scenario apart from check box groups and multiselect inputs in forms, it is one to take note of when using $_GET and $_POST.

$HTTP_RAW_POST_DATA

This SuperGlobal provides direct access to the raw POST data stream. This is common when streaming binary data to a server. The value of this variable is a byte stream. To replicate this in a form submission, we need to override the default encoding to text/plain or some other value. By default, form submission will automatically encode form fields prior to submission.

$_FILES

This SuperGlobal provides access to any files uploaded as part of a "multipart/form-data" encoded form submission. This variable is a map of maps of the files. The first level keys are the name of the form file input field, whereas the second provide information on the filename, size, type, and other details. Figure 13.9 shows the results of uploading an image file.

$_FILES

Submit a file using this form to view FILE details

File Submission Form		$_FILES values	
Field name	Input	Variable and Value	
file1	/home/kfbishop/Documents/ Browse...	$_FILES['file1']['name']	Matt_Flame.png
		$_FILES['file1']['type']	image/png
		$_FILES['file1']['tmp_name']	/tmp/MultiPart5464677753134198106
		$_FILES['file1']['error']	0
		$_FILES['file1']['size']	531909

Submit this FILE UPLOAD

Figure 13.9   snoop.php—$_FILES SuperGlobal sample

$_COOKIE

The $_COOKIE SuperGlobal provides access to a map of the cookie data sent along with the request. The keys for the $_COOKIE variable vary based on the cookies stored on your browser for the domain.

$_REQUEST

The $_REQUEST SuperGlobal contains a combination of the $_GET, $_POST, and $_COOKIE variables. Be aware that any keys that are duplicates within the three groups will be dropped.

XML Processing Using PHP and WebSphere sMash

The WebSphere sMash implementation of PHP provides a couple of simple XML accessor methods that can be utilized to integrate with XML-based resources. The xml_decode() method will read and parse an XML document and return a map of variables that can be accessed directly using normal PHP syntax. The converse method of the xml_encode() method takes a PHP map and transforms it into an XML document. With that said, you probably don't want to bother with these, as they don't deal with common XML issues such as CDATA blocks and namespaces.

There is another solution standard to PHP called SimpleXML (http://www.php.net/manual/en/book.simplexml.php), which makes it a snap to process XML data. The following sample PHP script will consume an RSS feed and display it on the browser. Listing 13.7 shows how we fetch a remote XML document, parse it using SimpleXML, and then output the result in a fairly nice structure. In this example, we pull in the Project Zero Blog feed and display the latest article to the user. This file is called /public/simple_xml.php in the Book.PHP.XML project.

Listing 13.7   Using SimpleXML to Process RSS Feed

```php
<?php
ini_set('display_errors',1);
$xml =
connection_get("http://www.projectzero.org/blog/index.php/feed/");
$rss = simplexml_load_string($xml['body']);
//var_dump($rss);
echo "<h1>";
echo $rss->channel[0]->title[0];
echo "</h1>";
$items=$rss->channel[0]->item;
echo "<h3>Article count: ".count($items)."</h3>";
echo "<hr/>";
foreach($items as $item) {
  //var_dump($item);
  echo "<h3><a href='".$item->link[0]."'>".
    $item->title[0].
    "</a></h3>".
    $item->description[0];
}
echo "<br/><hr/>RSS Version: ".$rss['version'];
?>
```

From an XML perspective, all this script does is parse an XML string into mapped array. This is performed by the simplexml_load_string() function. The rest is normal XML and data access processing. The input to the load function is the "body" member of the results of the connection_get command. This command fetches the contents of a URL and returns a three element mapped array, consisting of the "status" of the call, the "headers," and finally the "body" string. This "body" content is what we pass into the xml load function. All nodes in an XML map are considered arrays, which you can iterate as you would any other list. Working with attributes is done by accessing them as a direct array member, as shown in the final line of the script. They call it SimpleXML for a reason. For more information on XML processing in PHP, refer to the online SimpleXML manual. The results of loading this script in your browser is shown in Figure 13.10.

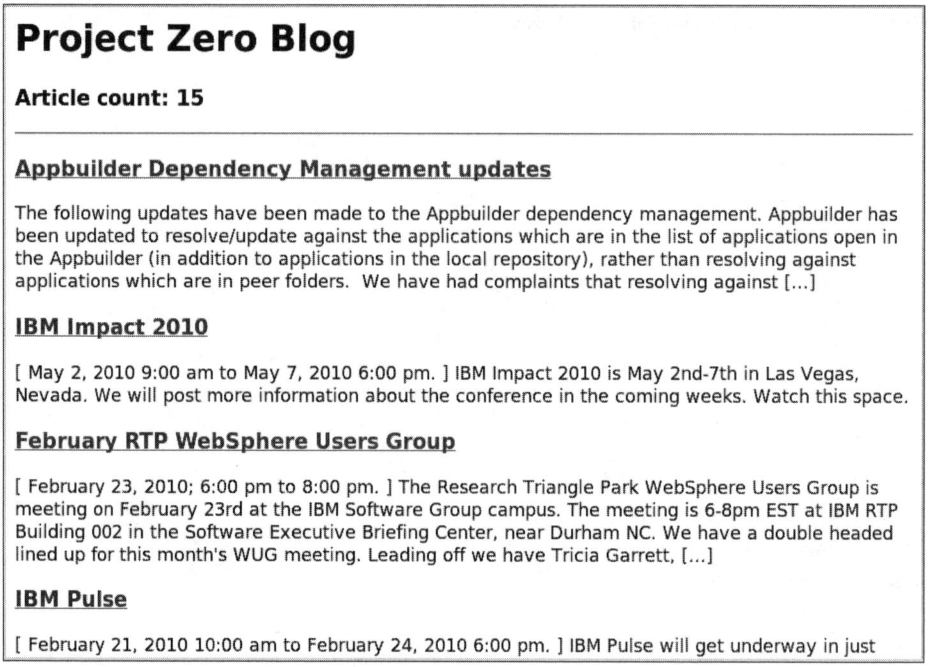

Project Zero Blog

Article count: 15

Appbuilder Dependency Management updates

The following updates have been made to the Appbuilder dependency management. Appbuilder has been updated to resolve/update against the applications which are in the list of applications open in the Appbuilder (in addition to applications in the local repository), rather than resolving against applications which are in peer folders. We have had complaints that resolving against [...]

IBM Impact 2010

[May 2, 2010 9:00 am to May 7, 2010 6:00 pm.] IBM Impact 2010 is May 2nd-7th in Las Vegas, Nevada. We will post more information about the conference in the coming weeks. Watch this space.

February RTP WebSphere Users Group

[February 23, 2010; 6:00 pm to 8:00 pm.] The Research Triangle Park WebSphere Users Group is meeting on February 23rd at the IBM Software Group campus. The meeting is 6-8pm EST at IBM RTP Building 002 in the Software Executive Briefing Center, near Durham NC. We have a double headed lined up for this month's WUG meeting. Leading off we have Tricia Garrett, [...]

IBM Pulse

[February 21, 2010 10:00 am to February 24, 2010 6:00 pm.] IBM Pulse will get underway in just

Figure 13.10   Results of a simple_xml request

There are few topics that should to be discussed on this sample. First, the `get_connection()` call requires the `zero:zero.php.connection` dependency. So, it needs to be added to the project, or else you will receive an error about a missing function. This dependency will likely not show up in your repository by default, so access the manage repository section, search for this module, and select the latest version. After it's been downloaded and added to your project, you'll be ready to pull in XML document from anywhere. Technically, you also need to enable the `zero.php.ConnectionExtension`, but it's enabled by default in all PHP application. For reference sake, this is defined in the `/config/php.ini` file in your project. Go ahead and make sure it's there, and also explore some of the other setting defined in this file:

```
extension = zero.php.ConnectionExtension
```

There are a few final items to take note of in this simple application. The first line enables error reporting to Standard Out, which when called by URL is the browser itself. Although this makes it easy to debug a misbehaving application, it is probably not appropriate for production applications. Get in the habit of wrapping complex logic in try/catch blocks and returning a friendly error message to your users. There are also a couple other commented debugging lines that can be useful for error resolution. The `var_dump()` function does exactly as you would expect and dumps the contents of a variable to Standard Out. The rest of this script should be self-explanatory. Experiment with pulling other XML documents and how to process and manipulate their content using PHP's SimpleXML.

WebSphere sMash PHP Extensions

WebSphere sMash provides many extensions to assist in the development of PHP-based applications. These extensions are enabled by defining them in the /config/php.ini file for the application. Each of the extensions shown next can be enabled by adding a line similar to that shown here in the php.ini file:

```
extension = zero.php.ExtensionName
```

If these extensions don't quite meet your needs, there is a process to create your own extensions for others to use. PHP Extensions were covered previously in this chapter.

The remainder of this chapter details the PHP extensions provided by WebSphere sMash. Becoming acquainted with these APIs can greatly improve your ability to write PHP applications that access relational databases, interact with remote resources, and provide application protection support and other helpful features. The following API groups are presented:

- **WebSphere sMash utilities**—Provides access to the global context (GC) and the virtual files system
- **URI utilities**—Provides access to build application-specific URIs
- **Java extensions**—Provides access to Java resources from PHP
- **Groovy extensions**—Provides access to Groovy resources from PHP
- **Remote connections**—Provides utilities to enable easy access to remote resources
- **JSON utilities**—Provides methods for processing JSON data
- **Active content filtering**—Provides protection from malicious incoming data
- **Cross-Site Request Forgery (CSRF)**—Provides programmatic protection from CSRF attacks
- **Login**—Provides ability to log into WebSphere sMash applications programmatically
- **Database access**—Provides a series of database-related functions broken down by: General, Query, Results, and Transactions
- **XML utilities**—Provides methods to process XML data

WebSphere sMash Utilities

Extension name: zero.php.ZeroExtension

The following functions provide support for accessing WebSphere sMash-specific concepts. These are used to access the global context, process included views, and access the virtual file system defined by WebSphere sMash (see Table 13.5).

Table 13.5   WebSphere sMash Utility Functions

Function	Description
DOCROOT	Returns the document root directory path of the Zero Application that is executing the calling script.
fire_event	Fires an event registered in the configuration file of the application. **Arguments:** String eventName—Name of the event to fire. Array args—Argument list to be passed into the event handler.
getVFile	Gets the absolute path of a file within the application's virtual directory stack. This is the flattened directory structure; the top-most file wins in conflicts, except for special files such as zero.config, which are logically merged together. **Arguments:** String vFile—Logical relative file based on the application's root location. **Returns:** String—Absolute path to the virtual file location. Returns NULL if vFile does not exist.
listFiles	List all the files under a virtual directory. The first file of a given name is added to the list, while any subsequent files with the same name are skipped. **Arguments:** String vDirectory—Logical relative directory based on the applications root location. **Returns:** Array of strings containing the vFile paths of all files in the merged logical vDirectory. Returns NULL if directory does not exist.
render_view	Helper function to render a view of data in the global context. Views are located relative to the /app/views vDirectory.
zcontains	Checks for the existence of a key within the given global context (GC). **Arguments:** String key—Key to check for existence. **Returns:** boolean—True if key exists; false otherwise.

Table 13.5 WebSphere sMash Utility Functions

Function	Description
zdelete	Deletes keys (and associated values) from the global context (GC). **Arguments:** String key—Global context key to be deleted. boolean deleteChildren—[Optional] If true, key is treated as a prefix or context qualifier, and any matching children keys will be deleted. False means exact match on key name. **Returns:** boolean—True if key(s) successfully deleted; false otherwise.
zdump	Dump the entire contents of the global context. **Arguments:** String key—The global context name to dump. **Returns:** String—Contents of global context being dumped.
zget	Returns a value form the global context based on the provided key. The key must contain the fully qualified "/zone/..." prefix. Example: "/request/headers/in/Content-Type" or "/user/myKey". To manually add new values to the global context, see zput(). **Arguments:** String key—Key to locate value upon. Must include full zone prefix. Object defaultValue—Value to return if key is not found in the requested zone. **Returns:** The value matching that key in the appropriate GC zone, the supplied default value if provided in the arguments, or NULL if not found.
zlist zlist_all	List all the global context paths at the specified key prefix. **Arguments:** String key—Key to search upon. May be full of partial, but must include the full zone prefix. boolean includePrefix—True causes results to be returned with the enclosing zone prefix; false strips the zone prefix from the results. Default is false. **Returns:** Array—List of matching key strings.

Table 13.5   WebSphere sMash Utility Functions

Function	Description
zpost zput	Provides for storing key/value pairs into the global context. The difference between the functions is that zput will replace an existing value located by the key, and zpost will append to an existing value, coercing it into an array if needed. **Arguments:** String key—Fully qualified key to use. Object value—The value to append to existing value at the specified key location. boolean binary—If true, do not automatically encode the value being stored. Default of false performs encoding.

URI Utilities

Extension name: zero.php.URIUtilsExtension

This extension provides functions that allow the developer to create WebSphere sMash-appropriate URIs. These URIs take into account any defined context root and virtual directory paths. The paths provided are validated, and any parameters are automatically encoded.

It is always best to use relative URIs when accessing local resources such as images, style sheets, and scripts. This prevents issues when dealing with reverse proxies and deployment time changes, such as port number or context root changes (see Table 13.6).

Table 13.6   URI Utility Functions

Function	Description
get_absolute_uri	Returns a fully qualified URI based on a relative path. The results will include the protocol, host, port, context root, URI path, and formatted parameters. If the path argument contains a leading slash, the returned URI is based from the application's root; otherwise, it is based relative to the calling script. **Arguments:** String path—URI path to convert to proper URI. Map params—[Optional] Any query parameters to include in URL (for example, "?key1=val1&key2=val2"). **Returns:** Proper URI based on defined path.

Table 13.6   URI Utility Functions

Function	Description
get_relative_uri	Returns a relative URI based on path. This is the preferred function to use if accessing resources within the same application. If the path argument contains a leading slash, the returned URI is based from the application's root; otherwise, it is based relative to the calling script. **Arguments:** String path—URI path to convert to application-specific URI. Map params—[Optional] Any query parameters to include in URL. **Returns:** Proper URI based on defined path.
get_requested_uri	Returns a proper URI based on the presumed URL used on the originating request. Reverse proxies and other external factors may alter the actual URL used to access the resource. **Arguments:** boolean includeQuery—True if the returned URI should include the query string portion of the URI (for example, "?key1=val1&key2=val2"). **Returns:** Full URI, with or without the additional query string appended.

Java Extensions

Extension Name: com.ibm.p8.engine.xapi.reflection.impl.JavaExtensionLibrary

This subsystem provides direct access to Java resources from PHP files (see Table 13.7). See the "PHP to Java Bridge" section of this chapter for more information on using Java from within PHP files.

Table 13.7   Java Bridge Functions

Function	Description
java_import	Provides a means to directly import Java classes into the PHP runtime. When imported, the class is available for instantiation and/or direct access to static members and functions.
	Arguments:
	String classname—The package and classname to be imported.
	Array interfaces—[Optional] List of interfaces to be defined that this class implements. Default is NULL.
	boolean includeBase—[Optional] PHP class to declare the same base class as the Java class being imported. Default is true.
	String importedName—[Optional] Name to be used in PHP to reference this class. Default is NULL, which is to use the classname without package names. Used to prevent potential naming conflicts in import.
	Boolean includeNestedClasses—[Optional] Include inner classes as part of import. Default is true.
	Returns:
	boolean—Did import succeed.

Groovy Extensions

Extension name: com.ibm.p8.engine.xapi.groovy.GroovyExtensionLibrary

The following functions provide facilities to access Groovy classes from within PHP (see Table 13.8). See the extended discussion later in this chapter on the PHP to Groovy bridge for more details.

Table 13.8   Groovy Functions for PHP

Function	Description
groovy_create_closure	Provides the ability to create a Groovy closure around an object/function.
	Arguments:
	Callback callback—PHP style callback (array containing an object and method/function name).
	Returns:
	Groovy closure object to pass to callback.

Table 13.8 Groovy Functions for PHP

Function	Description
groovy_eval	Executes a simple Groovy code block on-the-fly. **Arguments:** String script—Groovy script string to be evaluated by Groovy runtime. **Returns:** Return value from script evaluation. Defaults return is a numeric value (0=success, non-0=fail).
groovy_import	Imports a Groovy class to be visible by the PHP runtime. Once imported, the Groovy class is treated as a PHP class with all members and functions available. The Groovy class is located by searching the include path of the PHP runtime (located in the php.ini). **Arguments:** String scriptname—The package and script name containing the Groovy class(es) to be imported. Array interfaces—[Optional] List of interfaces to be defined that this class implements. Default is NULL. boolean includeBase—[Optional] PHP class to declare same base class as the Groovy class being imported. Default is true. String importedName—[Optional] Name to be used in PHP to reference this class. Default is NULL, which is to use the classname without package names. Used to prevent potential naming conflicts in import. **Returns:** boolean—Did import succeed.

Remote Connections

Extension name: zero.php.ConnectionExtension

This extension assists in making connections to remote resources (see Table 13.9).

Table 13.9   Connection API Functions

Function	Description
connection_get	Provides the ability to perform a GET request on a remote resource. Custom headers may be sent as well.
	Arguments:
	String URL—Full URL of remote resource.
	Map headers—[Optional] Map of key/value headers to send with request.
	Returns:
	Map response, with the following keys:
	status—Response status code value (for example, 200).
	body—Main response data.
connection_post	Provides ability to perform POST request on a remote resource.
	Arguments:
	String URL—Full URL of remote resource.
	Map headers—[Optional] Map of key/value headers to send with request.
	String body—Contents to be POSTed to remote resource.
	Returns:
	Map response, with the following keys:
	status—Response status code value (for example, 200).
	body—Main response data.

JSON Utilities

Extension name: zero.php.JSONExtension

This extension provides facilities for working with JSON data. Methods are provided for reading and writing JSON. JSON is often used when working with RESTful resources (see Table 13.10).

Table 13.10   JSON Utility Functions

Function	Description
json_decode	Decodes a JSON-encoded string.
	Arguments:
	String json—String containing serialized JSON structure.

Table 13.10   JSON Utility Functions

Function	Description
json_encode	Encodes a complex structure (maps, arrays, strings, ints, and so on) into a serialized JSON string. **Arguments:** Object val—Object to be encoded.

Active Content Filtering

Extension name: zero.php.ACFExtension

This extension provides protection from malicious incoming data. Active Content Filtering (ACF) provides methods to scan and cleanse data for <script> tags and other potentially harmful string structures (see Table 13.11).

Each of these functions take the following arguments:

String | Stream input—Source string to be processed.

String contentType—[Optional] Type of content (for example, text/html).

String encoding—[Optional, default="UTF-8"] Encoding of input data.

String filterRuleFile—[Optional] File containing rules for this ACF process.

Table 13.11   ACF Functions

Function	Description
acf_process	Processes a string for ACF content, returning the cleansed string.
acf_process_stream	Processes an input stream for ACF content, removing any active content.
acf_validate	Processes a string for ACF content, returning any active content located.
acf_validate_stream	Processes an input stream for ACF content, returning any active content located.

Cross-Site Request Forgery

Extension name: zero.php.CSRFExtension

This extension provides programmatic protection from Cross-Site Request Forgery (CSRF); see Table 13.12. Consult the Project Zero website for more information on CSRF procedures.

Table 13.12   CSFT Functions

Function	Description
csrf_protected_form_field	Creates a hidden form field that contains the CSRF token to be verified against the submission URI. **Arguments:** String uri—URI to be verified against CSRF.
csrf_protected_uri	Validates a URI is pointing to the originating server. **Arguments:** String uri—URI to be verified against CSRF.

Login

Extension name: zero.php.LoginServiceExtension

This sub-system provides the ability to log into a WebSphere sMash application programmatically. This can be used for system-level processing that needs to occur without user interaction (see Table 13.13).

Table 13.13   Login Service Functions

Function	Description
zero_login	Logs in a user programmatically. **Arguments:** String username—Username to be authenticated. String password—Password for the user to be authenticated.
zero_logout	Logs out current user. No arguments defined for this method.

Database Access

Extension name: zero.php.QueryExtension

This subsystem provides methods for accessing relational data sources. There are functions are broken down by: General, Query, Results, and Transactions.

Database General Functions

The following functions shown in Table 13.14 illustrate common data functions available for database data inspection.

Table 13.14   Database General Functions

Function	Description
dataIsValid data_is_valid	Validates if manager has configuration that can connect to a database. **Arguments:** Manager mgr—DataSource manager to use. **Returns:** True if successfully connected to the database; false otherwise.
dataLastError data_last_error	Returns information about the last error. **Returns:** Map of last error, or NULL if no previous error. Keys in map are: type—"WARNING", "SEVERE", or "FATAL" functionName—Function causing error. message—Error message.
dataManager dataNewManager data_manager data_new_manager	Creates a new manager from a DataSource. The DataSource is indicated in one of two ways. The first way is to pass a resource that is returned from the dataSource API. The second way is to pass a string key that corresponds to a set of database parameters in the zero.config file. **Arguments:** DataSource resource or String dataSourceKey. **Returns:** Manager—Handle to the DataSource Manager.

Table 13.14   Database General Functions

Function	Description

`dataSource`
 	
`dataNewDataSource`
 	
`data_new_data_source`
 	
`data_source`
	Creates and returns a DataSource of the given type. The type argument has three possible meanings, which are tested in the order shown. As soon as one of the mechanisms is successful at creating a DataSource, the function returns it.
	
	The type name has been previously registered with an IDataSourceProvider instance. See `DataSourceFactory.`
	`registerProvider()` for details.
	
	The type name is the fully qualified class name of a DataSource implementor. The class will be instantiated with the default constructor, and the params will be set on the created DataSource object. Note that parameter keys are expected to map one-to-one with setter methods on the object.
	
	The type name, when appended to the string "zero.data.php.datasource", forms a fully qualified class name of an IDataSourceProvider implementor. The IDataSourceProvider will be instantiated and registered with the type name.
	
	Arguments:
	String type—The DataSource type to create.
	
	Array params—List of parameters to pass into the DataSource constructor.
	
	Returns:
	DataSource—DataSource instance, or NULL if fail to create new DataSource.

`dataStringAsByteArray`
`data_string_as_byte_array`
 	
`bytes`
	Returns the string argument as a string data resource. This kind of resource is used in situations where a BLOB is expected by the SQL engine.
	
	Arguments:
	String string—Source string to be processed as Blob.
	
	Returns:
	Array—Byte string to be treated as Blob by Database.

Database Query Functions

Table 13.15 shows the functions used to perform database queries.

Table 13.15 Database Query Functions

Function	Description
dataExec data_exec	Executes any SQL statement. SELECT operations are handled by queryArray, while all other operations are handled by update. **Arguments:** Manager mgr—DataSource manager to use. String sql—SQL statement to process, with optional '?' tokens. Array params—Parameters to use in SQL token replacement. **Returns:** Result whose type depends on the SQL statement used. For SELECT, an array of values. For others, an int indicating the number of rows altered. Value may be NULL on invalid parameters, or false if an error occurs.
dataExecOpt data_exec_opt	An optimized form of the exec API that behaves like query-First for SELECT statements and updateMany for other statements. **Arguments:** Manager mgr—DataSource manager to use. String sql—SQL statement to process, with optional '?' tokens. Array params—Parameters to use in SQL token replacement. **Returns:** Result whose type depends on the SQL statement used. For SELECT, a map of key/value pairs matching selection requests. For others, an array of ints indicating the number of rows altered. Value may be NULL on invalid parameters, or false if an error occurs.

Table 13.15   Database Query Functions

Function	Description
dataInsert data_insert	Executes UPDATE and INSERT statements and returns generated column values. The values of the generated keys are returned as strings that can be coerced to another type if needed. **Arguments:** Manager mgr—DataSource manager to use. String sql—SQL statement to process, with optional '?' tokens. Array columns—Columns that contain generated keys. Array params—Parameters to use in SQL token replacement. **Returns:** The generated keys as strings, or false on error.
dataExec data_exec	Executes any SQL statement. SELECT operations are handled by queryArray, while all other operations are handled by update. **Arguments:** Manager mgr—DataSource manager to use. String sql—SQL statement to process, with optional '?' tokens. Array params—Parameters to use in SQL token replacement. **Returns:** Result whose type depends on the SQL statement used. For SELECT, an array of values. For others, an int indicating the number of rows altered. Value may be NULL on invalid parameters, or false if an error occurs.

Table 13.15 Database Query Functions

Function	Description
dataExecOpt data_exec_opt	An optimized form of the exec API that behaves like query-First for SELECT statements and updateMany for other statements. **Arguments:** Manager mgr—DataSource manager to use. String sql—SQL statement to process, with optional '?' tokens. Array params—Parameters to use in SQL token replacement. **Returns:** Result whose type depends on the SQL statement used. For SELECT, a map of key/value pairs matching selection requests. For others, an array of ints indicating the number of rows altered. Value may be NULL on invalid parameters, or false if an error occurs.
dataQuery data_query	Executes an SQL query (SELECT) and uses the result handler to create the return value. The result handler can have one of two forms, which are listed next. PHP callback function—Indicated by passing the function name. PHP ResultHandler resource. **Arguments:** Manager mgr—DataSource manager handle. String sql—SQL statement to process, with optional '?' tokens. ResultHandler handler—Custom callback or resultHandler referenced from dataNewResultHandler call. Array params—Parameters to use in SQL token replacement. **Returns:** Results from ResultHandler processing.

Table 13.15   Database Query Functions

Function	Description
dataQueryArray data_query_array	Executes a SQL query (SELECT) and returns an array of results where each element represents a single row. The rows themselves are key/value maps. **Arguments:** Manager mgr—DataSource manager handle. String sql—SQL statement to process, with optional '?' tokens. Array params—Parameters to use in SQL token replacement. **Returns:** Array of result rows, containing map of column names and values.
dataQueryArrayByFactory data_query_array_by_factory	Executes a SQL query and uses the factory callback function to create the return value. The callback function will be called once per row. The result of each callback will be placed in an array and returned to the caller of this API. **Arguments:** Manager mgr—DataSource manager handle. String sql—SQL statement to process, with optional '?' tokens. Callback factory—Class with callback function to process ResultSet rows. Array params—Parameters to use in SQL token replacement. **Returns:** Array of result rows, containing map of column names and values.
dataQueryFirst data_query_first	Executes a SQL query and returns the first result row as a map. **Arguments:** Manager mgr—DataSource manager handle. String sql—SQL statement to process, with optional '?' tokens. Array params—Parameters to use in SQL token replacement. **Returns:** Map of column names and values.

Table 13.15 Database Query Functions

Function	Description
dataQueryFirstByFactory data_query_first_by_factory	Executes a SQL query and uses the factory callback function to create the return value. The result of the query will contain at most one row. The callback function will be called exactly once. The callback must be called "callback," take a single ResultSet argument, and whose response will be returned to the initial caller as the result. **Arguments:** Manager mgr—DataSource manager handle. String sql—SQL statement to process, with optional '?' tokens. Callback callback—Function to pre-process the result record from a query. Array params—Parameters to use in SQL token replacement. **Returns:** Return value from callback function.
dataQueryIterator data_query_iterator	Executes a SQL query and returns an Iterator resource. The Iterator can be manipulated using the dataIterator APIs. Each iterated element represents a single row from the query result. **Arguments:** Manager mgr—DataSource manager handle. String sql—SQL statement to process, with optional '?' tokens. Array params—Parameters to use in SQL token replacement. **Returns:** Iterator of maps of results row.
dataQueryIteratorByFactory data_query_iterator_by_factory	Executes a SQL query and uses the factory callback function to create the return value as an Iterator. The callback must be called "callback," take a single ResultSet argument, and whose response will be returned to the initial caller as the result. The callback is called once per resultset record. **Arguments:** Manager mgr—DataSource manager handle. String sql—SQL statement to process, with optional '?' tokens. Callback callback—Function to preprocess result record from query. Array params—Parameters to use in SQL token replacement. **Returns:** Iterator of return values from callback function

Table 13.15   Database Query Functions

Function	Description
dataQueryResults data_query_results	Executes a SQL query and returns a ResultSet resource, which can be accessed using the dataResultSet APIs. **Arguments:** Manager mgr—DataSource manager handle. String sql—SQL statement to process, with optional '?' tokens. Array params—Parameters to use in SQL token replacement. **Returns:** ResultSet of queried records, or NULL if no matching records.
dataUpdate data_update	Executes a SQL update, such as INSERT, UPDATE, or DELETE. **Arguments:** Manager mgr—DataSource manager handle. String sql—SQL statement to process, with optional '?' tokens. Array params—Parameters to use in SQL token replacement. **Returns:** int—Number of records updated as part of the SQL alter statement. A false is returned if an error occurred.
dataUpdateMany data_update_many	Executes a batch SQL update. The SQL statement is executed once for each parameter list entry. **Arguments:** Manager mgr—DataSource manager handle. String sql—SQL statement to process, with optional '?' tokens. Array params—Array of Parameter maps to use in SQL token replacement. **Returns:** int array—Matching list of number of records updated as part of each SQL alter statement. A false is returned if an error occurred.

Database Results Functions

Functions used to process data returned by query functions are shown in Table 13.16.

Table 13.16 Database Results Functions

Function	Description
dataBlobGetBytes data_blob_get_bytes	Returns the contents of the Blob resource as a string. **Arguments:** Blob handle—The source Blob. int position—Starting byte position to access. Int length—Number of bytes to process. **Returns:** String containing returned value.
dataBlobLength data_blob_length	Returns the length of the Blob resource data. **Arguments:** Blob handle—The source Blob to process. **Returns:** The length of the Blob as a double.
dataBlobSetBytes data_blob_set_bytes	Sets the byte contents of the Blob resource. **Arguments:** Blob handle—The source Blob. int position—Starting byte position to access. String bytes—The bytes to inject into the Blob. int offset—[Optional] Offset within input bytes to process. Default is 0. Int length—[Optional] Number of bytes in input string to write. Default is length of input string. **Returns:** Number of bytes written as an int, or –1 on error.
dataClobGetString data_clob_get_string	Returns the contents of the Clob resource as a string. **Arguments:** Clob handle—The source Clob. **Returns:** String contents of the Clob.

Table 13.16   Database Results Functions

Function	Description
dataClobLength data_clob_length	Returns the length of the Clob resource data. **Arguments:** Clob handle—The source Clob to process. **Returns:** The length of the Clob as a double.
dataBlobGetBytes data_blob_get_bytes	Returns the contents of the Blob resource as a string. **Arguments:** Blob handle—The source Blob. int position—Starting byte position to access. Int length—Number of bytes to process. **Returns:** String containing returned value.
dataBlobLength data_blob_length	Returns the length of the Blob resource data. **Arguments:** Blob handle—The source Blob to process. **Returns:** The length of the Blob as a double.
dataIteratorHasNext data_iter_has_next	Returns true if there is a next item on the Result. **Arguments:** Iterator handle—Iterator to test for more values. **Returns:** True if there are more values; false otherwise.
dataIteratorNext data_iter_next	Returns the next item, and removes it from the Iterator. **Arguments:** Iterator handle—Iterator to retrieve values from. **Returns:** Next item in Iterator.
dataIteratorRemove data_iter_remove	Removes the next item from the Iterator. **Arguments:** Iterator handle—Iterator containing values.

Table 13.16 Database Results Functions

Function	Description
`dataNewResultHandler` `data_new_result_handler`	Creates an instance of ResultHandler for use with the data-Query API. Provides for custom handling of result sets. **Arguments:** String name—Fully qualified class name of a ResultHandler instance. **Returns:** Resource that can be passed into dataQuery calls.
`dataResultSetAbsolute` `data_rs_absolute`	Sets the current row index relative to either the beginning or the end of the ResultSet. **Arguments:** ResultSet rs—ResultSet to alter. int row—Row reference to set pointer location. Positive number references form beginning of RS, negative walks backwards from end of RS. **Returns:** boolean—True if pointer adjustment worked; false otherwise.
`dataResultSetClose` `data_rs_close`	Closes the ResultSet resource. **Arguments:** ResultSet rs—resultSet handle to release. **Returns:** boolean—True if close worked; false otherwise.
`dataResultSetGetColumnCount` `data_rs_get_column_count`	Returns the number of columns in the ResultSet resource. **Arguments:** ResultSet rs—ResultSet to process. **Returns:** Number of columns in ResultSet, or -1 on error
`dataResultSetGetColumnName` `data_rs_get_column_name`	Returns the name of the given column in the ResultSet. **Arguments:** ResultSet rs—ResultSet to process. int index—Column index to process. **Returns:** String containing name of the column, based on table column name or field alias from query, or NULL on error.

Table 13.16   Database Results Functions

Function	Description
`dataResultSetGetObject` `data_rs_get_object`	Returns the value of the given column. **Arguments:** ResultSet rs—ResultSet to process int or String column—Column to process. May be index based (starting at 1), or accessed by name. **Returns:** Column value as an object with no data type coercion implied.
`dataResultSetGetRow` `data_rs_get_row`	Returns the index of the current row. The index of the first row is 1. **Arguments:** ResultSet rs—ResultSet to process. **Returns:** int—index of current row pointer within the ResultSet, or -1 on error.
`dataResultSetNext` `data_rs_next`	Move the internal position of the ResultSet resource to the next row. **Arguments:** ResultSet rs—ResultSet to process. **Returns:** boolean—True if next row, or false at end of ResultSet list.
`dataResultSetPrevious` `data_rs_previous`	Move the internal position of the ResultSet resource to the previous row. **Arguments:** ResultSet rs—ResultSet to process. **Returns:** boolean—True if previous row, or false at beginning of ResultSet list.

Database Transaction Functions

Database transactions are used to perform multiple data manipulations statements as a single unit of work. Table 13.17 lists the functions available to provide transaction support.

Table 13.17   Database Transaction Functions

Function	Description
dataBeginTransaction data_begin_transaction	Enters transaction mode with the given Manager. This mode is exited by calling either dataCommitTransaction or dataRoll-backTransaction. **Arguments:** Manager mgr—The Data manager to operate on. **Returns:** boolean—true = Successful transaction creation; false on failure.
dataCommitTransaction data_commit_transaction	Commits the current transaction and then exits transaction mode. A transaction must already have been started via dataBeginTransaction. **Arguments:** Manager mgr—DataSource manager under transaction. **Returns:** True on success or false on error.
dataEndTransaction data_end_transaction	Rolls back and ends the current transaction. No writes are persisted as part of the transaction. A transaction must already have been started via dataBeginTransaction. **Arguments:** Manager mgr—DataSource manager under transaction. **Returns:** True on success or false on error.
dataIsInTransaction data_is_in_transaction	Access function to determine if Data manager has an active transaction. **Arguments:** Manager mgr—DataSource manager to use. **Returns:** True if mgr is within a transaction. False otherwise.

Table 13.17   Database Transaction Functions

Function	Description
`dataRollbackTransaction` `data_rollback_transaction`	Rollback the current transaction and then exits transaction mode. The caller should have called dataBeginTransaction before calling this API. **Arguments:** Manager mgr—Database manager holding active transaction. **Returns:** boolean—True on successful transaction rollback, or false on error.
`dataTransaction` `data_transaction`	Executes the given callback as a database transaction. If any errors occur, the entire transaction will be rolled back. The callback must accept two parameters: the DataSource manager, and an optional userData that is user defined (obviously), and handled by the callback function. Under normal circumstances, the callback is not required to return a value. However, there are two ways for the callback to explicitly fail the transaction. The callback can either throw an exception, or return false. If either of these occur, the transaction is rolled back; otherwise, it will be committed. **Arguments:** Manager mgr—DataSource manager to process the transaction. Callback callback—Function to process the full transaction data. Object userData—[Optional] User-defined parameter data to be passed into the callback function. **Returns:** boolean—True if the transaction completed and was properly committed. False otherwise.

XML Utilities

Extension name: zero.php.XMLExtension

These functions provide simple access to XML data. This XML support is very limited, and its use beyond basic reading and writing of simple xML documents is discouraged. You should use the PHP built-in SimpleXML facilities. See the XML example later in this chapter.

Table 13.18 XML Utility Functions

Function	Description
xml_decode	Decodes an XML-encoded string into a SimpleXML-like object structure that can be processed using natural PHP conventions. Failures on decoding result in an XMLEncodingException. **Arguments:** XML string **Returns:** Object of decoded string.
xml_encode	Encodes an object into a string that represents a decodable XML object. Valid input includes primitive type and arrays. If invalid, input data will result in a XMLEncodingException. **Parameters:** Object key—The object to be XML encoded. Boolean idRefs—True will generate ID references for each node. False will not generate ID references. String xmlRoot—Value to use as the root element node for the XML document. **Returns:** XML string.
getAttribute	Returns the value of the attribute based on the provided key for an element. **Arguments:** String name—Name of attribute for this element. **Returns:** String value.
getAttributes	Return the complete array of attribute name value pairs on a given element. **Returns:** Array of key/value pairs.

Conclusion

PHP combined with WebSphere sMash forms an environment that is much more than the sum of its parts. PHP is an easily accessible web scripting language that promotes rapid development and short time to market. WebSphere sMash provides an excellent application server environment with convenient and easy bridging between PHP and Java/Groovy. The combination of PHP and WebSphere sMash creates an outstanding web development environment, merging ease of use and enterprise-level power.

Get Started with Groovy

Groovy is an object-oriented, dynamically typed scripting language for Java developers. Java developers should feel comfortable using Groovy because it perpetuates Java's syntax and semantics. Groovy also provides a more succinct syntax that results in code much smaller than comparable Java code. A developer can mix Java and Groovy style syntax, which allows Java developers to ease themselves into using Groovy style syntax. This chapter introduces you to the Groovy syntax to facilitate your understanding of Groovy code snippets throughout the text of this book.

Before we dive into syntax, let's start with a simple Java class that prints a message to stdout (standard out) and then rewrites it in a Groovy way (see Listing A.1).

Listing A.1   Simple Java Class

```
public class HelloGroovy
{
  public static void main(String[] args)
  {
    System.out.println("Hello Groovy World!");
  }
}
```

This code prints "Hello Groovy World!". This is perfectly acceptable Groovy code, but let's refine it and make it as Groovy as possible. The first thing we can do to make this code more Groovy is to remove the class definition. We can also remove the special main method. Groovy has added println() to java.lang.Object, so there's no need to have the System.out in front of it.

Groovy also makes semicolons and parentheses optional. Both can still be used, if needed—for example, if you wanted to put two statements on one line, you'd need to separate them with a semicolon. Taking all this into account, we end up with a Groovy script that looks like this:

```
println "Hello Groovy World!"
```

This code is compact with only the minimum needed to get the job done. There is a subtle difference between this Groovy code and the preceding Java code. The Groovy code is a script and is implicitly compiled to a class with the same name as the file in which the script is defined. You can see this by adding a line to your script, as follows:

```
println this.class
```

Default Imports

Groovy makes several packages available by default beyond the usual java.lang that Java imports by default. The result of these imports is that you can use many more classes without explicit imports. Listing A.2 shows the list of default imports for Groovy.

Listing A.2   Default Imports

```
import java.lang.*
import java.util.*
import java.io.*
import java.net.*
import java.math.BigInteger
import java.math.BigDecimal
import groovy.lang.*
import groovy.util.*
```

This gives the developer a wide variety of commonly used classes available by default.

Dynamic Typing

Groovy is a dynamically typed language. It does not require that you explicitly declare the type of a variable. Furthermore, variables can change types within your code (see Listing A.3).

Listing A.3   Dynamic Variable Types

```
class BarClass{
  def var = "this is bar"
}
bar = new BarClass()
println bar.var.class
bar.var = 42
println bar.var.class
```

This code starts by defining a class named BarClass with a variable named var. Notice that the variable isn't typed but uses the keyword def to define the variable. The output from this script shows us that the variable starts out as type java.lang.String and then becomes java.lang.Integer. This can be both helpful and frustrating, so you might want to be careful when naming your variables. You should also note that when you are writing a script and not a class, you can leave out the def keyword. In the preceding code, notice that the bar script variable is not typed, nor is it defined with the def keyword. This is perfectly acceptable Groovy code. However, using the def keyword can prove to be useful in avoiding erroneously reusing variable names.

GStrings and Heredocs

Groovy strings provide a method for string concatenation that is much easier than Java string concatenation. GStrings use embedded expressions to achieve this (see Listing A.4).

Listing A.4   Embedded Expressions

```
def pi = 3.1415
def foo = "PI equals $pi"
```

This exemplifies the simplest use of GString expressions by using curly braces. We can do much more complicated expressions, however, as shown in Listing A.5.

Listing A.5   More Embedded Expressions

```
def pi = 3.1415
def foo = "2PI equals ${pi*2}"
println "${foo.toUpperCase()}"
```

We can also let our string span multiple lines with heredocs. In Groovy, heredocs are delimited with triple quotes (see Listing A.6).

Listing A.6   Groovy Heredocs

```
def pi = 3.1415
def foo = """This is a paragraph using
Expressions like pi = $pi
Spanning multiple lines."""
```

With GStrings and heredocs, Groovy provides a powerful set of string tools that are easy to use.

Embedded Quotes

Quotes can be embedded in strings with Groovy in a natural way. If you want to embed double quotes, you can use single quotes to define the string. Likewise, the same is true if single quotes are to be embedded. Groovy also supports the usual escaping of quotes (see Listing A.7).

Listing A.7   Escaping Quotes

```
println 'double "quotes" are easy'
println "or \"escape\" them"
println "single 'quotes' are easy too"
```

Single and double quotes can be used within heredocs, as shown in Listing A.8.

Listing A.8   Quotes in Heredocs

```
println """
"double quotes"
'single quotes'
"""
```

Getters and Field Pointers

When class variables are defined in Groovy, we can access those fields using the "." (dot) operator. We can modify that behavior or retrieve the variable by providing our own getter method (see Listing A.9).

Listing A.9   Changing Default Variable Access

```
class BarClass{
  def var = "this is bar"
  def getVar(){
    return "**$var**"
  }
}
def bar = new BarClass()
println bar.var
```

The output from this code would be "**this is bar**". Although this can be useful, there may be times when you would want to get access to the fields, bypassing the getter. To do this, you need to create a field pointer, as shown in Listing A.10.

Listing A.10   Field Pointer

```
class BarClass{
  def var = "this is bar"
  def getVar(){
    return "**$var**"
  }
}
def bar = new BarClass()
println bar.@var
```

The output of this code is "this is bar", which is the exact text in the variable bypassing the getter method. We can also assign this field pointer to a variable and use the variable to access the field (see Listing A.11).

Listing A.11   Assigning a Field Pointer to a Variable

```
...
def varPtr = bar.@var
println varPtr
```

What might be a bit confusing is that this does not work for setters. We cannot use varPtr to set bar.var. Likewise, you cannot access a custom setVar method with the dot operator; you must explicitly call your custom setVar method.

Parentheses and Method Pointers

We noted earlier that parentheses are optional, but this isn't true in all cases. No-arg methods require that parentheses be present, as shown in Listing A.12.

Listing A.12   No-arg Method

```
def foo = "Hello Groovy World!"
println foo.toUpperCase()
```

It is possible to overcome this by using a method pointer. To do this, you define a variable that is the pointer to the method using the ampersand (see Listing A.13).

Listing A.13   Setting a Method in a Variable

```
def foo = "Hello Groovy World!"
def fooUpper = foo.&toUpperCase()
println fooUpper
```

Return Statements

Return statements are also optional for methods. The last line in a method is an implicit return statement. As shown in Listing A.14, you can use return or safely leave it off.

Listing A.14   Implicit Return Statement

```
class FooClass
{
   Def doIt()
   {
      "last line"
   }
}
foo = new FooClass()
println foo.doIt()
```

This script, of course, prints "last line" to stdout. Any return type is allowed; it's just a matter of which is the last line in the method. If the last line cannot be evaluated, a null is returned. Listing A.15 will always return null.

Listing A.15   Another Implicit Return Statement

```
class FooClass
{
   Def doIt()
   {
      if(true){"last line"}
   }
}
foo = new FooClass()
println foo.doIt()
```

If we want to return the string, we must explicitly use the `return` statement, changing the `if` statement to the following:

```
if(true){ return "last line"}
```

Exception Handling

Exceptions are another optional part of Groovy. You can choose to catch exceptions or not depending on if the code is interested in the exceptions. Unlike Java, Groovy doesn't require that checked exceptions get handled in the code. All exceptions are unchecked in Groovy. The decision about the importance of an exception is left completely to the developer.

Safe Dereferencing

In Java, there is one unchecked exception that is often caught or defended against by developers: the dreaded NullPointerException (NPE). In Java, a developer would typically use an `if` statement guard to protect against NPEs, as shown in Listing A.16.

Listing A.16 Protecting from NullPointerExceptions in Java

```
if(null != foo)
{
  foo.doSomething();
}
```

Groovy provides a nifty bit of syntactic sugar to defend against NPEs—the safe dereferencing or "?" operator:

```
foo?.doSomething ()
```

The "?" operator dispatches calls only when the object is not null. So, the toUpperCase method will only get executed if foo is non-null. This makes defensive programming fast and easy. The usual `if` statement guard a developer might use in Java is traded for a single character.

Operator Overloading

Groovy brings operator overloading to Java. Table A.1 describes the overloaded operators and the methods that they map to.

All the comparison operators handle nulls gracefully so that NullPointerExceptions don't get thrown.

Table A.1 Overloaded Operators

(Source: http://groovy.codehaus.org/Operator+Overloading)

Operator	Method
a + b	a.plus(b).
a – b	a.minus(b)
a * b	a.multiply(b)
a ** b	a.power(b)

Table A.1   Overloaded Operators

(Source: http://groovy.codehaus.org/Operator+Overloading)

Operator	Method
a / b	a.div(b)
a % b	a.mod(b)
a | b	a.or(b)
a & b	a.and(b)
a ^ b	a.xor(b)
a++ or ++a	a.next()
a-- or --a	a.previous()
a[b]	a.getAt(b)
a[b] = c	a.putAt(b, c)
a << b	a.leftShift(b)
a >> b	a.rightShift(b)
~a	a.bitwiseNegate()
-a	a.negative()
+a	a.positive()
a == b	a.equals(b) or a.compareTo(b) == 0 **
a != b	! a.equals(b)
a <=> b	a.compareTo(b)
a > b	a.compareTo(b) > 0
a >= b	a.compareTo(b) >= 0
a < b	a.compareTo(b) < 0
a <= b	a.compareTo(b) <= 0

Boolean Evaluation

Groovy boolean evaluation is much different than Java. In Groovy, expressions get automatically evaluated to a boolean `true` or `false`. The best way to show how things evaluate is by way of demonstration. In Listing A.17, the following evaluate to `true`.

Listing A.17   Evaluate to true

```
if(1) //true
if(-1) //true, all non-zero values evaluate to true
if(!null) //true, non-null values are true
if("foo") //true

foo = ["a","b","c"]
if(foo)  //true, non-empty lists, maps and arrays evaluate to true
```

In Listing A.18, the following evaluate to `false`.

Listing A.18   Evaluate to false

```
if(0)  //false
if(null) //false
if("") //false, empty strings and string buffers evaluate to false

foo = []
if(foo)  //false
```

This should give you a feel for how Groovy evaluates truth.

Closures

Groovy's definition of a *closure* is essentially a named block of code. Listing A.19 is a Groovy closure in its simplest form.

Listing A.19   Very Simple Closure

```
def foo = { println "I'm a foo" }
foo()
```

Unsurprisingly, this code produces `"I'm a foo"` printed to standard out. Groovy closures can also accept parameters; by default, there is a single parameter named `"it"` (see Listing A.20).

Listing A.20   Default "it" Variable

```
def foo = { println "I'm a $it" }
foo "bar"
```

Groovy closures can also accept named parameters, as shown in Listing A.21.

Listing A.21   Named Parameters

```
def foo = { a, b ->
  println "$a + $b = ${a+b}"
}
foo 3, 4
```

Finally, closure parameters can be preloaded by using curry (see Listing A.22).

Listing A.22   Using Curry

```
def foo = { a, b ->
  println "$a + $b = ${a+b}"
}
def addTwo = foo.curry(2)
addTwo 4
```

Curry will accept any number of parameters, preloading the closure parameter's starting with the leftmost defined.

Lists

Groovy offers convenient syntax for list creation and manipulation (see Listing A.23).

Listing A.23   List Creation

```
def people = ["alice", "bob", "claire"]
println people.class
```

The output of this code snippet shows us that by default, a list of type java.util.ArrayList is created. We can manipulate the type by using the as operator (see Listing A.24).

Listing A.24   Manipulating the Type of a List

```
def people = ["alice", "bob", "claire"] as Set
def people = ["alice", "bob", "claire"] as String[]
```

Empty lists can be created by just using the square brackets:

```
def emptyList = []
```

We can add to a list by using the overloaded left shift operator or the += operator (see Listing A.25).

Listing A.25   Adding to a List

```
def people = ["alice", "bob", "claire"]
people << "davide"
people += "earl"
println people
```

This code snippet will output the following:

```
["alice", "bob", "claire", "davide", "earl"]
```

The += operator will also concatenate two lists, as shown in Listing A.26.

Listing A.26   List Concatenation

```
def people = ["alice", "bob", "claire"]
def morepeople ["davide", "earl"]
people += morepeople
println people
```

This code snippet will output the following:

```
["alice", "bob", "claire", "davide", "earl"]
```

Retrieving elements from the list can be accessed in either an array style or a list style (see Listing A.27).

Listing A.27   List Element Access

```
def people = ["alice", "bob", "claire"]
println people[1]
println people.getAt(1)
```

As expected, this code snippet will output "bob" twice. You can remove the last item in the list using the pop method, as shown in Listing A.28.

Listing A.28   Using the pop Method

```
def people = ["alice", "bob", "claire"]
println people.pop()  //prints "claire"
println people  //prints ["alice", "bob"]
```

Likewise, lists can be sorted and reversed with methods of the same name (see Listing A.29).

Listing A.29   Sorting and Reversing a List

```
def people = ["bob", "alice", "claire"]
people.sort()
println people //prints ["alice", "bob", "claire"]
println people.reverse()  //prints ["claire", "bob", "alice"]
```

Note that the sort method makes a change to the list, whereas the reverse method returns the reversed list.

join is a convenient method that returns a string concatenation of all the elements in a list separated by any string you pass it (see Listing A.30).

Listing A.30   Using the join Method

```
def people = ["alice", "bob", "claire"]
println people.join() //prints alicebobclaire
println people.join(",")  //prints alice,bob,claire
```

Another convenient method is findAll. This method takes in a closure, which is used to match items in a list and returns a list with all the matching items (see Listing A.31).

Listing A.31   Using the findAll Method

```
def people = ["alice", "bob", "claire"]
println people.findAll{ it.startsWith "c" } //prints ["claire"]
```

Other methods that are available are max, min, and sum—they do what you might expect (see Listing A.32).

Listing A.32   Using the min, max, and sum Methods

```
def scores = [70, 60, 90]
println scores.min() //prints 60
println scores.max() //prints 90
println scores.sum() //prints 220
```

collect is another convenient method that returns a new list modified by the closure it is passed (see Listing A.33).

Listing A.33   Using the collect Method

```
def scores = [70, 60, 90]
println scores.collect{ it += 5 } //prints [75, 65, 95]
```

The flatten method flattens multidimensional lists. It returns a new flattened list, leaving the original list alone, as seen in Listing A.34.

Listing A.34   Using the flatten method

```
def scores = [[70, 60, 90], 80, [70, 50]]
println scores.flatten() //prints [70, 60, 90, 80, 70, 50]
```

Groovy adds an additional operator called the spread operator, "*", to our list of tools. The spread operator spreads the elements of a list over the parameters of a method call (see Listing A.35).

Listing A.35   Using the Spread Operator

```
def order(first, second, third)
{
  println "1: $first"
  println "2: $second"
  println "3: $third"
}
def params = ["Rowan", "Claire", "Sophia"]
order(*params)
```

Finally the spread-dot operator provides a quick way to iterate over a list, applying the same method to each item in the list, and returns the results in a new list (see Listing A.36).

Listing A.36   Using the Spread-Dot Operator

```
def params = ["Rowan", "Claire", "Sophia"]
params*.toLowerCase() //prints ["rowan", "claire", "sophia"]
```

As you can see, Groovy provides quite a number of convenient methods for manipulating lists.

Maps

As with lists, Groovy provides convenient syntax for dealing with maps (see Listing A.37).

Listing A.37   Creating a Map in Groovy

```
def gifts = [rowan: "legos", claire: "puppy", sophia: "doll"]
println gifts.get("rowan")
println gifts.sophia
```

The creation of a map is very easy, as is access to map elements. To create an empty map, we need only the following:

```
def emptyMap = [:]
```

Adding elements to a map is just as easy as accessing elements (see Listing A.38).

Listing A.38   Adding Elements to a Map

```
def gifts = [rowan: "legos", claire: "puppy", sophia: "doll"]
gifts.put("mom", "diamonds")
gifts.dad = "socks"
```

To concatenate two maps, Groovy enables you to use the overloaded += operator, as shown in Listing A.39.

Listing A.39   Map Concatenation

```
def aMap = [one: "1", two: "2"]
def anotherMap = [three: "3", four: "4"]
aMap += anotherMap
println aMap
```

Finding keys and values are still done in the familiar Java ways (see Listing A.40).

Listing A.40   Retrieving Keys and Value from a Map

```
def aMap = [one: "1", two: "2"]
aMap.keySet() //returns ["one", "two"]
aMap.containsKey("one")  //returns true
aMap.values()  //returns ["1", "2"]
aMap.containsValue("3") //returns false
```

Ranges

Ranges are a new datatype that Groovy offers. Ranges can be of any class that implements the comparable interface: the next method and the previous method. The simplest range is an integer range such as 0..4. This range is the integers from 0 to 4 inclusive. Another simple range is a range of characters, such as 'a'..'c', which is the characters a, b, and c. A more sophisticated range would be a date range, as shown in Listing A.41.

Listing A.41   Creating a Date Range

```
def today = new Date()
nextWeek = today + 6
def dateRange = today..nextWeek
dateRange.each{ println it }
```

This code prints today's date and the next six days. The each method iterates through each element in the range, executing the block defined.

Looping

Looping can be done in the usual Java ways—for example, using a `for` loop (see Listing A.42).

Listing A.42   Java for Loop

```
for(int i = 0; i < 5; i++)
{
  println i
}
```

This code outputs the numbers 0 through 4. You can also use the normal `while-do` and `do-while` loops. Groovy provides other looping mechanisms. The `for` loop can use the range operator to iterate over the range 0..4 (see Listing A.43).

Listing A.43   The for Loop Using a Range

```
for(i in 0..4)
{
  println i
}
```

Again, this code outputs the numbers 0 through 4. There also are other looping mechanisms provided by Groovy, as shown in Listing A.44.

Listing A.44   Using the upto Method for Looping

```
0.upto(4)
{
  println it
}
```

It should be noted that there are no primitives in Groovy—everything is an object. In this case, the "0" is an integer object that Groovy has extended with the `upto` method. At this point, you might worry about calling a Java method that takes a primitive. Groovy handles all the conversions for you under the covers, so there are no issues to worry about. The `upto` method again iterates over the range 0 to 4, executing the code block at each iteration. Here again, we're using the `it` default variable, which is what the `upto` method is iterating over. If our intention is to execute a block of code five times, there is an even easier way to do this in Groovy (see Listing A.45).

Listing A.45   Looping Over a Code Block with the Times Method

```
5.times()
{
  //do something
}
```

The `times` method does exactly what you'd think it would do. It executes the code block as many times as is specified—five times in this case. In addition to the looping constructs we've already seen, we also have the ability to skip count (see Listing A.46).

Listing A.46   Looping Using the step Method

```
0.step(10,2){}
5.step(100, 5){}
```

The `step` method allows you to count by 2s, 5s, or anything. The `in` operator is overloaded to operate over lists much like an iterator works in Java (see Listing A.47).

Listing A.47   Iterating over a List

```
def foo = ["one", "two", "three"]
for(i in foo)
{
  println i
}
```

This allows us easy access to any list without using the usual boilerplate code of getting an iterator and then stepping through each element. A final looping construct that we should look at is each (see Listing A.48).

Listing A.48   Iterating Using the each Method

```
["one", "two", "three"].each{ println it }
(1..3).each{ println it }
```

The each method operates on lists and ranges, iterating over each element in the list or range. Groovy also provides an easy way to name the variable instead of using the default it. You may have noticed that we're actually passing each a closure so we can use closure syntax to name the variable (see Listing A.49).

Listing A.49   Named Variables with each

```
["one", "two", "three"].each{ num ->
  println num
}
```

Perhaps you need to iterate over a list with an index; this is also easily done in Groovy (see Listing A.50).

Listing A.50   Using eachWithIndex

```
["one", "two", "three"].eachWithIndex{ num,i ->
  println "$i. $num"
}
```

As we can see, Groovy provides a rich variety of looping constructs that should meet any need.

Optional Parameters

Another nice feature of Groovy is the ability to have optional parameters with default values (see Listing A.51).

Listing A.51   Optional Parameters with Default Values

```
def purchase(item, quantity = 1)
{
  println "You have purchased $quantity $item"
}
purchase "coat"
purchase "socks", 2
```

The defined method matches both calls; in the first case, it outputs "You have purchased 1 coat". This uses the default value for quantity. The second call specifies a value for quantity and outputs "You have purchased 2 socks".

This concludes our quick overview of Groovy. As you can see, it's designed to be simple for Java programmers to pick up, while still offering a lot of nice scripting features to make everyday tasks easier.

Index

IBM Training:

A bright choice for your business *and* your career.

Completing *Getting Started with IBM WebSphere sMash* was a great start toward building a solid set of IBM WebSphere® skills. For your next step, reinforce and extend what you've learned in this book with training from IBM.

You've come this far, now continue your skill development with this IBM WebSphere course:

Developing RESTful Applications with WebSphere sMash (Course code ZU000)

Learn how to expose content as RESTful services in IBM WebSphere sMash. Additionally, learn to use dynamic scripting languages, such as PHP and Groovy, to rapidly develop, test, debug and deploy applications to IBM WebSphere sMash.

- This specific course is available as a self-paced virtual class with hands-on labs.

- Additional courses are also available for IBM WebSphere application development for Java®, web services and XML.

To enroll in this course and learn more about other application development courses in your country, visit

ibm.com/training/websphere/books

Energize your career

FREE Online Edition

Your purchase of **Getting Started with IBM WebSphere sMash** includes access to a free online edition for 120 days through the Safari Books Online subscription service. Nearly every IBM Press book is available online through Safari Books Online, along with more than 5,000 other technical books and videos from publishers such as Addison-Wesley Professional, Cisco Press, Exam Cram, O'Reilly, Prentice Hall, Que, and Sams.

SAFARI BOOKS ONLINE allows you to search for a specific answer, cut and paste code, download chapters, and stay current with emerging technologies.

Activate your FREE Online Edition at
www.informit.com/safarifree

> **STEP 1:** Enter the coupon code: TFQCIWH.

> **STEP 2:** New Safari users, complete the brief registration form.
> Safari subscribers, just log in.

If you have difficulty registering on Safari or accessing the online edition, please e-mail customer-service@safaribooksonline.com